Discrepant Histories
Translocal Essays on Filipino Cultures

Discrepant Histories
Translocal Essays on Filipino Cultures

Edited by
V<small>ICENTE</small> L. R<small>AFAEL</small>

TEMPLE UNIVERSITY PRESS
PHILADELPHIA

Temple University Press, Philadelphia 19122

Published 1995

Published in the Republic of the Philippines by Anvil Publishing, Inc.

This book is printed on acid-free paper.

Printed in the Republic of the Philippines.

ISBN 1-56639-355-8 cloth
ISBN 1-56639-356-6 paper

CIP data available from the Library of Congress.

In the series, *Asian American History and Culture,* edited by Sucheng Chan
and David Palumbo-Liu.

The following publishers have generously given permission to reprint the following
articles from copyrighted works:

Benedict Anderson, "Cacique Democracy in the Philippines: Origins and Dreams,"
New Left Review 169 (1988): 3-33. Copyright 1988 by *New Left Review.*

Reynaldo C. Ileto, "Cholera and the Origins of the American Sanitary Order in the
Philippines," from *Imperial Medicine and Indigenous Society,* edited by David Arnold
(Manchester: Manchester University Press, 1988): 125-147. Reprinted with
permission of St. Martin's Press, Incorporated.

Warwick Anderson, "'Where Every Prospect Pleases and Only Man Is Vile': Laboratory Medicine as Colonial Discourse," *Critical Inquiry* 18.3 (1992): 506-529.
Copyright 1992 by University of Chicago.

Vicente L. Rafael, "Nationalism, Imagery, and the Filipino Intelligentsia in the
Nineteenth Century," *Critical Inquiry* 16.3 (1990): 591-611. Copyright 1990 by
University of Chicago.

Jean-Paul Dumont, "Ideas on Philippine Violence: Assertions, Negations and
Narrations." *Paths to Terror: Domination, Resistance, and Communal Violence,*
edited by Carol Nordstrom and JoAnn Martin (Berkeley: University of California
Press, 1992): 133-153. Copyright 1992 by The Regents of the University of
California.

Neferti Xina M. Tadiar, "Manila's New Metropolitan Form," *differences: A Journal of
Feminist Cultural Studies* 5.3 (1993): 154-178. Copyright 1993 by Brown University.

For Regine, Mishka, Javier, Mara, and Janina
and
For Carol, Yoshiko, and Jack

ACKNOWLEDGMENTS

Some of the essays in this book first appeared in the following publications which are hereby gratefully acknowledged.

"Cacique Democracy in the Philippines: Origins and Dreams." *New Left Review,* 169, May-June 1988. 3-33.

"Cholera and the Origins of the American Sanitary Order in the Philippines." *Imperial Medicine and Indigenous Societies.* David Arnold, ed. Manchester: Manchester University Press; and New York: St. Martin's Press, 1988. 125-48.

"'Where Every Prospect Pleases and Only Man is Vile': Laboratory Medicine as Colonial Discourse." *Critical Inquiry,* 18, 1992, University of Chicago, 506-29.

"Nationalism, Imagery, and the Filipino Intelligentsia in the Nineteenth Century." *Critical Inquiry,* v. 16 no. 3, Spring 1990, 591-611.

"Filipinos in the United States and their Literature of Exile." *Reading the Literature of Asian America.* Shirley Geok-Lim and Amy Ling, eds. Temple University Press, 1992. 49-78.

"Ideas on Philippine Violence: Assertions, Negations, and Narrations." *The Paths to Domination, Resistance and Terror,* Carol Nordstrom and JoAnn Martin, eds. Berkeley: University of California Press, 1992. 133-53.

"Manila's New Metropolitan Form." *differences: A Journal of Feminist Cultural Studies,* v. 5 no. 3, 1993. 154-78.

All the other essays have not been previously published.

The editor would also like to acknowledge the assistance of the Program for Cultural Studies, East-West Center, for the fellowship and space to complete this collection of essays. Many thanks as well to the work and encouragement of Karina Bolasco, RayVi Sunico, Janet Francendese, David Palumbo-Liu, David Lloyd, and Ken Wissoker.

TABLE OF CONTENTS

Part IV. AESTHETICS AND POLITICS OF THE EVERYDAY

NOTES ON THE CONTRIBUTORS

BENEDICT ANDERSON is Aaron L. Binenkorb Professor of International Studies at Cornell University, where he is also Director of the Modern Indonesian Project. He is the author of *Java in a Time of Revolution, In the Mirror: Literature and Politics in Siam in the American Era, Imagined Communities: Reflections on the Origins and Spread of Nationalism* and *Language and Power: Exploring Indonesian Political Cultures.*

WARWICK ANDERSON is Assistant Professor in the Department of the History of Science, Harvard University. He received his Ph.D. from the University of Pennsylvania and also holds a medical degree from the University of Melbourne. He is finishing a book on American colonial medicine in the Philippines.

FENELLA CANNELL is Lecturer at the Department of Anthropology, at the London School of Economics and Political Science. She has previously taught at Cambridge University. Currently, she is writing an ethnography of everyday life in a Bikol town.

OSCAR V. CAMPOMANES is Assistant Professor in the English Department, University of California at Berkeley. He has recently completed his Ph.D. in American Studies at Brown University and is writing a book on U.S. colonial discourse on the Philippines.

JEAN-PAUL DUMONT is the Clarence J. Robinson Professor of Anthropology at George Mason University and the author of several books in English and French, including *Visayan Vignettes: Ethnographic Traces of a Philippine Island* and *The Headman and I.* He is presently at work on an ethnography of Bohol.

REYNALDO C. ILETO is Professor of History at the James Cook University in Townsville, Australia. He is the author of several essays on the Philippines and the highly acclaimed books, *Magindanao, 1860-1888: the Career of Datu Uto of Buayan,* and *Pasyon and Revolution: Popular Movements in the Philippines, 1840-1940.*

MARTIN F. MANALANSAN IV is completing his Ph.D. in Anthropology at the University of Rochester and has been working with the Gay Men's Health Center in Manhattan. He is writing an ethnography of Filipino gay immigrants in the U.S.

VICENTE L. RAFAEL is Associate Professor in the Department of Communication, University of California at San Diego. He is the author of several essays on the Philippines and *Contracting Colonialism: Translation and Christian Conversion in Tagalog Society Under Early Spanish Rule.*

MICHAEL SALMAN is Assistant Professor in the History Department, University of California, Los Angeles. He received his Ph.D. in American History from Stanford University and is completing two books on the American colonization of the Philippines with special focus on the debates around slavery and the impact of abolitionist ideology on U.S. policies.

NEFERTI XINA TADIAR is completing her Ph.D. in English at Duke University and is associated with the faculty of the Department of English at the University of the Philippines. She is currently finishing her dissertation on modes of subject formation in Philippine literature since the 1970s.

Introduction

Writing Outside:
On the Question of Location

VICENTE L. RAFAEL

THIS COLLECTION BRINGS TOGETHER ESSAYS ON THE PHILIPPINES WRITTEN approximately from the late 1980s to the early 1990s by scholars based in English language Western institutions, including one in Australia. Seven of these pieces have appeared in academic journals or anthologies dealing with subjects other than the Philippines published in the United States or England, while three of them appear in print for the first time in this volume. None of them, however, has been previously published in the Philippines itself, the country to which they explicitly refer. The simultaneous publication of this collection in the Philippines by Anvil Publishing and in the United States by Temple University Press serves a dual purpose. It is designed to make these writings available to audiences in the Philippines who otherwise would have limited access to the Western publications which put out these essays or are likely to do so. It is also meant to make accessible to a mixed readership in the U.S. and elsewhere texts which may be useful in thinking through issues of colonialism, nationalism, neocolonialism and the post-colonial condition as these occur in specific sites and travel across indeterminate points in the world.

The essays are organized less around a single theme or a unified agenda as they are permeated by sustained engagements with questions of power, representation, and agency within the context of the colonial legacies of modernity in the Philippines. They also share a cross-disciplinary protocol, poaching their critical vocabularies from varieties of structuralist, post-structuralist, Marxist, feminist, and phenomenological approaches. There is less interest in these essays with debating theories as with translating such debates across the borders that separate area studies from the disciplines, locating them on the matrices of specific colonial, national, immigrant, and local formations. In this sense, they are obliquely allied with, though not entirely absorbed by, the hybrid and highly charged field that has come to be known in the United States as "cultural studies."[1]

And while not all the essays are explicitly historical, they are affiliated in their skepticism toward historicist approaches which, in their obsession with matters of periodization, tend towards dehistoricizing the terrain of their investigations. Rather than ask about the past as such, these essays inquire about the conditions of possibility which make the past thinkable as simultaneously constitutive and disruptive of the present. For in their own ways, these essays postulate the imperative to defamiliarize received ideas about the Philippines, seeing the archipelago as a site of different and often contentious projects—political, economic, and cultural—whose borders are historically constructed and so remain spatially unstable. Indeed, they participate to varying degrees in rendering those borders that comprise the Philippines and the "West" fluid and indeterminate. How so and to what effects?

Written by scholars based outside the national order of the Philippines (with its own distinct academic culture, circuits of publicity, and politics of scholarship), the papers in this collection necessarily papers address multiple audiences. For this reason, they tend to take the reality of the Philippines anew, framing and reframing what seems obvious and even banal to a Philippine audience for the sake of making the country legible within and across the different textual conventions of such academic practices as social history, comparative literature, feminist theory, and cultural anthropology. One effect of constantly having to resituate the Philippines outside the constraints of a nationalist imaginary is to call attention to the frayed and porous passages between what is "inside" and "outside" not only of the Philippines but also of that which is commonly thought of as the "West." Similarly, part of the significance of stitching these pieces together may lie with the ways in which they engage the conventions of modern area studies from the perspective of questions relating to location and locality so compellingly thematized by practitioners of cultural studies. Area studies, as it was formulated in the midst of the Cold War in the United States, was meant to treat nation-states as elementary units of analysis and to see areas themselves as stable entities securely representable on maps and in the workings of bureaucratic machineries. Cultural studies, with its roots in oppositional knowledge and practices in England and later on in the U.S., has taken on a currency in a post-Cold War era and is characterized (if in fact it is possible to typify such broad and shifting sets of critical practices) by a deep ambivalence toward the possibilities of stabilizing areas of knowledge, much less crediting imperialist and nationalist claims for such totalities. The post-Cold War study of areas, therefore, bumps up against the skepticism of cultural studies regarding the categorical privilege of the nation-state.

Situated on such a juncture, these essays implicitly raise the question of what it might mean to write about the Philippines from the "outside." In what ways has that outside been historically a constitutive feature of the "inside" of the nation? To what extent are the related histories of colonialism and nationalism the result of, as well as the cause of, the migrations and movements of Filipinos within and outside of the Philippines? Indeed, how does it happen that the very notion of "Filipino" takes on a sociological density only in and through that history of displacement, conquest, resistance, and in relation to an always elusive outside? And how do those unequal and still ongoing movements and attachments between inside and outside (for example the closure of the two largest overseas U.S. military bases, Clark Field and Subic Bay, simultaneous with the emergent plight of Filipino-American children left behind by departing U.S. servicemen; the massive outflow of Filipino laborers, especially domestic workers to virtually all parts of the world coincident with the emergence of Filipinos as the largest "Asian-American" group in the United States in the late 20th century) imply a new geography of knowledge and different channels and modes of scholarly production about the Philippines? Negotiating between and among epistemological regimes, how can this migratory scholarship participate in the task of reconfiguring the relationship between and among the "Third" and the "First" worlds, and all others beyond and in between?

Herein lies another quality that binds these essays to one another: their ability if not their vocation to travel, crossing borders that constitute areas of knowledge and experience. For not only can these texts be read profitably by those with an obvious focus on Asian, Asian-American, and Philippine studies. Because they are joined to conversations opened up by new areas of studies in the humanities and social sciences—conversations which spill across national boundaries yet invariably refer to them—they can also be read symptomatically as attempts to localize and thereby undercut the globalizing pretensions of the terms of such discussions. By focusing on the complex histories of societies that comprise the Philippines, they reassess the stakes in cultural studies debates around colonialism and nationalism, relativizing their reach and clarifying their limits and particularity in the West.

At the same time, these essays speak to current conditions in the Philippines. Such conditions include among others, political and economic inequality of staggering proportions, the policing of everyday life, ecological havoc, uncontrolled population growth, ceaseless flows of transmigrant laborers, and a spiralling national debt. Subjected to three colonial regimes over four hundred years, then to a succession of nationalist and neocolonial governments, to over a decade of Martial Law dictatorship along with an ever-deepening bondage to the International Monetary Fund and the World Bank, and lately with the election of Fidel Ramos and the reintegration of the Marcoses into Filipino elite circles, the return to what Benedict Anderson calls "cacique democracy," the archipelago has also been the site of recurrent peasant rebellions, ethnic and religious secessionist movements, anticolonial guerrilla warfare, rightwing coup attempts, and everyday modes of oppositional practices among different subaltern groups. The Philippines then has never been a static entity, a nation-state with a stable polity. Indeed, the outlines of its territorial borders recognizable on standard maps have always been a function of administrative exigencies on the part of both colonial and national state bureaucracies. The reality of the Philippines has always exceeded these artificial boundaries, evading their essentializing claims and regulatory compulsions.

By problematizing received notions of the Philippines and Filipinos, these essays point out the arbitrariness of those boundaries. In the pages that follow, there is a sense that the Philippines is as much a sovereign nation in the global imaginary as much as it is a series of relations anchored to crisis and contingency.

However, just as these essays resituate the Philippines, they also imply a necessary reorientation of the "West." No longer conceivable as simply a stable place from which other places are seen and assessed, nor an advancing frontier of progress into which other areas are incorporated, the "West" can be thought of, as Edouard Glissant has suggested, as a set of highly volatile and contested projects.[2] The formation of the West has historically entailed practices often steeped in violence and seduction that have left their undeniable imprints on the non-Western world. Projecting itself as the home of an expansive, mobile, and desirable culture, the West has historically warred on those it regards as its others as much as it has been at war with the others who inhabit, and so are constitutive of, its sites.

Written out of these clusters of contradiction, the papers in this collection reflect and refract the formations of the Philippines as simultaneously implicated in the reformulations of the West. Betwixt and between zones of multicultural formations and cross-disciplinary practices, these texts are tokens of displaced scholarship which are themselves about the specific and highly localized modalities of displacements wrought by the forces of modernity working across national boundaries and historical periods. In lieu of chronologies and templates, they offer chronotopes, that is, densely crafted and ironizing descriptions of such areas as colonial and national technologies of power, literary artifacts of memory and exile, languages and politics of identity and violence, and gendered imaginings of nationhood and disease. In their diversity, these essays are explicitly partisan and therefore fragmentary accounts which do not aspire to become part of a definitive whole, or even for canonical status in the area of Philippine/ Southeast Asian studies. Instead, they offer the beginnings of a more circumscribed but no less necessary project of charting the implosions of the Philippines in the "West" and vice versa, tracing the unequal and disparate crossings, exiles, and migrations of one into the other that make for incommensurable exchanges and surprising appropriations. As such, they evoke the circuits of longing and love, of resistances and recognitions that bind the inside of one to the outside of the other.

"Cacique Democracy in the Philippines: Origins and Dreams" by Benedict Anderson forms a point of departure, or perhaps more appropriately, of dispersal, in this collection. Originally published in the British journal, *New Left Review*, Anderson's essay sets recent Philippine history in broad relief, comparing the rise of Filipino elite nationalism to those of Latin America and Southeast Asia. Drawing attention to the enormous historical significance of a Chinese mestizo minority able to articulate their economic and political interests with those of successive colonial states, Anderson shows the ethnic specificity of the Filipino ruling class that sets it apart from its regional neighbors. Profiting from the anti-sinicism and the religious, residential, and mercantilistic policies of Spain, from the administrative and ideological requirements of the United States, from the militaristic nationalism of the Japanese, and from the postwar reconstruction needs of the Republic and Cold War policies of the United States, the mestizo elite formed themselves into an oligarchy whose interests came to dominate the workings of the colonial and national state. It was only with the ascendance of the Marcoses in the mid-1960s that the calculus of power shifted, as Martial Law enabled Ferdinand and Imelda to force the oligarchs to serve the state. Yet, Martial Law amounted to oligarchical rule by other means, so that the end of the dictatorship and the rise of Corazon Aquino (and more recently Fidel Ramos) has resulted in the return to "cacique democracy." In this succinct and incisive account, Anderson provides us with a sharply drawn image of Philippine politics as a "well-run casino" with Filipino national elites as brokers between their fragmentary polities and a New World Order. Indeed, it is this idea of power as the capacity to lay claim over the site of circulation and thereby broker the exchange between the inside and the outside that will, as we shall see, form a persistent motif in some of the papers that follow.

The next three essays are joined by their historical focus—the period of United Sates rule in the Philippines—and by their analytical concerns—the explication of technologies of colonial rule. Such technologies included militarized measures for instituting public health and disease control, highly specialized laboratory experiments and scientific papers on tropical medicine, and reformatory prisons and model penal colonies. Insofar as these mechanisms of colonial rule impinged directly on the individual bodies of both the colonizers and colonized, they in fact drew their authority from their capacity to mystify such processes of individuation as "natural" and self-evident.

In "Cholera and the Origins of the American Sanitary Order in the Philippines," Reynaldo Ileto argues for the salience of seeing the Filipino-American war of 1899-1902 and the war against the cholera epidemic of 1902-1904 within a single historical optic. Both were fought and commanded by virtually the same American military personnel; and both were ordered towards establishing the basis of colonial authority in terms of disciplined and hygienic subjects receptive to tutelary interventions. Yet the coercive imposition of a sanitary order by way of quarantines, forcible isolation of infected peoples, burning of houses, wholesale evacuation of villages, and so forth met with all kinds of oppositions in the form of evasions, concealments of the sick, and continued use of local curers among the Filipinos. As Ileto points out, where colonial public health measures were designed to standardize the definition of illness, regiment treatments, and individualize the disposal of the dead, Filipinos struggled to keep "death and dying a social event," resorting to traditional curing rites and healers. Amid the triumphalist accounts of the victory over cholera among the colonizers, the colonized insisted on reasserting local notions of bodily order that eluded sanitary incorporation.

Ileto's attempt at demythologizing the benevolent intentions of American sanitation is complemented by Warwick Anderson's nuanced analysis of the medical laboratory as integral to the formation of colonial hegemony in his paper, "'Where Every Prospect Pleases

Only Man is Vile': Laboratory Medicine as Colonial Discourse." Anderson is interested in the various ways by which the language of medical science formulated in the laboratory of the Bureau of Science in Manila rendered United States imperialism simultaneously powerful and benign. As a privileged site for producing the "truth" about the "tropics," the colonial laboratory contributed to biologizing the social and historical contexts of domination. In the voluminous scientific papers produced by the Bureau, what eventually emerged were "fabricated and rationalized images" of Filipino bodies as carriers of foreign antibodies and germs which threatened white bodies; and of American bodies as both a vulnerable and resilient racial type capable of guarding against the invisible foreign parasites lurking in the tropics and lodged in native bodies. As vital instruments for defining the categories of sociality ranging from working conditions to the organization of residential and commercial spaces and the consolidation of racial hierarchies, the laboratory and the scientific paper served as densely technical and highly formalized nodes in the network of colonial knowledge and the transaction of American power in the Philippines.

Colonial medicine offered the prospect of turning all of colonial society into one huge laboratory where the bodies of both ruler and ruled would be reduced into the categories of science. In his essay, "'Nothing Without Labor': Penology, Discipline and Independence in the Philippines Under United States Rule," Michael Salman advances a related argument with regard this time to the colonial prison. Drawing on the writings of Michel Foucault, Salman traces the ways by which colonial penology was deployed by both American and Filipino colonial officials as an "interpretive metaphor" in the structuring of colonial society. Like laboratories, prisons were sites for producing the idea of an ordered and disciplined subjectivity, one that would in time become an agent in the administration of the very means of its subjugation. As Salman writes, "The prison, an asylum to segregate criminals from their environment, highlights the alienating quality of colonialism as a project of cultural disparagement, rejection, and reformation." For the prison is above all an ambiguous operation charged with punishment and reform, administering brutality *and* humanitarianism. It is this articulation of the prison with colonial society that Salman evokes in his description of Bilibid Prison and the

Iwahig Penal colony. Modeled after Indian reservations and new penal institutions in the United States, the Iwahig prison became a simulation of colonial society, complete with their own local governments, schools, and homesteads which inmates could farm with their families. But as Salman shows, the penal colony became a screen on which to project ideas about colonial society itself as a "reformative asylum" designed to uplift formerly insurgent natives under the tutelary gaze of white supervision. As such, the Philippines was governed by a "carceral continuum" where bondage was a sign of benevolence and colonial incarceration coextensive with democratic tutelage.

Colonial violence constituted the possibilities for both the consolidation and negation of colonial rule. In rationalizing the terror of the new and the foreign, colonialism set about constructing different social orders, novel grammars of identity, and thus alternative ways for conceptualizing and acting upon history and destiny. The dialectical counterpoints to colonial rule, nationalism and diaspora, are the subjects of the next three essays, linked by their overlapping concerns with language, literature, and loss.

"Nationalism, Imagery, and the Filipino Intelligentsia of the Nineteenth Century" by Vicente L. Rafael begins with an extended gloss on Benedict Anderson's massively influential book, *Imagined Communities: Reflections on the Origins and Spread of Nationalism*.[3] Stressing the importance of nationalism's modernity—that is, the historically specific ways in which the nation emerges on the conjunction of language, death, and community—Rafael examines the contradictions that inhere in the relationship between imagination and imagery in the writings and photographs of Jose Rizal. Specifically, he inquires into the difference between the textual and photographic means for reproducing a sense of national longing on the part of Rizal, popularly regarded as the "father of the Filipino nation." By reading across a disparate series of Rizal's writings—letters to his mother, a formative essay on nationalism, passages from his travel diaries, and autobiographical fragments—Rafael points out the divided notion of the nation in Rizal's texts. The nation is both a gendered figure available to the appropriative gestures of the patriot-son and a phantom presence that exceeds the patriot's ability to localize its boundaries. Turning to the circulation of the photographs of Rizal and his fellow nationalists,

Rafael sees a similar project at work: that of promoting a radical estrangement between colonizer and colonized on the one hand, and that of providing memory traces of absent patriots to the motherland on the other. However, unlike Rizal's writings, Rizal's photographs cannot be fully assimilated into a nationalist narrative. As images on a flat surface, they seem impervious to the work of mourning that pervades Rizal's writings, and thus persist as ghostly presences at a remove from nationalism's hermeneutic pull.

Exiled in Europe and later on in Dapitan, Rizal exemplified (though he certainly did not originate) a Filipino style of imagining nationhood on the register of loss that turned writing into a work of mourning. The Filipino and Filipino-American writers discussed by Oscar Campomanes in his essay, "Filipinos in the United States and their Literature of Exile" in some ways bear witness to the resilience of that style. Critically situated in relation to dominant understandings of "Asian-American" and "immigrant" literature in the United States, Campomanes' essay argues that the colonial history of the Philippines and the unique conditions of the Filipino diaspora in the United States set apart their writings from other immigrant groups in the United States. Characterizing their literature as "exilic," he goes on to show the "motifs of departure, nostalgia, incompletion, rootlessness, leavetaking, and dispossession" recurring in the works of two generations of Filipinos in the U.S. In the literature of the first and second generation of writers, the United States rarely emerges as a "promised land." Rather the Philippines serves as the locus of utopic longings precisely in and through its absence. Exile forged out of colonial and neocolonial conditions furnish these writers with a grammar with which to escape assimilation in the United States even as they inhabit the unbridgeable distance between their words and the place of their longing.

That ambivalence towards the "outside," whether in the form of the dominant American social order which consigns them to its margins or the Philippine homeland which now appears exterior to their experience, also marks the culture of Filipino "gay" immigrants in New York city as described in Martin Manalansan's ethnography, "Speaking of AIDS: Language and the Filipino 'Gay' Experience in America." Drawing from his experience as an AIDS activist with the

Gay Men's Health Center in Manhattan, Manalansan examines the ways by which Filipino "gays" deal with the AIDS pandemic by, among other things, having recourse to the linguistic resources of the *bakla* (loosely translated, male transvestite) culture which they brought with them from the Philippines. He begins by drawing a set of insightful distinctions between the Western notion of gay identity, tied as it is to a generalized anxiety about stable ontologies, and the Filipino conception of the *bakla* which, by stressing the performative aspects of gender differences, parodies as it reinscribes the gap between the masculine and the feminine. Manalansan outlines the colonial lineage of *bakla* culture, pointing to the institutionalized transvestitism in Spanish Catholic rituals and the camp aesthetic of United States Hollywood culture. The vernacular of the *bakla, swardspeak,* entails what we might think of as the camp appropriation of the dominant languages of Spanish, English, and Tagalog. Speaking it entails a certain linguistic dexterity that in ironizing hegemonic languages holds out the possibility of transforming its speakers into figures in control of ambiguity rather than its mere effects. Manalansan argues that it is precisely this capacity of *swardspeak* to figuratively displace the totalizing effects of dominant discourses that makes it a potent resource for Filipino "gays." Confronted with the eminently contractable AIDS virus, they translate and so localize its universalizing effects within an immigrant geography. Far from being a "deviation" from a Filipino immigrant aesthetic, the *bakla* vernacular may very well be its most instructive expression.

The ironizing and resignification of marginality constitutes an aesthetic of everyday life that Filipino immigrant culture seems to share with those of certain rural communities outside of Manila. But in Metro Manila itself, the state and the discourse of nationalist development predicated on "free markets" has tended to generalize conditions of marginality resulting in the unregulated flow of rural populations into the capital. It is the everyday articulations of self, society, and state—always conflictual and historically permeated with memories and experiences of violence—that are explored by the remaining three essays.

In "The Power of Appearances: Beauty, Mimicry and Transformation in Bikol," Fenella Cannell writes a richly textured ethnogra-

phy of notions of "beauty" and practices of imitation among rice-
growing peasants of a small Bikol town. Cannell notes that "Bikolano
people of all classes are in fact extremely interested in thinking about
the Philippines with reference to a somewhere else. Usually that somewhere else is America, and usually the comparisons stress that the
'outside' or distant place—the imagined America—is a place of power,
wealth, cleanliness, beauty, glamor, and enjoyment." The practices of
imitation such as everyday joke-telling, amateur singing contests, and
elaborate *bakla* beauty pageants, are ways of performing one's ability
to establish a relationship of proximity to this outside. Imitation among
Bikolanos, as Cannell argues, is not simply a matter of reproducing
Western models but of an "ironic exploration of the possibility of
accessing the power of the imagined American world." The practice
of mimicry thus entails entertaining phantasms of self-transformation
regardless of one's place in the social hierarchy. It is for this reason
that male transvestite beauty contests are widely popular in the Bikol
area. Like all other cultural cross-dressers such as clergy, shamans,
and Chinese mestizos, the *bakla* serves as a powerful medium, a compelling mimic of things "Western." As a highly skilled impersonator,
the *bakla* exemplifies a popular yet risky desire to conjugate the "inside" and "outside" with one's altered body, thereby bridging the gap
between the relative impoverishment of Bikol society and the utopic
possibilities held out by an imaginary "America." As such, the aesthetics of imitation also implies a politics of cultural displacement.
Such a politics requires an alertness to the appearance of signs which
come from the outside—those traces of a colonial relationship embedded in popular music, movies, and print media—along with the cultiva-
tion of one's ability to reappropriate and recontextualize these. In so
doing, one establishes a relationship of proximity to the sources of
power and beauty, thereby recontextualizing one's sense of marginality.

Analogous to the performance of mimicry in Bikol are the notions of violence among the people of the Visayan island of Siquijor
as described in Jean-Paul Dumont's essay, "Ideas on Philippine Violence: Assertions, Negations, and Narrations." Conducting his fieldwork during and immediately after the period of Martial Law, Dumont
is initially struck by the seeming contradiction between the historical

prevalence of violent occurrences in the country and the frequent disclaimers among Siquijorians that such violence and disorder exist at all. Amid stunning social inequalities and the widely visible abuses of the Marcos dictatorship, people in the island claimed to get along, and were intent on denying, especially to a foreign anthropologist, the existence of violence in their community. Yet, such a disavowal, as Dumont argues, was ideological. Stories about accidents, illness, and death suggested that violence was indeed woven into the everyday lives of the Siquijorians. One source of violence was the spirit world which demarcated an outside realm that visited illness and death upon the island. By locating violence in this realm, Siquijorians seemed to be claiming that they were objects rather than perpetrators of violence. Dumont historicizes such a disavowal, pointing out that violence was traditionally handed down from the colonial and national governments, the control of which was way beyond the immediate reach of the people. Hence, this disavowal of violence encodes an obsession with anticipating its possible appearance. As Dumont suggests in his discussion of people's responses to the national elections of 1986, to speak about violence as if it were absent is to inoculate oneself from its actual occurrence. Alongside this ideology of violence is thus a range of subtle, everyday forms of resistance—jokes, ironic asides, gleeful punning regarding government programs, national leaders, and the like—which acknowledged the power of the outside while displacing its hold on oneself.

The post-Marcos years has not meant the end of state violence, but has in fact resulted in sustained attempts to manage and rationalize its effects in the name of "national development." In "Manila's New Metropolitan Form," Neferti Tadiar analyzes the contradictions spawned by recent policies of deregulated capitalist development on the one hand, and the deregulated flows of labor into Metro Manila on the other. She focuses on the ways everyday forms of violence, which not only accompany development but are the development process itself, play themselves out in the notions and uses of urban space. Taking the nationalist elite's desire for modernity as a historical framework, Tadiar reads the emergence of flyovers—vertical structures designed to bypass busy intersections and allow for smooth flow of traffic—as attempts to control the collective movements of masses of people and accommodate the pressures that they bring about. For nationalist elites and representatives of the state, along with private investors, managing the traffic of vehicles becomes a way of representing as well as realizing their management of the economy, particularly the traffic in local labor and global capital. Flyovers serve not only as a metaphor for this desire for rationality but also the material medium of what Tadiar refers to as this desire's "mode of production." But as with development schemes in general, the nationalist conflation of "democracy" and "free markets" creates massive dislocations and seemingly chaotic conditions of excess in the form of unemployment and pools of cheap labor. These in turn generate a political economy of flexible labor regimes: informal networks of hiring and working practices that elude regimentation and discipline. The state itself, characterized by recurring oscillations between "drives" against such human excess (as in "clean up drives" against squatters, prostitutes, and sidewalk vendors) and periods of laxity, negligence, and graft fall prey to this contradiction "between ideal images" and "illegitimate desires" that Tadiar sees as analogous to the pathological condition of bulimia, the bouts of excessive eating and stomach purgings that plague certain women.

This notion of state bulimia opens the door for a gendered analysis of the relations among state power, urban space, and global capital. Following the gendered discourse of modernization, the nation-state tends to project itself as the masculine caretaker of its domestic affairs, thereby feminizing its population and, as Tadiar argues, projecting attributes of female sexuality—its fluidity, its excessiveness but also its procreativeness and maternality—onto its labor force. Yet, from the perspective of global capital, both the nation-state and its labor force are expected to be "female-like," compliant, and hospitable to its penetration and circulation, thereby reversing the state's perception of itself. Caught up in this ambivalent "political-libidinal dynamics of capitalism and nationhood," it is small wonder that the state's attempts at a more liberalized, flexible mode of authoritarianism cannot but reproduce the very excess of traffic in bodies and refuse that it had sought to contain. Indeed, the developmentalist desire encoded in flyovers has already been thwarted as traffic in Metro Manila today is far worse than it has ever been in living memory. And the state's response—to build yet even more roadways and overpasses (financed overwhelmingly with foreign capital) would seem to reiterate Tadiar's diagnosis of the bulimic constitution of state power. In this highly nuanced description of Metro Manila's emergent urban forms, Tadiar engages in a double critique of both the current versions of power in the Philippine nation-state and the often universalizing tendencies of Western theories of urban space.

This collection on the Philippines is neither programmatic nor comprehensive. It would have been important to have essays on non-Christian peoples that comprise a sizeable minority of the population, on the importance of women's movements both in the country and elsewhere, and on contending Christianities and the vicissitudes of Church-State relations. Similarly, there is no real discussion of the organized left, or what's left of it; or the changing right and its military nexus; or middle class political culture in the wake of the Aquino regime. More urgently, essays on environmental issues, ecological politics, and the social aftermath of Mt. Pinatubo's continuing catastrophe would have been timely. One could come away from this volume overwhelmed, as I am, with a sense of what's missing, of what hasn't been or can't as yet be written about, of what might perhaps evade full disclosure and defy scholarly understanding. That is, one would feel inadequate to the task of approaching that which lies outside of one even as one fitfully inhabits its traces and lives out its discrepant histories. If this collection has somehow stirred a sense of the strange elusiveness along with the unexpected familiarity of the Philippines then it would have exceeded its objectives.

NOTES

---

1. See for example the essays in Lawrence Grossberg, Carey Nelson and Paula Treichler, editors, *Cultural Studies*, New York: Routledge, 1992, for lively and varied discussions and exemplifications of this field. And for a recent critical commentary on the intellectual and political stakes in cultural studies, see Frederic Jameson, "On 'Cultural Studies'," *Social Text*, 34, 1993, 17-52.

2. Edouard Glissant, *Carribean Discourse; Selected Essays*, translated by J. Michael Dash, Charlottsville: University of Virginia Press, 1992.

3. London: New Left Books, 1983; second edition, London: Verso, 1992.

Part 1

The Routes of Power

ONE

Cacique Democracy in the Philippines: Origins and Dreams

BENEDICT ANDERSON

ABOUT THIS TIME LAST YEAR, PRESIDENT CORAZON AQUINO TOLD A MOST instructive lie. Addressing the Filipino-Chinese Federated Chambers of Commerce on 9 March 1987, she described her appearance before them as a "homecoming," since her great-grandfather had been a poor immigrant from southeast China's Fukien province.[1] Doubtless her desperate need—given the Philippines' near-bankrupt economy and \$28 billion external debt [2]—to inspire feelings of solidarity and confidence among a powerful segment of Manila's business class made some embroidery understandable. But the truth is that the president, born Corazon Cojuangco, is a member of one of the wealthiest and most powerful dynasties within the Filipino oligarchy. Her grandfather, putative son of the penniless immigrant, was Don Melecio Cojuangco, born in Malolos, Central Luzon in 1871. A graduate of the Dominicans' Colegio de San Juan de Letran and the Escuela Normal, and a prominent *agricultor* (i.e. hacendado) in the province of Tarlac, he was, in 1907, at the age of 36, elected to the Philippine

Assembly, the quasi-legislature established by the American imperialists in that year. [3] One of his sons (Corazon's uncle) became governor of Tarlac in 1941, another (her father, Don José) its most prominent congressman. In 1967, one of his grandsons (her cousin), Eduardo 'Danding' Cojuangco, became governor of Tarlac with Ferdinand Marcos's backing, and went on to count among the most notorious of the Marcos cronies. Another grandson (her younger brother), José 'Peping' Cojuangco, was in those days one of Tarlac's congressmen, and is today again a congressman—and one of the half-dozen most powerful politicians in the country. Her marriage to Benigno Aquino, Jr., who was at a various periods governor of Tarlac and senator, linked her to another key dynasty of Central Luzon. Benigno Aquino, Sr., had been a senator in the late American era and won lasting notoriety for his active collaboration with the Japanese Occupation regime. At the present time, one of her brothers-in-law, Agapito 'Butz' Aquino, is a senator, and another, Paul, the head of Lakas ng Bansa (one of the three main "parties" in her electoral coalition); an uncle-in-law, Herminio Aquino, is a congressman, as are Emigdio 'Ding' Tanjuatco (cousin), and Teresita Aquino-Oreta (sister-in-law). [4] A maternal uncle, Francisco 'Komong' Sumulong, is majority floor-leader of the House of Representatives. Nor was Corazon herself, on becoming president, quite the simple housewife of her election broadsheets. For thirteen years she had served as treasurer of the Cojuangco family holding company, which controls a vast financial, agricultural, and urban real estate empire. [5]

Yet there is a core of truth in President Aquino's claims of 9 March 1987 and this core offers a useful guide to understanding the peculiarities of modern Philippine politics. The "-co" suffix to her maiden name is shared by a significant number of other dynasties within the national oligarchy: Cuenco, Tanjuatco, Tiangco, Chioco, etc. It originates from the Hokkienese k'o, a term of respect for older males; and it shows that her family originated among the Chinese mestizos who bloomed economically under the Spanish colonial regime and consolidated their wealth with political power under the Americans. [6] It is the dominance of this group which decisively marks off the Philippines from Spanish America (mestizos frequently in power, but not Chinese mestizos) and the rest of Southeast Asia (Chinese mestizos, indeed any mestizos, removed from political power, with the ambiguous exception of Siam). How did this happen?

Spanish Colonialism, the Church, and the Mestizo Elite

By the time the Spanish arrived to conquer, in the 1560s, the empire of Felipe II had reached its peak, and the islands, named after him, were the last major imperial acquisition. Iberian energies were absorbed in Europe and the Americas. The few Spaniards who did travel on to the Philippines found little on the spot to satiate their avarice. The one substantial source of rapid wealth lay not in mines but in commerce with Imperial China. Manila quickly became the entrepot for the "galleon trade," by which Chinese silks and porcelains were exchanged for Mexican silver, to be resold, at colossal profit, across the Pacific and eventually in Europe. It was not a business that required much acumen or industry; one needed merely to be in Manila, to have the right political connections, and to work out relationships with the Chinese traders and artisans who flocked to the entrepot.[7]

The absence of mines, and, until much later, of hacienda-based commercial agriculture, meant not only a concentration of the Spanish in the Manila area, but the lack of any sustained interest in massive exploitation of the indigenous (or imported) populations as a labor force. At the same time, the fact that the pre-Hispanic Philippines (in contrast to Burma, Siam, Cambodia, Vietnam, or Java) lacked any states with substantial military or bureaucratic power meant that relatively little force was required for the initial conquest and for its subsequent consolidation. Small garrisons, scattered here and there, generally sufficed.[8] Hence, *in the provinces*, to a degree unparalleled anywhere in the Americas except Paraguay, Spanish power in the Philippines was mediated through the Church.

The ardently Counter-Reformation clerics were fortunate in finding the great bulk of the indigenous population to be "animists." Buddhism and Hinduism had not reached so far. And though Islam was sweeping in from what today is Indonesia, it had consolidated itself only in parts of Mindanao and adjacent southern islands. There it could be contained, if never subdued.[9] Meanwhile a vast proselytization was launched which has resulted in the contemporary Philippines being 90 percent Christian.[10] (Only in twentieth-century Korea has Christianization in Asia been comparably successful.) The most noteworthy feature of this campaign was that it was conducted, most arduously, not through the medium of Spanish, but through the dozens of local languages. Till the very end of the Spanish regime no more than five percent of the local population had any facility with the colonial language. Spanish never became a pervasive lingua franca, as it did in the Americas, with the result that, certainly in 1900, and to a lesser extent even today, the peasants and fishermen in different parts of the archipelago could not communicate with one another: only their rulers had a common archipelago-wide speech.

Two other features of clerical dominion had lasting consequences for the evolution of the Philippine social structure. On the one hand, the quarrelling Orders, parcelled out among the various islands by Felipe II in the sixteenth century, pioneered commercial agriculture in the later eighteenth century, at the prodding of Carlos III's last, enlightened governor, José Basco y Vargas (1777-87). It was they who built what, in effect, were the first great haciendas. But these "conglomerates" remained institutional, rather than family (dynastic) property. The friars might liberally father children on local women, but they could not marry the women, or bequeath property to the progeny. In due course, the conquering Americans would dispossess the friars of their lands, as the eighteenth-century Bourbons had dispossessed the Jesuits; and these lands would fall like ripe mangoes into the hands of the likes of President Aquino's immediate ancestors.[11] The Philippines thus never had a substantial *criollo* hacendado class.

On the other hand, the Church, at least in its early days, had serious dreams of Christianizing the Celestial Empire. From the start it set eagerly to converting those whom the Spanish generally referred to as *sangleyes*.[12] Usually unlucky with the itinerant fathers, they were spectacularly successful with the children fathered on local mothers. Spanish colonial law helped by assigning these children a distinct juridical status as mestizos (in due course the word meant, typically, not the offspring of Spaniards and "natives," but of Chinese and local women). Christianized through their mothers, organized in their own guilds (*gremios*), compelled to avoid political transvestitism by wearing a distinctive costume and coiffure, these children, and their intermarrying further descendants, came to form a distinct stratum of colonial society. In some cases, perhaps only the "-co" suffix to their names betrayed distant celestial origins.

They might, however, have remained a marginal and stigmatized group, had it not been for the services of British imperialism. When Madrid joined in the Seven Years' War, London responded, *inter alia*, by occupying Manila in 1762 and holding it for the next two years. The local *sangleyes*, frequent victims of Iberian extortion and contempt, rallied to the invaders, who, when they retired, insouciantly left these humble allies to the vengeful mercies of their erstwhile oppressors. Most were then expelled from the Philippines, and further immigration was legally barred for almost a century. Into the vacuum created by the expulsions came the mestizos, who took over much of local trade, and began, following the friars' example, to move into small-scale latifundism.[13]

But they were, world-historically, several generations behind their ladino confreres in the Americas. Among them there were still no great rural magnates, no lawyers, few priests or prominent exporting merchants; above all there was no intelligentsia. The Church, characteristically reactionary, controlled printing and what miserable travesty of educational institutions existed. Hence the great nationalist upheaval that rocked the Americas between 1810 and 1840 had no counterpart in the archipelago until the 1880s.

The nineteenth century, nonetheless, was kind to the mestizos. One might have expected Spaniards to flock there after the loss of the Americas. But the last galleon had sailed in 1811. Spain itself was wracked with ceaseless conflict. And Cuba was so much closer, so infinitely richer. New people arrived, but the ones who mattered were not Spaniards but Anglo-Saxons (British and Americans) and, once again, *sangleyes*, by now, of course, "Chinese." In 1834 Manila was fully opened to international trade, and Cebu City and other smaller ports followed in due course; the ban on Chinese immigration was abolished. Chinese discipline, austerity, and energy quickly drove the mestizos out of inter-island trade and small-scale urban business. On the other hand, the internationalization of the economy after 1834 offered the mestizos—now a quarter of a million strong in a four million population—new opportunities in the countryside, in combination with British and American trading houses. These businesses saw the possibilities in full-scale commercialization of Philippine agriculture, and thus provided the necessary capital and commercial outlets to permit the mestizos to become, for the first time, real hacendados.

Nothing better illustrates this interplay between Anglo-Saxons, mestizos, and Chinese than the modern history of the island of Negros, today the "sugar island" par excellence of the Philippines. Almost uninhabited when British interests set up the first sugar mill there in 1857, the island's population had increased almost tenfold by the end of the century, and 274 steam mills were in operation.[14] If the British supplied capital, transoceanic transport, and markets, it was mestizos from Panay and Cebu, threatened by the Chinese influx into the port-cities of Cebu City and Iloilo, who managed the transfer of the peasant labor needed to grow and process cane. In no time at all, these frontier capitalists turned themselves, on the Spanish model, into "feudal" hacendados in the *nouveau riche* grand style. Thus, in the summer of 1987, when talk of land reform was in the Manila air, Congresswoman Hortensia Starke, one of the great sugar planters of Western Negros, could tell the newspapers: "Your land is like your most beautiful dress, the one that gives you good luck. If someone takes it from you, he only wants to destabilize you, to undress you."[15]

The Growth of National Sentiment

The next step was to get educated. A serious education was not easy to acquire in the colony, where the Church was violently opposed to any inroads of liberalism from Madrid and controlled most local schools. But the mestizos' growing wealth, the internationalization of the economy, and the steamship combined to make it possible for a number of young mestizo males to study in Europe. Quickly termed *ilustrados* (enlightened ones), they created during the 1880s the colony's first real intelligentsia, and began a cultural assault on benighted clericalism and, later, on Spanish political domination.[16] No less significant was the fact that, going to the same schools, reading the same books, writing for the same journals, and marrying each other's sisters and cousins, they inaugurated the self-conscious consolidation of a pan-Philippine (except for the Moro areas) mestizo stratum, where their elders had formed dispersed clusters of provincial caciques. It was these people who, at the very end of the century, began calling themselves "Filipinos," a term which up till then had designated only Spanish creoles.[17]

Wealthy and educated they might now be, but they had no political power. Late nineteenth-century Spain was too feeble economically and too divided politically to cope intelligently with rising mestizo demands. Repression was the order of the day, culminating in the execution in 1896 of the brilliant mestizo polymath José Rizal, whose two great, banned novels, *Noli Me Tangere* and *El Filibusterismo*, mercilessly satirized, in Spanish, clerical reaction, secular misrule, and the frequent opportunism and greed of his own class.[18]

Yet, not unsurprisingly, the inevitable insurrection did not originate with the *ilustrados*. In 1892, Andrés Bonifacio, an impoverished autodidact from the Manila artisanate, formed a secret revolutionary society with the mellifluous Tagalog name of Kataastaasang Kagalanggalang na Katipunan ng mga Anak ng Bayan (The Highest and Most Respectable Society of the Sons of the People—Katipunan for short), after the Masonic model.[19] The Katipunan's title already implied its reach and limitations. The use of Tagalog, rather than a Spanish understood only by a tiny elite, showed Bonifacio's intention of appealing to, and mobilizing, the *indio* masses. On the other hand, in those days Tagalog was spoken only by the masses of Central and Southern Luzon, and was incomprehensible in Mindanao, the Visayas, and even Ilocano-speaking northwestern Luzon.[20] In August 1896, Bonifacio launched an ill-prepared insurrection in Manila, which was quickly suppressed; but the movement spread rapidly in the surrounding provinces, where leadership was increasingly taken over by youthful mestizos.[21] Preoccupied by the revolutionary movement that had broken out in Cuba in February 1895, the Spanish fairly quickly gave up the struggle. In 1899, a Republic of the Philippines was proclaimed under the leadership of 'General' Emilio Aguinaldo, a youthful caudillo from the province of Cavite (who had had Bonifacio judicially murdered in 1897).[22]

It was, however, a fragile Republic, with more than a few similarities to Bolívar's abortive Gran Colombia. It had no purchase on the Muslim southwest; parts of the Visayas seemed likely to go their own independent way; and even in Luzon, mestizo leadership was contested by a variety of religious visionaries and peasant populists carrying on the tradition of Bonifacio's radicalism.[23] Moreover, the mestizo generals themselves (who included the grandfathers of both Ferdinand Marcos and Benigno Aquino, Jr.) began to follow the pattern of their American forebears, by setting themselves up as independent caudillos. Had it not been for William McKinley, one might almost say, the Philippines in early twentieth century could have fractured into three weak, caudillo-ridden states with the internal politics of nineteenth-century Venezuela or Ecuador.

But the McKinley Administration, egged on by William Randolph Hearst, went to war with Spain in April 1898, claiming sympathy with Filipino (and Cuban) revolutionaries. A week later Admiral Dewey destroyed the Spanish fleet in Manila Bay; and by the Treaty of Paris signed in December, the Philippines was ceded to the Americans. From that point, "pacification" replaced "sympathy." By 1901 Aguinaldo had surrendered, with most other caciques following suit, though peasant resistance continued in some areas until 1910.

U.S. Colonization and the National Oligarchy

The American colonization changed everything.[24] In the first place, it ensured the political unification of the archipelago by smashing, often with great brutality, all opposition.[25] (Even the Muslim areas, which Spain had never wholly subdued, were fully subjected to Manila, thereby probably losing their last chance at sovereign independence.) Secondly, it vastly improved the economic position of the mestizos. The American regime decided to expropriate much (about 400,000 acres) of the rich agricultural land hitherto held by the Orders, and to put it up for public auction. The mestizos, well-off hacendados even in late Spanish times, were the group with the money and the interest to take advantage of this opportunity, and most of the former ecclesiastical property fell into their hands. Still more important, after 1909, by the terms of the Payne-Aldrich Act, the Philippines were enclosed within the American tariff wall, so that their agricultural exports had easy, untaxed access to the world's largest national market—where, in addition, prices, especially for sugar, were often well above world norms.

But it was above all the political innovations of the Americans that created a solid, visible "national oligarchy." The key institutional change was the stage-by-stage creation of a Congress-style bicameral legislature, based, in the lower house at least, on single-district, winner-take-all elections.[26] The new representational system proved perfectly adapted to the ambitions and social geography of the mestizo *nouveaux riches*. Their economic base lay in hacienda agriculture, not in the capital city. And their provincial fiefdoms were also protected by the country's immense linguistic diversity. They might all speak the elite, "national" language (Spanish, later American), but they also spoke variously Tagalog, Ilocano, Pampango, Cebuano, Ilongo, and a dozen other tongues. In this way competition in any given electoral district was effectively limited, in a pre-television age, to a handful of rival local caciques. But Congress, which thus offered them guaranteed access to national-level political power, also brought them together in the capital on a regular basis. There, more than at any previous time, they got to know one another well in a civilized "ring" sternly refereed by the Americans. They might dislike one another, but they went to the same receptions, attended the same churches, lived in the same residential areas, shopped in the same fashionable streets, had affairs with each other's wives, and arranged marriages between each other's children. They were for the first time forming a self-conscious *ruling* class.[27]

The timing of American colonization also had a profound formative influence on the emerging oligarchy and its style of rule. The America of 1900-1930 was the America of Woodrow Wilson's lamented "congressional government." The metropole had no powerful centralized professional bureaucracy; office was still heavily a matter of political patronage; corrupt urban machines and venal court-house rural cliques were still pervasive; and the authority of presidents, except in time of war, was still restricted. Hence, unlike all the other modern colonial regimes in twentieth-century Southeast Asia, which operated through huge, autocratic, white-run bureaucracies, the American authorities in Manila, once assured of the mestizos' self-interested loyalty to the motherland, created only a minimal civil service, and quickly turned over most of its component positions to the natives. In 1903, Filipinos held just under half of the 5,500 or so positions in this civil service. By the end of the "Filipinizing" governor-generalship of (Democrat) Francis Harrison in 1921, the proportion had risen to 90 per cent (out of a mere 14,000 jobs); and by the mid-thirties Americans held only 1 percent of civilian bureaucratic posts, most of them in the educational field.[28] (American power depended on military dominance and the tariff.) As in the United States, civil servants frequently owed their employment to legislator patrons, and up to the end of the American era the civilian machinery of state remained weak and divided.

The new oligarchs quickly understood how the congressional system could serve to increase their power. As early as Harrison's time, the Americans acquiesced in the plundering of the Central Bank of the Philippines. House Speaker Sergio Osmeña, Sr., and his friends helped themselves to huge, virtually free loans for financing the construction of sugar centrals, and cheerfully ignored the subsequent bankrupting of the bank of issue. In a more general sense, congressional control of the purse, and of senior judicial appointments, taught the oligarchy that the "rule of law," provided it made and managed this law, was the firmest *general* guarantee of its property and political hegemony. (As we shall see, it was Marcos's suspension of the "rule of law" that aroused the alarm and hostility of significant portions of the oligarchy in the 1970s and early 1980s.)

One final feature of the American political system is worth emphasizing: the huge proliferation of provincial and local elective offices—in the absence of an autocratic territorial bureaucracy. From very early on mestizo caciques understood that these offices, in the right hands, could consolidate their local political fiefdoms. Not unexpectedly, the right hands were those of family and friends. Brothers, uncles, and cousins for the senior posts, sons, and nephews for the junior ones.[29] Here is the origin of the "political dynasties"—among them the Aquinos and Cojuangcos—which make Filipino politics so spectacularly different from those of any other country in Southeast Asia.

Those were palmy days. But after 1930 the clouds began to gather. As the Depression struck the United States, Washington came under increasing pressure from trade unions and farm organizations (who opposed the influx of Filipino labor and agricultural products) to impose independence on the colony. Though the caciques could not decently say so in public, independence was the last thing they desired, precisely because it threatened the source of their huge wealth: access to the American market. Besides, they had now switched from Spanish to English, and their children were going to school in Manhattan and Boston. And they lacked the monarchical residues which, suitably transformed, underpinned the imagined 'national traditions' of Khmer, Burmese, and Indonesians: the mestizos had no Angkor, Pagan, or Borobudur at their service. It was thus with real reluctance that in 1935 they accepted commonwealth status. The one evident plus was the initiation of a Filipino chief executive. The urbane, rascally mestizo Manuel Quezon became Commonwealth president.[30]

The Japanese Occupation and After

Six years later, in December 1941, the armies of Imperial Japan struck south. In a matter of weeks most of the Americans were sent packing, including General Douglas MacArthur, who carted President Quezon and Vice-President Osmeña along with him.[31] The rest of the oligarchy (one of two celebrated exceptions aside) bustled to collaborate with the invaders. Among the most prominent of these collaborators were Corazon Aquino's father-in-law (who became speaker of the occupation assembly and director-general of the pro-Japanese "mass organization" Kalibapi) and the father of her vice-president (Don José Laurel, Sr., who in 1943 became president of the puppet republic then inaugurated by Tokyo).[32]

But collaboration could do nothing to save the hacienda-based export economy. Japan would permit no exports to America, and American bombers and warships ensured, after 1942, that few crops would reach Japan. The treasured "rule of law" began to break down as anti-Japanese guerrilla bands, sometimes led by the small Socialist and Communist parties, expanded in the remoter rural areas, as inflation soared, and as Japanese exactions increased. Former tenants and landless laborers were emboldened to squat on hacienda lands and grow, not sugar, but crops needed for their everyday survival. Many refused now to pay the old brutal rents, and had the insolence to threaten the bailiffs who demanded them. Above all in the Central Luzon of the Cojuangcos and Aquinos, where rural poverty and exploitation were most acute, such peasants joined hands with the guerrillas in forming the Hukbalahap armies which harassed the Japanese and assassinated such collaborators as they could reach.[33] Unsurprisingly, many of the oligarchs abandoned their haciendas to their unlucky bailiffs and retreated to Manila, where they turned their experienced hands to war-profiteering.[34]

One might have expected the returning Americans to punish the oligarchs for their collaboration with the enemy. Senior officials in Washington indeed made noises to this effect. But the on-the-spot Liberator was, of course, MacArthur, who had close personal and business ties with the prewar oligarchy, and who, like Lyautey in Morocco, enjoyed playing lordly proconsul to native houseboys.[35] Quezon having meanwhile met his incautious Maker, MacArthur in 1946 arranged the election of his old mestizo friend (and prominent collaborator) Manuel Roxas as first president of the now sovereign Republic of the Philippines.[36]

Roxas had only two years in power before he joined Quezon, but they were exceptionally productive years. An amnesty was arranged for all "political prisoners" (mainly fellow-oligarchs held on charges of collaboration). In 1947, an agreement was signed permitting the U.S. to retain control of its twenty-three (large and small) land, sea, and airbases for a further ninety-nine years (this was what, as in 1900, most mattered to Washington).[37] And the Constitution of 1935 was so amended as to give American citizens 'parity' access to the resources of the newly sovereign Republic (in return for which the oligarchy was granted continuing access, for a defined period, to the protected American market).[38] There was an additional bonus in this move, since it guaranteed activation for the Philippines of the Tydings Rehabilitation Act, which offered $620,000,000 to those Americans and Filipinos who could demonstrate that they had lost a minimum of $500 as a result of the war.[39] (Since the average annual per capita income of Filipinos was then a quarter of this sum, the major Filipino beneficiaries of Senator Tydings' generosity were the caciques.)

The next aim was to restore fully the pre-war agrarian and political order. For three basic reasons this goal proved difficult to achieve. First was the price of independence itself: removal of the American ringmaster for domestic political competition, severe weakening of the state's capacity for centralized deployment of violence,[40] a fisc no longer externally guaranteed, and a war-ravaged and near-bankrupt economy. Second was the appearance, in Central Luzon at least, of an emboldened peasantry backed by armed Hukbalahap forces, which, denied access to constitutional participation by Roxas's maneuvers, had little reason to make accommodations. Third was a rapid expansion of the suffrage that UN membership, in those innocent days, made it impossible to deny.

The Heyday of Cacique Democracy

Hence it was that in the last year of Roxas's life the Philippines saw the first conspicuous appearance of the country's now notorious "private armies." Drawn from lumpen elements in both Manila and the countryside, these armed gangs, financed by their hacendado masters, terrorized illegal squatters, peasant unions, and left-wing political leaders, with the aim of restoring uncontested cacique rule.[41] The term "warlord" entered the contemporary Filipino political vocabulary. Unsurprisingly the new warlords found that their private armies were also highly functional for a now unrefereed electoral politics. The presidential elections of 1949, won by Roxas's vice-presidential successor Elpidio Quirino,[42] were not merely corrupt in the pre-war style, but also extremely bloody and fraudulent: not so much because of central management, as because of the discrepancy between state power and cacique ambitions under conditions of popular suffrage and acute class antagonism.[43] (Characteristic of the time was what Nick Joaquín, the country's best-known writer, called the "bloody fiefdom" of the Lacson dynasty in the sugar-planter paradise of Western Negros. Manila was virtually impotent vis-à-vis Governor Rafael Lacson's murderous "special police" and "civilian guards.")[44]

This was not what the Americans had bargained for. Besides, China had just been "lost," Vietnam seemed likely to go the same way, and major Communist insurrections had broken out in neighboring Malaya and Burma. Colonel Edward Lansdale was dispatched to restore order through the agency of Quirino's secretary of defense, Ramon Magsaysay, one of the few prominent politicians of the era who did not have cacique origins. Thanks to a mere million dollars in military and other aid, the physical isolation of the Philippines, the restricted Luzon base of the Hukbalahap, and the errors of the Huk leaders themselves,[45] Lansdale prevailed. By 1954, the Huk rebellion had been crushed, thousands of impoverished Luzon peasants transmigrated to "empty" Mindanao[46] (where they soon came into violent conflict with the local Muslims), and Magsaysay maneuvered into the presidency.[47]

The period 1954-1972 can be regarded as the full heyday of cacique democracy in the Philippines.[48] The oligarchy faced no serious domestic challenges. Access to the American market was declining as post-independence tariff barriers slowly rose, but this setback was compensated for by full access to the state's financial instrumentalities. Under the guise of promoting economic independence and import-substitution industrialization, exchange rates were manipulated, monopolistic licenses parcelled out, huge, cheap, often unrepaid bank loans passed around, and the national budget frittered away in pork barrel legislation.[49] Some of the more enterprising dynasties diversified into urban real estate, hotels, utilities, insurance, the mass media, and so forth. The press, owned by rival cacique families, was famously free.[50] The reconsolidated, but decentralized, power of the oligarchy is nicely demonstrated by the fact that this press exposed every possible form of corruption and abuse of power (except for those of each paper's own proprietors), but, in the words of historian and political scientist Onofre Corpuz: "Nobody in the Philippines has ever heard of a successful prosecution for graft."[51] It was in these golden times that Corazon Aquino's father, Don José Cojuangco, acquired 7,000 hectares of the 10,300 hectare Hacienda Luisita in Tarlac, and turned its management over to his energetic son-in-law Benigno 'Ninoy' Aquino, Jr.[52]

But cacique democracy contained within itself the seeds of its own decay, and these began visibly sprouting towards the end of the 1960s. Uncontrolled and parasitic plundering of state and private resources tilted the Philippines on its long plunge from being the most "advanced" capitalist society in Southeast Asia in the 1950s to being the most depressed and indigent in the 1980s. By the end of the golden era, five percent of the country's income earners received, probably, about 50 percent of total income. At the same time, over 70 percent of state revenues came from regressive sales and excise taxes, and a mere 27.5 percent from income taxes—largely paid by foreign corporations.[53] Combined with a characteristically tropical-Catholic birthrate of over 3 percent (which since 1850 had increased the islands' population eightfold), the result was a massive pauperization of the unprivileged. [54]

Ferdinand Marcos: The Supreme Cacique

Cacique democracy in the independent Philippines also led to secular changes in the operation of the political system. The oligarchs more and more followed Chairman Mao's advice to walk on two legs. Manila was where the president resided and where Congress met, where pork barrel funds were dealt out, where licenses and loans were secured, where educational institutions proliferated, and where imported entertainments flourished. The dynasts began leaving their haciendas in the hands of sons-in-law and bailiffs and moving into palatial new residential complexes on the outskirts of the old capital. Forbes Park was the first, and still the most celebrated, of these *beaux quartiers*, which remain sociologically unique in Southeast Asia. Elsewhere in the region luxurious houses are jumbled together with the dwellings of the poor.[55] But the golden ghetto of Forbes Park was policed, as a complex, by armed security guards; access even to its streets required the production of identification papers.

This partial move to Manila combined with demographic increase and the postwar expansion of the suffrage to monetarize political life. It was less and less possible to win elections, even provincial elections, on a forelock-tugging basis. The costs of campaigning increased exponentially in the 1960s, not least because the period saw the renewed growth of the private armies. In contrast to the late 1940s, these armed groups were now deployed mainly in intra-oligarchy competition.[56] Corazon Aquino's husband was conforming to general practice in the late 1960s when he campaigned for a senatorial seat in a black Mercedes ringed with Armalite-toting bodyguards.[57] With splendid, grumbling insouciance, Senator Sergio 'Serging' Osmeña, Jr., on losing the 1969 presidential race to Ferdinand Marcos, complained: "We were outgunned, outgooned, and outgold."[58] By then, at forty per hundred thousand head of population, the Philippines had one of the highest murder rates in the world.

So the stakes slowly grew, and American-era inhibitions slackened. The crux was the presidency, which always had the potentiality of dislocating cacique democracy. We noted earlier that the stability of the system, and the solidarity of the oligarchy, depended on the Congress, which offered roughly equal room at the top for all the competing provincial dynasties. The one-man office of president was not, however, divisible, and came to seem, in the era of independence, a unique prize. The shrewder, older oligarchs had foreseen possible trouble and had borrowed from the U.S. the legal provision that no president could serve for more than two terms—so that the office could sedately circulate within the charmed circle. But it was only a matter of time before someone would break the rules and try to set himself up as Supreme Cacique for Life. The spread of military juntas and one-party dictatorial regimes throughout the Third World in the 1960s made a break of this kind seem more normal: indeed it could even be justified opportunistically as a sign of liberation from "Western" ideological shackles.

The final destabilizing factor was education. As noted earlier, in Spanish times educational facilities were extremely limited, and the only "national" language available was Spanish, to which, however, no more than five percent of the indigenous population had access. Secular, twentieth-century American imperialism was a different sort of beast. Immensely confident of Anglo-Saxon world hegemony and the place of English as the language of capitalism and modernity, the colonial regime effortlessly extruded Spanish[59] and so expanded an English-language school system that by 1940 the Philippines had the highest literacy rate in Southeast Asia.[60] After independence, the oligarchy, like other Third World oligarchies, found that the simplest way of establishing its nationalist credentials was to expand cheap schooling. By the early 1960s university degrees were no longer a ruling class near-monopoly.

The huge expansion of English-language education produced three distinct, politically significant, new social groups. Smallest was a radical intelligentsia, largely of bourgeois and petty-bourgeois urban origins, and typically graduates of the University of the Philippines. Among them was Nur Misuari, who in the later 1960s formed the Moro National Liberation Front in the Muslim southwest. Still better known was José Maria Sison, who broke away from the decrepit post-Huk Communist party to form his own, and, borrowing from the Great Helmsman, founded the New People's Army which was, until recently, a nationwide presence and the major antagonist of the oligarchy.[61] (The spread of English, and, later, of "street Tagalog," in nationalist response to American hegemony, has made possible an archipelago-wide *popular* communication—below the oligarchy—that was inconceivable in the era of Bonifacio or the Hukbalahap.)

Next largest in size was a *bien-pensant* proto-technocracy, which also included graduates from American universities. Drawn from much the same social strata as the radical intelligentsia, it was enraged less by the injustices of cacique democracy than by its dilettantism, venality, and technological backwardness. This group also deeply resented its own powerlessness. When Marcos eventually declared Martial Law in 1972 and proclaimed his New Democracy, it flocked to his standard, believing its historic moment had come. It stayed loyal to him till the early 1980s, and long remained crucial to his credibility with Washington planners, the World Bank and the IMF, and foreign modernizers all and sundry.

Largest of all—if not that large—was a wider urban bourgeois and petty-bourgeois constituency: middle-level civil servants, doctors, nurses, teachers, businessmen, shopkeepers, and so on. In its political and moral outlook it can perhaps be compared with the Progressives (definitely not the Populists) of the United States in the period 1890-

1920. In the 1960s it made its political debut in campaigns for honesty-in-government, urban renewal, crackdowns on machine and warlord politics, and the legal emancipation of municipalities and the new suburbs. As might be expected, this group was both anti-oligarchy and anti-popular in orientation. Had it not been English-educated, and had not President Kennedy secured a major change in American immigration laws, it might have played a key role in Philippine politics in the 1970s and 1980s. But these factors offered it enticing alternatives, such that, by the mid-1980s, well over a million Filipinos (mainly from this stratum) had emigrated across the Pacific, most of them for good.[62] This bourgeois hemorrhage in the short run weakened a significant political competitor for the oligarchy, but in the longer run cost it an important political ally—one reason why the Aquino government has so little room for maneuver.

The Marcos regime, which began to entrench itself long before the declaration of Martial Law in 1972, was an instructively complex hybrid.[63] From one point of view, Don Ferdinand can be seen as the Master Cacique or Master Warlord, in that he pushed the destructive logic of the old order to its natural conclusion. In place of dozens of privatized "security guards," a single privatized National Constabulary; in place of personal armies, a personal Army; instead of pliable local judges, a client Supreme Court; instead of a myriad pocket and rotten boroughs, a pocket or rotten country, managed by cronies, hitmen, and flunkies.

But from another viewpoint, he was an original; partly because he was highly intelligent, partly because, like his grotesque wife, he came from the lower fringes of the oligarchy. In any case, he was the first elite Filipino politician who saw the possibilities of reversing the traditional flow of power. All his predecessors had lived out the genealogy of mestizo supremacy—from private wealth to state power, from provincial bossism to national hegemony. But almost from the beginning of his presidency in 1965, Marcos had moved mentally out of the nineteenth century, and understood that in our time wealth serves power, and that the key card is the state. Manila's Louis Napoléon.

Marcos Settles In

He started with the Army, which until then had been politically insignificant.[64] The size of the armed forces was rapidly increased, the amplitude of its budget multiplied, and its key posts allotted to officers from the Ilocano-speaking northwestern Luzon from which Marcos himself originated. The final decision to declare martial law, for which plans had been prepared months in advance, was taken in concert with the military high command—Corazon's cousin Eduardo 'Danding' Cojuangco and Defense Secretary Juan 'Johnny' Ponce Enrile being the only civilian co-conspirators.[65] The civil service followed, particularly that ambitious sector identified earlier as candidate-technocrats. The state would save the country from what Marcos identified as its prime enemies—the Communists and the oligarchy.

Marcos exploited state, rather than hacienda, power in two other instructive ways. The first was to deal with the Americans, the second with his fellow-oligarchs.

He understood, more clearly than anyone else—including the Filipino Left—that for Washington the Philippines were like Cyprus for London. The huge bases at Subic and Clark Field had nothing to do with the defense of the Philippines as such, and everything to do with maintaining American imperial power along the Pacific Rim. It followed that Manila should treat them as luxury properties, for the leasing of which ever more exorbitant rentals could be charged.[66] So too the Philippine Army. Raymond Bonner's book, *Waltzing with a Dictator*, amply documents how Marcos, at considerable personal profit, rented a (noncombattant) army engineering battalion to Lyndon Johnson, who in 1965 was busy hiring Asian mercenaries to bolster the "international crusade" image desired for the American intervention in Vietnam. Next to the South Koreans, he got, mercenary for mercenary, the best price in Asia. (In this effort he had considerable help from his egregious wife, who splashed her way into high-level Washington circles in a way that no Dragon Lady had done since the shimmering days of Madame Chiang Kai-shek.[67]) But he also had the imaginative insolence to try to do to the Americans what they had so long been accustomed to doing to the Filipinos. According to Bonner, Marcos contributed a million dollars to each of Richard Nixon's presidential election campaigns—with, of course, "state money"—thereby joining that select group of Third World tyrants (Chiang Kai-shek, Pak Chung Hee, Reza Pahlavi, Rafael Trujillo, and Anastasio Somoza) who played an active role in the politics of the metropole.[68]

As far as the oligarchy was concerned, Marcos went straight for its jugular—the "rule of law." From the very earliest days, Marcos used his plenary Martial Law powers to advise all oligarchs who dreamed of opposing or supplanting him that property was not power, since at a stroke of the martial pen it ceased to be property.[69] The Lopez dynasty (based in Iloilo) was abruptly deprived of its mass media empire and its control of Manila's main supplier of electricity.[70] The 500 hectare Hacienda Osmeña was put up for "land-reform" somewhat later on.[71] There was no recourse, since the judiciary was fully cowed and the legislature packed with allies and hangers-on. But Marcos had no interest in upsetting the established social order. Those oligarchs who bent with the wind and eschewed politics for the pursuit of gain were mostly left undisturbed. The notorious "cronies" were, sociologically, a mixed bag, including not only relatives of Ferdinand and Imelda, but favored oligarchs and quite a few "new men."

At its outset, the Martial Law regime had a substantial, if restricted, social base. Its anti-Communist, "reformist," "modernizing," and "law and order" rhetoric attracted the support of frustrated would-be technocrats, much of the underempowered urban middle class, and even sectors of the peasantry and urban poor. Shortly after winning absolute power he announced that the state had seized no less than 500,000 guns from private hands, raising hopes of a less visibly dangerous public life.[72] A limited land-reform succeeded in creating, in the old Huk stamping-grounds of Central Luzon, a new stratum of peasant-owners.[73] But as time passed, and the greed and violence of the regime became ever more evident, much of this support dried up. By the later 1970s the technocrats were a spent force, and the urban middle class became increasingly aware of the decay of Manila, the devastation of the university system, the abject and ridiculous character of the monopolized mass media, and the country's economic decline.

The real beneficiaries of the regime—aside from the Marcos mafia itself[74]—were two military forces: the National Army and the New People's Army. Martial Law in itself gave the former unprecedented power. But Marcos also used favored officers to manage properties confiscated from his enemies, public corporations, townships, and so forth. The upper-echelon officers came to live in a style to which only the oligarchy had hitherto been accustomed.[75] Military intelligence became the regime's beady eyes and hidden ears. Legal restraints on military abuses simply disappeared. And there was only one master now to determine postings and promotions. To be sure, the Old Cacique packed the leadership with pliant placement from his Ilocano-speaking homeland, but there was still plenty to go round.

On the other hand, the dictatorship encouraged a rapid growth, and slower geographic spread, of the Communist guerrilla forces. No less significant than their expanding rural support was their organized reach into urban areas. One of the most striking features of the last years of the regime was the gradual adoption of a nationalist-Marxist vocabulary by notable sections of the bourgeois intelligentsia, the lower echelons of the Church hierarchy, and the middle class more generally.[76] Only the militant Left appeared to offer some way out.

The story of the unraveling of the regime following the brazen assassination of Benigno Aquino, Jr., at Manila's airport on 21 August 1983 is too well known to need detailing here. More important is an understanding of the regime that has replaced it.

Riding the 'People Power Revolution'

The initial coalition behind the dead man's widow was wide and (variably) deep: she was then above all Corazon Aquino rather than Corazon Cojuangco. It was based on a huge groundswell of revulsion against the Old Cacique and his *manileña* Miss Piggy. It included, from the right, ambitious middle-ranking and junior officers of the National Army, frustrated finally by the old regime's visible decay and the ethnic nepotism of its premier danseur; the ever-hopeful technocracy and the non-crony segments of Manila's business community; almost all factions of the Church; the middle class; the non-

NPA sectors of the intelligentsia; sundry self-described "cause-oriented groups" which regarded themselves as the vanguard of a newly-legal Left; and the oligarchs.

The coalition was far too diverse and incoherent to last very long. Two years after the "People Power Revolution," it has become far narrower and, as it were, more densely packed. First to go were its right and left wings. For the cowboy activists of the Reform the Armed Forces Movement (RAM), who had played a pivotal role in February 1986 by betraying Marcos, the only genuinely tolerable successor to the old regime was a military junta, or a military-dominated government under their leadership. But this course had no serious domestic support, and was, for a Washington basking in Port au Prince TV glory, in any case out of the question. Besides, cold-eyed realists in the Reagan Administration perfectly understood that the Philippine military was far too factionalized, incompetent, corrupt, vainglorious, and ill-trained to be given any blank cheques.[77] A series of risible brouhahas, culminating in the Gregorio ('Gringo') Honasan coup de force of 28 August 1987, only confirmed the soundness of this judgment. On the left, the situation was more complex. Far the most powerful component within it was the NPA, which had greatly benefited from the Martial Law regime, and had now to decide how to respond to the new constellation of forces. The issue of whether frontally to oppose the Aquino regime, or try substantially to alter its internal equilibrium, was seriously debated in 1986-87. For a complex of reasons, too intricate to detain us here, and the wisdom of which is yet to be determined, the die was cast, early in 1987, for confrontation.[78] The immediate consequence was the collapse of the legal Left, and the manifest enfeeblement of the "cause-oriented groups," which, by the time of the Honasan comedy, had lost almost everything but their causes. Out of these developments emerged the real, unbalanced, and uneasy partners of the contemporary Aquino coalition: the oligarchy, the urban middle class, and the Church.

During the new regime's first year, when the elan of the "People Power Revolution" remained quite strong, the coalition's junior partners were optimistic. The restoration of an open-market press, greatly expanded freedom for assembly and organization, and the crumbling of the crony monopolies and monopsonies, filled the various sectors of the middle class with giddy exhilaration. They could be fully themselves once again. Business confidence would be restored and the Philippines rerouted onto the path of progress. Good Americans were on their side. Honest technocratic expertise would at last be properly appreciated and rewarded. The intelligentsia (or at least major parts of it) now felt free to detach itself from the radical Left; it had a new home on television and radio, and in the press.

Furthermore, President Aquino's inner circle included not only Cardinal Sin but a number of idealistic human-rights lawyers and left-liberal journalists and academics. And Corazon herself, perhaps taking a leaf out of the Book of Modern Kings, made every effort to appear in public *en bonne bourgeoise*. Tita ('Auntie') as she was now called, was a brave, pious, unpretentious housewife who wanted only what was best for her nephews and nieces. The treasurer of Don José Cojuangco's holding company and the coheiress of Hacienda Luisita remained mostly invisible. There was a touching confidence that the country's problems were on their way to sensible solution. She had opened talks with the NPA and with the Muslim insurrectionaries. A major land-reform—which would not affect the middle class, but which promised to undermine the NPA's expanding rural base—would be enacted. The Americans would provide substantial sums in support of restored constitutional democracy. And People Power would, through free and honest elections, create a progressive legislative partner for the President, giving the middle class its long-dreamed-of chance to lead the country. In substantial measure the ecclesiastical leadership shared these hopes, trusting that the new situation would permit the Church to become once again ideologically united and organizationally disciplined.[79] The catchword of the era was "democratic space," which is perhaps most aptly translated as "middle class room for maneuver between the military, the oligarchy, and the Communists."

The second year of the new regime dashed most of these illusions. The talks with Muslim and Communist leaders broke down for essentially the same reason: the Aquino regime found itself in no position to make any attractive concessions. Haunted by nationalist dreams, even those Muslim leaders who seemed prepared to accept "autonomy," rather than independence, still demanded a Muslim autonomous zone remembered from the American colonial era. Yet ever since the Lansdale-Magsaysay regime had begun transmigrating potential and actual Hukbalahap peasant supporters to "empty" lands in Mindanao, the island had been rapidly "Christianized," by spontaneous migrants, land speculators, logging and mining conglomerates, large-scale commercial agribusinesses, and so on. Even had it wished—which it did not—to accede to Muslim dreams, this would have required the Aquino government either forcibly to relocate these tens, if not hundreds, of thousands of "Christians" (but where to?) or to leave them to the political mercies of justifiably angry Muslims. It lived by its own American-era dreams—a United Philippines—and besides, the Army, which had suffered far more severe casualties fighting the Muslims than combatting the Communists, would not have stood for "weakness." With the NPA the same was true. There was nothing President Aquino could offer the Communists which they did not already have or which the Army would be likely to permit.[80]

Nor were the Americans much help. The Reagan Administration was preoccupied with its own survival, and a dozen 'more important' foreign policy tar-babies. Its own financial recklessness meant that it had now very little to offer the Philippines even in military aid (which remained a pittance, more or less what it wished to give the Nicaraguan "contras"). Talk of a "Marshall Plan" for the Philippines vanished with the noise of escaping steam. And the overseas middle class stayed put. Its members might periodically return home with armfuls of presents for the relatives, but they had decided that the future of the bourgeoisie in the Philippines was too uncertain to be worth any substantial investments.[81] In the first year of the regime there had been much bold talk of liquidating the American bases, but by the second it was already clear that they would stay put: the Aquino government felt it could not afford seriously to antagonize Washington, and besides, it could not contemplate the loss in income and jobs that closure would imply. (In the 1980s, the U.S. military was still the second largest employer—after the Filipino state—in the country.) The one important service the Americans did provide was explicit political support in the face of the various *buffa* coup attempts that anticlimaxed in the 'Gringo' ringer of August 1987.

The pivotal issue for the regime coalition was, however, the "restoration of democracy," signalled by the 11 May 1987 elections for a reanimated Senate and House of Representatives, and the 18 January 1988 elections for provincial governors, mayors and other local power-holders. The middle-class hope was that these elections would not only set the provisional Aquino government on a firm constitutional base, but would forcefully demonstrate to the Army and the Communists where the popular will lay. Moreover, it would translate People's Power into sufficient institutional power to carry out the domestic reforms deemed essential to the future leadership prospects of the middle class.

The Caciques Claim Their Own

It was now and here that the senior partners in the ruling coalition finally made themselves felt. During the first year the oligarchy had had its uneasy moments. Corazon herself might be sound enough, but some of her closest advisers were not; the mass media, for the moment still dominated ideologically by middle-class urban reformists, kept up a constant drumfire in favor of a land-reform that hopefully would destroy the basis of NPA rural power. Even the World Bank, along with senior Japanese and American officials, was arguing the same logic. And, pending the elections, the president held plenary powers. Who could be sure that in a moment of frailty she might not do something fatal?

The alarm was real, if probably ill-founded. COLOR (Council of Landowners for Orderly Reform—500 magnate members) was hastily established; it sent Corazon resolutions signed with (happily, its own) blood, threatening civil disobedience in the event of serious land-reform. A Movement for an Independent (Sugar) Negros appeared, claiming to be ready to offer armed resistance to impending Manilan injustice.[82] Lawyers were said, by the press, to be "going crazy," reclassifying agricultural lands as "commercial-industrial," signing off surplus plots to infant relatives, fraudulently antedating mortgages, etc.[83]

What was needed in 1986, as in 1916 and 1946, was cacique democracy. If elections could be promptly and freely held, the oligarchy could hope to return to its pre-1972 control of "the rule of law," and put everyone—the middle class, the military, their tenants, and the "rabble"—in their respective places.

On 11 May 1987, national-level elections were held for twenty-four senatorial, and two hundred congressional seats. The outcome turned out to be eminently satisfactory. To quote a well-informed Filipino study: 'Out of 200 House Representatives, 130 belong to the so-called "traditional political families," while another 39 are relatives of these families. *Only 31 congressmen have no electoral record prior to 1971* and are not related to these old dominant families . . . Of the 24 elected senators, there are a few non-traditional figures but the cast is largely made up of *members of prominent pre-1972 political families.*'[84] Newly-elected Senator John Osmeña—grandson of Commonwealth vice-president Sergio Osmeña, Sr., and nephew of defeated 1969 presidential candidate Sergio Osmeña, Jr.—told the press: "One member of the family who does not do good is one too many, but 10 members in the family doing good are not even enough."[85]

The results were widely interpreted as a triumph for Corazon Aquino in so far as 23 of the 24 victorious senatorial candidates ran as her supporters and as members of various nominal parties in her electoral coalition.[86] Something comparable occurred in the Lower House.[87] But probably the outcome is better designated as a triumph for Corazon Cojuangco. The study quoted above notes that: "Of the 169 representatives who belong to the dominant families or are related to them, 102 are identified with the pre-1986 anti-Marcos forces, while 67 are from pro-Marcos *parties or families.*" A shake in the kaleidoscope of oligarchic power.

Not that the shrewder caciques failed to recognize certain new realities, including the genuine popular appeal of the President herself. (A significant number of Marcos collaborators swung over to her bandwagon.) When Congress finally opened in the late summer of 1987, it proclaimed itself committed to land reform, and appointed 'outsiders' to the chairmanships of the Senate and House committees in charge of agrarian affairs. But within days the chairman of the House Committee on Agrarian Reform, Representative Bonifacio Gillego, an ex-military intelligence official converted to "social democracy," was bemoaning the fact that seventeen of the twenty-one members of his committee were landlords—including presidential brother José

Cojuangco, presidential uncle-in-law Herminio Aquino, and the virago of Negros, Hortensia Starke.[88]

A fuller revival of the ancient regime came with the provincial and local elections which opened on 18 January 1988, and which found 150,000 candidates competing, *a l'américaine*, for close to 16,500 positions—an average of nine aspirants per plum.[89] These elections were of such an exemplary character that they deserve comment in their own right. In some places they represented happy reconsolidations. On the island of Cebu, for example, Emilio 'Lito' Osmeña, brother of Senator John, won the island's governorship, while his cousin Tomas ('Tommy'), son of Sergio 'Serging' Osmeña, Jr., defeated a candidate from the rival mestizo Cuen-*co* dynasty to become mayor of Cebu City.[90] A little to the north, in the fiefdom of the Duranos, the eighty-two-year-old Ramon Durano, Sr., ran successfully for mayor of Danao City, with the backing of one violent son, Jesus 'Don' Durano, against the opposition of another. The night after the election, losing candidate Thaddeus 'Deo' Durano, waylaid by intra-family assassins, ended up in critical condition in a Cebu City emergency ward.[91] The old warlord, who for the duration of Martial Law was a key Marcos henchman on Cebu, this time ran on the ticket of the PDP-Laban, the machine of President Aquino's brother José Cojuangco—who successfully recruited many other Marcos caciques under his sister's banner. Similar victories occurred in Olongapo—downtown from the Subic Naval Base—where Richard Gordon, husband of Congresswoman Katharine Gordon, became mayor; in Western Negros, where Congressman José Carlos Lacson was now joined by governor-elect Daniel Lacson, Jr.; and so on. . . .

Not that the old dynasties had things entirely their own way by any means. In some areas close to metropolitan Manila, middle-class reformists mobilized popular elements as well as "minor" dynasties to break up old fiefdoms. The Laurel machine in Batangas collapsed, to the embarrassment of the ineptly scheming vice-president, Salvador 'Doy' Laurel. The Rizal empire of Corazon's uncle, Congressman Juan 'Komong' Sumulong, was decimated. In Pampanga, out went the Nepomucenos, Lazatins, and Lingads. In the Iloilo fiefdom of the Lopezes, Olive Lopez-Padilla, daughter of one-time Vice-President Fernando Lopez and sister of Congressman Albertito Lopez, ran for governor on the wonderful vulgarian-hacendado slogan of "Bring Iloilo back to the Lopezes," but was nonetheless soundly thrashed.[92] In Mindanao's Cagayan de Oro, the Fortich dynasty, described by *The Manila Bulletin* as having run the place "since the beginning of the century," was humiliated.[93] No less interesting were certain military participations. In the Cagayan valley of northeastern Luzon, ex-Lieutenant-Colonel Rodolfo Aguinaldo, a key member of the Honasan rebel group, out-intimidated the local caciques (Dupayas and Tuzons) to seize the governorship. In Marcos's old base in Northern Ilocos, the vice-governorship was won, from military prison, by ex-Colonel Z—once the dreaded chief of the Metropolitan Command Intelligence Security Group under Marcos, a thug widely suspected of helping to mastermind the assassination of Corazon's husband, and a major participant in the abortive coups of January and April 1987.[94]

Even the NPA was indirectly drawn in. It was widely, and credibly, reported that in many areas where it had politico-military ascendancy, the movement charged candidates substantial fees for permission to campaign unmolested, and, here and there, lent unofficial support to sympathetic local aspirants.[95] Not that the civil war seriously let up. A day or two after the polls closed, Hortensia Starke's Hacienda Bino was burned to the ground, and the Hacienda La Purisima of Enrique Rojas, a top official of the National Federation of Sugar Planters, barely escaped the same fate.[96]

Politics in a Well-Run Casino

These variable outcomes need to be viewed in a larger framework for their implications to be well understood. The key facts to be borne in mind are these: No less than 81 percent of the country's 27,600,000 eligible voters voted.[97] One or other elective post was available for every 1,400 voters. The average number of contestants per post was roughly nine. In most places the contests were "serious" in a rather new way—forty-one candidates were assassinated by rivals (*not* the NPA) in the course of the brief campaign.[98] In different ways, and to different extents, almost all political leadership, from right to left, participated and could imagine that they had, up to a certain point, benefited. Everywhere, local patronage machines were replacing the centralized Marcos-era appointive *apparat.*

In any well-run casino, the tables are managed in the statistical favor of the house. To keep drawing customers, the owners must provide them with periodic, even spectacular, successes. A win is a splendid confirmation of the player's skill and heaven's favor. A loss demonstrates his/her misfortune or ineptitude. Either way, it's back to the tables as soon as possible. So with the blackjack of cacique democracy. Each local triumph for reform promises a rentier future; each loss signals miscalculations or ill luck. At the end of the week or the year, however, the dealer is always in the black.

The truth is that American electoralism remains powerfully attractive, even when, perhaps especially when, married to Spanish caciquism in a geographically fragmented, ethnolinguistically divided, and economically bankrupt polity. It disperses power horizontally, while concentrating it vertically; and the former draws a partial veil over the latter. "Anyone" can get elected: look at the high, uncoerced turnout; look at the number of competing candidates (you too can run); look at the execrable colonels (better they campaign in the provinces than plot in the capital); look at the (probably temporary) fall of the Laurels and the Nepomucenos; look at the NPA's electoral levies, which, from a certain angle, can be aligned with the election-time exactions of the warlords.[99] Precisely because the competition is violently real, it is easy to be persuaded to cheer for, as it were, Arsenal or Chelsea, without reflecting too hard on the fact that both are in the First Division, and that one is watching the match from the outer stands, not playing in it.

But, of course, by no means everyone enjoys spectator sports. Shortly after the 18 January 1988 elections a curious reporter went to interview employees at the Cojuangcos' Hacienda Luisita who had just voted massively for Arsenal. What difference had it made to their lives that Tita Cory had become President? "We used to get rice and sugar free, now we must pay. We used to get free water from the pumps in our yards. Now we must pay for pumped-in water because molasses from the sugar mill has seeped into our wells." Daily wages? They had been raised by ₱2.50 ($0.12) for field-hands, and ₱8 ($0.40) for mill-workers. Level of employment? Usually from two to four days a week, in good times. One elderly man spoke of trying to survive by busing to additional work in the neighboring province of Pampanga: transportation costs took ₱23 from the daily wage of ₱40, leaving him a net of ₱17 ($0.85). It still made sense to go. The reporter was told that a worker, who had been quoted in an international magazine as saying that on the hacienda horses ate better than the hands, had been 'summoned' by management. He had had to retract the slander. But one of the interviewees concluded: "Of course it is true. The horses get Australian grain and eggs, while we hardly have the meat."[100] All those interviewed either refused to give their names, or asked not to be identified.

NOTES

1. *Philippine Star Week*, 8-14 March 1987.

2. In July 1987 she estimated that debt payments would consume 40 percent of government revenues and 27 percent of all export earnings for the following six years. The economic growth rate in 1986 was 0.13 percent. *Philippine Daily Inquirer*, 28 July 1987.

3. *Philippine Daily Inquirer*, 12 February 1987; and information kindly supplied by Philippine historian Michael Cullinane. He ran as a candidate of the Progresistas, the most openly American-collaborationist of the parties of that era. The above article implausibly suggests that Melecio's grandfather, a certain 'Martin' Cojuangco, was the real immigrant founder of the dynasty.

4. Emigdio is secretary-general of the Lakas ng Bansa. José 'Peping' Cojuangco is chairman of another main coalition component, the PDP-Laban.

5. *Time*, 5 January 1987.

6. On this stratum the *locus classicus* remains Edgar Wickberg, *The Chinese in Philippine Life, 1850-1898*, New Haven 1965.

7. On the galleon trade, see William L. Schurz, *The Manila Galleon*, reprint edition, New York 1959. Furthermore, responding to pressure from enlightened clerics and officials appalled by the savage extortions of the settlers in the Americas, Madrid attempted to make amends in the Philippines by (fitfully) barring the residence of private Spaniards in the provinces.

8. There is a sizeable literature on the Spanish Philippines, but see especially, James L. Phelan, *The Hispanization of the Philippines: Spanish Aims and Filipino Responses, 1565-1700*, Madison 1959; Nicholas P. Cushner, *Spain in the Philippines: From Conquest to Revolution*, Quezon City 1971; Renato Constantino, *The Philippines: A Past Revisited*, Quezon City 1975, Parts 1 and 2; and the many impressive essays in Alfred W. McCoy and Ed. C. de Jesus, eds., *Philippine Social History: Global Trade and Local Transformations*, Quezon City 1982.

9. Drawing on their experiences in the Iberian peninsula, the Spaniards termed these Southeast Asian Muslims 'Moors' (*'Moros'*). The name has, after four centuries, stuck. Those Muslims today seeking independence from the Philip-

pines are loosely united in what they call the Moro National Liberation Front. The ghost of Felipe II must be amused.

The best historical-anthropological sources on the 'Moros' are: P.G. Gowing, *Muslim-Filipinos—Heritage and Horizon*, Quezon City 1979; Cesar Adib Majul, *Muslims in the Philippines*, Quezon City 1973, and his *The Contemporary Muslim Movement in the Philippines*, Berkeley 1985; and T.J.S. George, *Revolt in Mindanao: The Rise of Islam in Philippine Politics*, Oxford 1980. Important monographs on two of the major ethno-linguistic groups within the Moro People are Thomas Kiefer, *The Tausug: Violence and Law in a Philippine Muslim Society*, New York 1972; and Reynaldo Clemeña Ileto, *Magindanao, 1860-1888: the Career of Dato Uto of Buayan*, Ithaca, N.Y.: Cornell University, Southeast Asia Program Data Paper no. 32, 1971.

10. The standard work is Horacio de la Costa, *The Jesuits in the Philippines, 1581-1768*, Cambridge 1961. But see also Gerald H. Anderson, ed., *Studies in Philippine Church History*, Ithaca, N.Y. 1969; and the brilliantly iconoclastic text of Vicente L. Rafael, *Contracting Colonialism: Translation and Christian Conversion in Tagalog Society under Early Spanish Rule*, Ithaca, N.Y. 1988.

11. In the provincial environs of Manila alone, the clerics had accumulated, by the end of the nineteenth century, over 500,000 acres of land. The basic text on these developments is Dennis Morrow Roth, *The Friar Estates of the Philippines*, Albuquerque 1977.

12. From the Hokkienese *sengli*, meaning "trader." It is a lesson for our nationalistic age that neither the Spaniards nor the Hokkienese could yet imagine "Chinese." In this regard, they lagged far behind the Amsterdam's United East India Company, the giant transnational of the seventeenth century, which devoted intense penal, juridical, and "sumptuary" effort to forcing targeted groups under its power to realize that they were, after all, *Chinees*.

13. The account in this and the following paragraphs is summarized from Wickberg, *The Chinese in Philippine Life*.

14. See David Steinberg, "Tradition and Response" in John Bresnan, ed., *The Marcos Era and Beyond*, Princeton 1986, p. 44. This text also contains important essays by Wilfredo Arce and Ricardo Abad on 'The Social Situation,' and by Bernardo Villegas on 'The Economic Crisis.'

15. *The Manila Chronicle*, 19 July 1987. She went on: "To give up the land is to go against everything you have been taught as a child. It is like changing your religion." Another Dragon Lady, coconut hacendada Congresswoman Maria Clara Lobregat, wailed: "The land has been there for years and years, and you develop

some attachment to it. It's like you have a house with many rooms and you are asked to share the rooms with others."

16. See especially Horacio de la Costa, *The Background of Nationalism and Other Essays*, Manila 1965; John N. Schumacher, *The Propaganda Movement: 1880-1895*, Manila 1973; Cesar Adib Majul, *Political and Constitutional Ideas of the Philippine Revolution*, Quezon City 1967; and Renato Constantino, *Insight and Foresight*, Quezon City 1977.

17. "These people" included, at the non-Europe-educated edge, Don Melecio Cojuangco.

18. Several English-language translations of these novels exist, the most recent by Leon Ma. Guerrero: *The Lost Eden*, Bloomington 1961; and *El Filibusterismo (Subversion)*, London 1965.

19. The standard nationalist texts on the Katipunan and the revolution it initiated are: Teodoro A. Agoncillo's *The Revolt of the Masses: The Story of Bonifacio and the Katipunan*, Quezon City 1956; and *Malolos: The Crisis of the Republic*, Quezon City 1960. Agoncillo's theses are undermined by Reynaldo Clemeña Ileto's masterly *Pasyón and Revolution: Popular Movements in the Philippines, 1840-1910*, Quezon City 1979, which is unquestionably the most profound and searching book on late nineteenth-century Philippine history. See also T.M. Kalaw, *The Philippine Revolution*, Kawilihan, Mandaluyong, Rizal 1969.

20. As late as 1960, fifteen years after American-style independence, and thirty years after it had been decided to promote Tagalog as an official, national lingua franca, less than 45 percent of the population understood the language—marginally more than the 40 percent claiming to understand English. See the 1960 census data cited in Onofre D. Corpuz's, *The Philippines*, Englewood Cliffs, N.J. 1965, p. 77.

21. See Milagros C. Guerrero, "The Provincial and Municipal Elites of Luzon during the Revolution, 1898-1902," in McCoy and de Jesus, eds., *Philippine Social History*, pp. 155-90; and Nick Joaquín, *The Aquinos of Tarlac, An Essay on History as Three Generations*, unexpurgated version, Manila 1986, Part One.

22. Teodoro A. Agoncillo, *The Writings and Trial of Andres Bonifacio*, Manila 1963, contains most of the relevant documents in Tagalog and in English translation.

23. See Ileto's often heart-rending account in *Pasyón and Revolution*.

24. The contrasting fates of the contemporary anticolonial movements in Cuba and the Philippines are instructive. In Cuba, American imperialism, claiming to side with the revolutionaries, ousted the Spaniards, established its own military rule for four years, and then installed a quasi-independent Republic, which, however, came under its full economic control. The island had far less strategic than pecuniary value. With the Philippines it was largely the other way round. Washington's strategists, giddy at their navy's first imperial circumnavigation of the globe, saw in the superb harbor of Manila Bay a perfect trans-Pacific "coaling-station" and jumping-off point for the penetration of China and the outflanking of Japan. These "bases" could only be secured—not least from rival imperialist powers—by political means, i.e., colonization. Ever since, American relations with the Philippines have ultimately centered on military considerations. A succinct account of the thinking behind the American intervention can be found in William J. Pomeroy, *American Neo-colonialism: Its Emergence in the Philippines and Asia*, New York 1970, chapters 1-2. In 1897, Captain Alfred Mahan had been appointed to McKinley's Naval Advisory Board, from which he peddled his imperial sea-power theories to substantial effect.

There is a vast literature on the American era. The classical text is Joseph Ralston Hayden, *The Philippines—A Study in National Development*, New York 1942. Peter W Stanley's penetrating and highly entertaining *A Nation in the Making: The Philippines and the United States, 1899-1921*, Cambridge (Mass.) 1974 and the later volume he edited, *Reappraising an Empire: New Perspectives on Philippine-American History*, Cambridge (Mass.) 1984 are the best modern guides. See also Norman G. Owen, ed., *Compadre Colonialism: Studies on the Philippines under American Rule*, Ann Arbor, University of Michigan Papers on South and Southeast Asia No. 3, 1971; and Theodore Friend's unintentionally revealing *Between Two Empires: The Ordeal of the Philippines, 1926-1946*, New Haven 1965. A useful recent text is Daniel B. Schirmer and Stephen R. Shalom, *The Philippines Reader: A History of Colonialism, Dictatorship and Resistance*, Boston 1987, chapters 1-2.

25. See Leon Wolff, *Little Brown Brother*, London 1960; and Russell Roth, *Muddy Glory: America's 'Indian Wars' in the Philippines, 1899-1935*, West Hanover, Mass. 1981. The newly-baptized "Filipinos" put up a stout resistance. The repression cost at least 5,000 American lives and 600,000,000 still-golden dollars. Probably the high price, and the "Indian-hunter" mentality of the troops dispatched, accounts for the savagery of the Americans. The killed-to-wounded ratio among Filipinos was 5 to 1. At least 20,000 died in action, and a further 200,000 from war-related famine and pestilence. General 'Jake' Smith, assigned to pacify recalcitrant Samar, told his men: "I want no prisoners. I wish you to kill and burn; the more you burn and kill the better it will please me." Samar was to be turned into "a howling wilderness." To the Fairfield, Maine, *Journal*, Sergeant Howard McFarlane of the 43rd Infantry wrote: "On Thursday, March 29, [1900] eighteen of my company killed seventy-five nigger bolomen and ten of the nigger

gunners . . . When we find one that is not dead, we have bayonets." Wolff, *Little Brown Brother*, pp. 360 and 305.

26. But with a highly restricted, property-based franchise. Even on the eve of World War II, only about 14 percent of the potential electorate was permitted to vote.

27. One gets a nice close-up feel for this change in Joaquín's *The Aquinos of Tarlac*, pp. 155-98.

28. See Teodoro A. Agoncillo, *A Short History of the Philippines*, New York 1969, p. 169; and David Wurfel, "The Philippines," in George McT. Kahin, ed., *Governments and Politics of Southeast Asia*, second edition, Ithaca, N.Y. 1964, pp. 679-777, at pp. 689-90.
Next door, in the Dutch East Indies, the colonial state of the 1930s had about 250,000 officials on its payroll, 90 percent of them "natives." See my "Old State, New Society: Indonesia's New Order in Comparative Historical Perspective," *Journal of Asian Studies*, XLII, 3 May 1983, p. 480.

29. Such policies did not always guarantee harmony. Members of these cacique dynasties frequently quarrelled and competed with each other in local elections. But it can safely be said that an oligarchy is truly in place when rulers and opposition leaders, ins and outs, all come from the same families.

30. See Friend, *Between Two Empires*, chapters 3-11, for an exhaustive account. The role of President Aquino's father-in-law is recounted in chatty detail in Joaquín's *The Aquinos of Tarlac*, chapters 3-5.

31. MacArthur had long-standing Philippine connections. His father, General Arthur MacArthur, had been second-in-command of the original American expeditionary force, and replaced his odious superior, General Elwell Otis, in May 1900. He stayed in power till 4 July 1901, when "civilian rule" replaced that of the soldiers. The MacArthur family also had substantial business investments in the archipelago.

32. For some amusing glimpses of these stately ruffians at work, see chapter 5 of Renato and Letizia Constantino, *The Philippines: The Continuing Past*, Quezon City 1978. The standard text on the Occupation remains David Joel Steinberg, *Philippine Collaboration in World War II*, Ann Arbor 1967. But see also Hernando J. Abaya, *Betrayal in the Philippines*, New York 1946; and Alfred McCoy's essay in the volume he edited entitled *Southeast Asia under Japanese Occupation*, New Haven, Yale University, Southeast Asia Studies, Monograph Series No. 22, 1980.

33. The classic text on the peasant resistance during the Japanese occupation, and its relationships with Socialist and Communist cadres, is Benedict J. Kerkvliet, *The Huk Rebellion*, Berkeley 1977. See also Eduardo Lachica, *The Huks: Philippine Agrarian Society in Revolt*, New York 1971; and "Documents—The Peasant War in the Philippines," *Philippine Social Sciences and Humanities Review*, XXIII, nos. 2-4, June-December 1958, pp. 375-436. (The documents, originally composed in 1946, offer valuable data on land concentration, peasant landlessness, tenancy rates, and exploitation of sharecroppers.) Note, in addition, the remarkable special issue of *Solidarity* (No. 102), 1985, devoted mainly to retrospective discussion of the Huk rebellion.

34. See Resil B. Mojares, *The Man Who Would be President: Serging Osmeña and Philippine Politics*, Cebu 1986, for example. This excellent text shows how while father Sergio Osmeña, Sr., was serving in Washington as vice-president in exile; son Sergio Jr., was making money hand over fist supplying the Japanese occupation regime in Manila.

35. See William Manchester's edifying *American Caesar: Douglas MacArthur, 1880-1964*, London 1979.

36. Quezon died in the United States in 1944, and was succeeded, ad interim, by his vice-president Sergio Osmeña, Sr. MacArthur had no time for Osmeña, whom he regarded as old, tired, and too Spanish in personal style.

37. Wurfel, "The Philippines," p. 761.

38. Stuck with the Constitution's quorum requirements for amendments, Roxas found no way to achieve the necessary change except by disqualifying, on charges of terrorism and electoral fraud, those opposition congressmen representing areas dominated by the Hukbalahap. See Kerkvliet, *The Huk Rebellion*, pp. 150-51.

39. See Friend, *Between Two Empires*, pp. 258-60.

40. The Philippine Army was still small, and "second army" in character. In other words, it belonged to that array of mercenary forces, racially segmented, poorly armed and trained, and deployed for "internal security" purposes, that we find throughout the late colonial world. (After independence, some of their former NCOs—such as Idi Amin, Sangoulé Lamizana, Suharto, Jean-Baptiste Bokassa, etc.—became colonels and generals in an unhappy trice.) The contrast is with the "first armies" of the industrial world, including that of the Soviet Union, which were self-armed, officered by military academy graduates, technologically sophisticated, amply financed, and capable of substantial external aggression.

41. More than anything else it was the ravages of the private armies that precipitated the open Hukbalahap insurrection against the state in 1948. See Kerkvliet, *The Huk Rebellion*, chapter 5, for a fine account.

42. His defeated opponent was none other than fellow-oligarch Don José Laurel, Sr., president of the wartime puppet Republic.

43. It is probably a general rule that *private* armies appear only under such conditions. The reappearance of these armies in President Aquino's presidency indicates the weakness of the state's army and a general social polarization.

44. Proximate ancestors of today's so-called "vigilantes." See *The Aquinos of Tarlac*, pp. 221ff.

45. Characteristically, even the Communist Party of the Philippines was vulnerable to caciquism. Among its top leaders in the late 1940s were Casto Alejandrino, scion of a large landowning family, and the brothers Lava, intellectuals of landowning origins (an uncle had been a colonel in Aguinaldo's Revolutionary Army). They eventually quarrelled violently with the Hukbalahap Supremo, Luis Taruc, who came from a family of tenant-farmers (both his grandfathers had been sergeants in the Katipunan army). No real surprise that the well-born stood to the militant left of the commoner. This information comes from the extraordinary, recent joint interview conducted by *Solidarity* editor F. Sionil José, with Casto Alejandrino, Jesus Lava, Luis Taruc, and Fred Saulo, and printed in the above-cited 1985 issue of *Solidarity*.

46. See the valuable, if ingenuous, text by former CIA officer Alvin Scaff, *The Philippine Answer to Communism*, Stanford 1955, chapters 3-6 especially.

47. Declassified documents cited in Raymond Bonner's *Waltzing with a Dictator: The Marcoses and the Making of American Policy*, New York 1987, give a nice picture of the Lansdale-Magsaysay relationship. During the 1953 election campaign Lansdale insisted that all Magsaysay's speeches be written by a CIA operative masquerading as a *Christian Science Monitor* correspondent. When he discovered that the candidate had had the impudence on one occasion to use a Filipino speech-writer, the enraged Quiet American walked into Magsaysay's office and knocked him out (pp. 39-40).

48. It was the time when Ferdinand Marcos and Corazon's husband, Benigno 'Ninoy' Aquino, Jr., came to national prominence.

49. See Frank H. Golay, *The Philippines: Public Policy and National Economic Development*, Ithaca, N.Y. 1961. See also the Villegas chapter in Bresnan, ed., *The Marcos Era*, especially pp. 150-55. This well-intentioned economist puts

it modestly thus: "If one were to look for a political explanation of this flawed economic policy, he could find it in the imperfections of a fledging democracy in which power was still concentrated in the hands of the former landed gentry who turned into manufacturing entrepreneurs during the fifties and sixties. The Philippine legislature, through which tariff, fiscal, and monetary reforms had to pass, was dominated by groups that represented the very industrial sector that had been pampered by overprotection."

50. The internationally celebrated symbol of this freedom was the muckraking *Philippines Free Press*. It is less well known that the Locsin family which ran it was violently opposed to any unionization of its staff, and used brazenly brutal methods to thwart it.

51. *The Philippines*, p. 86.

52. See Joaquín, *The Aquinos of Tarlac*, pp. 273-86, for a sly account. Luisita is certainly the most famous hacienda in the Philippines today, and still, pending land-reform, in the hands of the Cojuangcos. Don José acquired it from a French-financed, Spanish-managed company, which became discouraged by persistent "labor unrest." In the mid-1950s, its sugar central serviced 1,000 sugar planters and its annual production was valued at eighteen million pesos.

53. Cf. Corpuz, *The Philippines*, pp. 77 and 105.

54. The Marcos era did not initiate this process, merely accelerated it. Today 70 percent of the population lives below the World Bank's lordly poverty line. A recent article in *The Philippine Daily Inquirer*, 17 January 1988, offers instructive comparative demographic data on Bangkok and Manila. Bangkok has 25 births per thousand population, and suffers 17.2 postnatal deaths among every 1,000 babies born alive; the figures given for Manila are 63.9 and 69.5 respectively.

55. I remember that in the Jakarta of the late 1960s naked slum children played football in the mud thirty yards from the house of a Supreme Court judge. Some of Bangkok's wealthiest families' homes are still located a stone's throw from stinking, cesspool infested squatter clusters. But the tendencies are in Manila's direction as new, segregated suburbs develop.

56. The best structural accounts of the system's entropy remain Thomas Nowak and Kay Snyder, "Clientelist Politics in the Philippines: Integration or Instability?" *American Political Science Review*, 68, September 1974; and their "Economic Concentration and Political Change in the Philippines," in Benedict J. Kerkvliet, ed., *Political Change in the Philippines: Studies of Local Politics Preceding Martial Law*, Honolulu 1974, pp. 153-241.

57. The *New York Times*, 9 August 1967. The same account describes Cojuangco financing of Aquino's political career, and the heavily guarded family compound (six California-style ranch houses grouped around a colossal swimming pool)—a useful antidote to the current martyrology surrounding the assassinated senator.

58. The *New York Times*, 16 November 1969. Marcos spent people's money so lavishly in this campaign that inflation increased 18 percent, the blackmarket value of the peso fell 50 percent, and he had to ask for a $100,000,000 prepayment of military-base rent from Washington. *Ibid.*, 6 December 1969. It surely helped his case that he had contributed $1,000,000 to Nixon's 1968 election campaign (according to Rafael Salas, his executive secretary from 1966 to 1969, as cited in Bonner, *Waltzing with a Dictator*, p. 141).

59. Virtually no Filipinos today speak Spanish, but a certain sham-aristocratic aura still surrounds the *idea* of Iberian culture. Older members of the oligarchy prefer to be addressed as Don and Doña. Ideologically, the hacienda remains un-Americanized. And children are still overwhelmingly baptized with Spanish names, even if later they acquire American or local nicknames (Juan 'Johnny' Enrile, Benigno 'Ninoy' Aquino).

60. According to Wurfel, *The Philippines*, pp. 691-92, by the early 1920s the funds spent on education had reached nearly half of annual government expenditures at all levels. Between 1903 and 1939 literacy rates doubled, from 20 percent to 49 percent. By the latter date nearly 27 percent of the population could speak English, a percentage larger than for any single local tongue, including Tagalog.

61. The NPA's top leadership was originally composed largely of University of the Philippines graduates. The same is true today, if to a lesser extent. This leadership appears still to think in English, to judge from the fact that many key party documents have no Tagalog versions.

62. "Before the revolution," so to speak, by comparison with the migration, "after the revolution," of comparable strata from Cuba, China, and Vietnam. There are instructive contrasts with other parts of Southeast Asia. The Suharto regime in Indonesia is far bloodier and more efficiently repressive than that of Marcos, but emigration has been small. Holland has a low absorptive capacity, and after 1945 Indonesians had abandoned Dutch for "Indonesian"—neither of them world-languages. Burma (till 1963) and Malaysia were English-educated, but since the late 1950s the regime in London has been increasingly hostile to colonial immigration.

63. There is no satisfactory overall study of the Marcos regime, *as a regime*. But there are any number of useful texts on its leading personalities and its policies. Bonner's book is not always accurate, but it is good, and extremely funny, on

the Marcoses' relationships with assorted American presidents and proconsuls. Otherwise, see: Gary Hawes, *The Philippine State and the Marcos Regime: The Politics of Export*, Ithaca, N.Y. 1987; David A. Rosenberg, ed., *Marcos and Martial Law in the Philippines*, Ithaca, N.Y. 1979; Alfred W. McCoy, *Priests on Trial*, Victoria 1984; R.J. May and Francisco Nemenzo, eds., *The Philippines After Marcos*, New York 1985; Walden Bello et al., *Development Debacle: The World Bank in the Philippines*, San Francisco 1982; Walden Bello and Severina Rivera, eds., *The Logistics of Repression: The Role of U.S. Assistance in Consolidating the Martial Law Regime in the Philippines*, Washington D.C. 1977; Filemon Rodriguez, *The Marcos Regime: Rape of the Nation*, New York 1985; Stephen R. Shalom, *The U.S. and the Philippines: A Study of Neocolonialism*, Philadelphia 1981; Robert B. Stauffer, "The Political Economy of a Coup: Transnational Linkages and Philippine Political Response," *Journal of Peace Research*, 11:3, 1974, pp. 161-77; Carolina G. Hernandez, "The Role of the Military in Contemporary Philippine Society," *Diliman Review* (January-February 1984); and the volume edited by Bresnan, cited above.

64. Following American constitutional practice, all military appointments at the rank of colonel or above had to be approved by Congress. Ambitious officers, aware of how bread is buttered, cosied up to powerful congressional politicians, who exploited their position to build personal cliques within the military by determining the territorial positioning of favored clients. Come election time, it was always handy to have the local commandant in one's pocket. The most substantial study of the Philippine military remains Carolina G. Hernandez, "The Extent of Civilian Control of the Military in the Philippines, 1946-1976" (Ph.D. thesis, State University of New York at Buffalo, 1979). It is especially interesting on Marcos's manipulation of budgets, promotions, and educational ideology to secure the installation of the dictatorship.

65. Bonner's account, based on declassified American documents, is the most detailed. *Waltzing with a Dictator*, chapters 5-6.

66. Subic Bay and Clark Field are the two bases that get the most publicity, but the base-complex as a whole includes, at one extreme, the ultra-secret San Miguel electronic eavesdropping facility, and at the other, the ultra-open Fort John Hay pleasure-dome. The latter, situated just outside the popular mountain resort of Baguio, technically belongs to the American Air Force, but in practice to Manila's rich. It is composed of almost nothing but swimming-pools, golf-courses, tennis-courts, bowling-alleys, movie-halls, diners, dance-clubs, and so on. Anyone can enjoy these amenities if they can pay in dollars. I recently visited the "base," and in the course of several hours' perambulations met not a single American, military or civilian, but saw hundreds of prosperous Filipinos amusing themselves.

67. *Ibid.*, chapter 3.

68. *Ibid.*, pp. 140-41.

69. The best account is Hawes, *The Philippine State.*

70. More precisely, Marcos seized Meralco, the holding company of a giant Lopez conglomerate that controlled the Manila Electric Company, the nation's second largest bank, plus oil pipelines, an oil refinery, and a major construction business.

71. Here I rely on an unpublished paper by Resil B. Mojares, "The Dream Lives On and On: Three Generations of the Osmeñas, 1906-1988," footnote 8.

72. See Lena Garner Noble, "Politics in the Marcos Era," in Bresnan, ed., *Crisis in the Philippines*, p. 85. While quite successful in the northern and central parts of the country, the arms sweep was a catastrophic failure in the Muslim southwest. It is clear that the large-scale insurrection of the Moro National Liberation Front launched shortly after the proclamation of Martial Law was precipitated by the fear that a disarmed Muslim population would be wholly at the mercy of Manila and the Christian majority.

73. See David Wurfel, *Philippine Agrarian Policy Today: Implementation and Political Impact*, Singapore: Institute of Southeast Asian Studies, Occasional Paper No. 46, 1977; and Ernesto M. Valencia, "Philippine Land Reform from 1972 to 1980: Scope, Process and Reality," in Temario Rivera, et al., eds., *Feudalism and Capitalism in the Philippines*, Quezon City 1982. For a recent array of perspectives, see the issue of *Solidarity* (Nos. 106-7, 1986) devoted wholly to the problems of agrarian reform.

74. The word is used advisedly. The one Hollywood blockbuster banned under Marcos was *The Godfather*. A crumb under the rhinoceros' hide.

75. The officers' Forbes Park, an exclusive new residential area amusingly entitled "Corinthian Gardens," was the one part of Manila to which, during a recent visit to the metropolis, I was unable to obtain even taxi-access.

76. The nationalism was important. It made generally popular the Left's depiction of Marcos as the *tuta* (running dog) of the Americans. Privately, of course, the Left's leadership was well aware that Marcos was actually the *least* docile of the country's presidents. This evaluation is confirmed by Bonner's book, which shows that Ferdinand was vastly more astute than his opposite numbers in Washington. He had Carter's vain mini-Kissinger, Assistant Secretary of State for East Asian and Pacific Affairs Richard Holbrooke, in his pocket and charged half a billion dollars for a new five-year bases agreement in 1971. Reagan, an old friend from the 1960s, bundled his fatuous vice-president off to Manila to inform Marcos

that "we love your adherence to democratic principle and to the democratic process." CIA Director Casey, in an earlier incarnation as chairman of the Export-Import Bank, had pushed through the bank's largest-ever foreign loan ($644,000,000) to finance a splashy nuclear power project in Central Luzon. (The project remains uncompleted though the interest on the loan accounts for about 10 percent of the Philippines' annual debt payments.) Marcos got $80,000,000 under the table from contractor Westinghouse, which simultaneously raised its estimates 400 percent. See *Waltzing with a Dictator*, pp. 307-9, and 265.

77. See Francisco Nemenzo's fine article, "A Season of Coups: Military Intervention in Philippine Politics," *Diliman Review*, 34, nos. 5-6, 1986, pp. 1, 16-25.

78. The core judgment was certainly based on estimates of Washington's long-term goals and amply justified by the course of events on Central and South America. A valuable introduction to the polymorphous culture of the Philippine Left is Randolph G. David, ed., *Marxism in the Philippines*, Quezon City 1984.

79. On Church politics, see Dennis Shoesmith's chapter in May and Nemenzo, ed., *The Philippines After Marcos*; and two texts by Robert Youngblood, "Church Opposition to Martial Law in the Philippines," *Asian Survey*, 18, May 1978, pp. 505-20; and "Structural Imperialism: An Analysis of the Catholic Bishops' Conference of the Philippines," *Comparative Political Studies*, 15, April 1982, pp. 29-56. See also *Touching Ground, Taking Root: Theological and Political Reflections on the Philippine Struggle*, Quezon City 1986, by Edicio de la Torre, who is among the most socially committed and thoughtful of contemporary Filipino clerics.

80. Her one important success was the "coming over" of Comrade/Father Conrado Balweg, a militant and charismatic (ex-) priest, who in the Marcos era had formed his own guerrilla force among the oppressed highland minorities of the Luzon Cordillera. The NPA, which had long featured him in its publicity as a popular hero and an example of Party-Church cooperation, while privately criticizing his womanizing and periodic "disobedience," now denounced him as an opportunist and counter-revolutionary. The Army continued to distrust and dislike him, not least because the condition of his "coming over," Aquino's promise to establish a genuinely "autonomous" Cordillera region, appeared to pave the way for sellouts in the Muslim southwest.
It is instructive that a very successful commercial film on Balweg appeared in 1987. The real Balweg is an extremely complex figure, but in the movie he appears as a surrogate for the Manilan liberal middle class, fighting heroically against both Army barbarity and Communist treachery—of course, for the People.

81. Nor were they really encouraged to return. There were few jobs for them in the Philippines, and their remittances did much to ease the foreign exchange

crisis faced by the government. The same was true of the huge wave of non-middle class Filipino migrants to Saudi Arabia and the Gulf in the late 1970s and early 1980s. It is likely that the Philippines is now among the largest net exporters of national personnel in the world.

82. *Philippine Daily Inquirer*, 23 July 1987.

83. *The Manila Chronicle*, 23 July 1987. One particularly panic-stricken cacique family was reported to have set up forty separate dummy corporations to retain its landholdings.

84. A survey conducted by the Institute of Popular Democracy, quoted in the *Philippine Daily Inquirer* of 24 January 1988. (Italics added to emphasize the 'comeback' nature of the new legislature.) I owe this reference and the one that follows to Mojares, "The Dream Lives On and On".

85. "Sonny move vs. Barcenas explained," *Sun Star Daily*, 29 October 1987. The Osmeñas had gone through difficult times under Martial Law. Sergio ('Serging') Osmeña, Jr., had been severely wounded in the notorious Plaza Miranda affair in 1971 (the grenading of an—oligarchic, but anti-Marcos—Liberal Party election rally in downtown Manila; Marcos declared it the work of the NPA, but it was widely believed that the killers were military men or convicts in Marcos's own pay). After the declaration of Martial Law he exiled himself to California, where he died in 1984. There John, after initially applauding Ferdinand's declaration, eventually wended his way, returning only after the Aquino assassination.

86. Vice-President Salvador 'Doy' Laurel's United Nationalist Democratic Organization (UNIDO); José 'Peping' Cojuangco's Philippine Democratic Party-Laban (PDP-Laban); Paul Aquino's Lakas ng Bansa (Strength of the Nation); and Senator Jovito Salonga's Liberal Party. Only the Liberals date back to the pre-martial law era.

87. The pro-government coalition won 150 out of 200 seats. The Left, running under the umbrella organization Alliance of New Politics, secured a mere two.

88. *The Manila Chronicle*, 25 July 1987.

89. *The Manila Bulletin*, 18 January 1988.

90. The Osmeña triumph represents the optimum outcome for a dynasty: it has a member in the national legislature, controls the provincial government, and runs the largest local commercial center. Note that Tomas's defeated rival, José

'Boy' Cuenco, is a younger brother of Senate President protem Antonino 'Tony' Cuenco, and grandson of former Senate President, (the late) Mariano Cuenco.

91. *Philippine Daily Inquirer*, 22 January 1988, and *The Philippine Star*, 23 January 1988.

92. *The Philippine Star*, 22 January 1988, and *The Philippine Daily Inquirer*, 21 January 1988. She meant, of course, "back" from Ferdinand and Imelda.

93. *The Manila Bulletin*, 21 January 1988.

94. See *The Philippine Daily Inquirer*, 22 January 1988, for an account of Abadilla's past, and *The Manila Times*, 19 January 1988, for a description of the torturer being flown, at state expense, from his Manila cell to a polling booth in Ilocos Norte. Corazon's advisers may have been pleased to see Aguinaldo "join the system"—and a long way from Manila. Even the case of Abadilla (whom Army leaders insisted would not be allowed to assume office) may have served the purpose of demonstrating how free the balloting really was.

95. The Army leaked a purported NPA circular warning that "all candidates wishing to campaign in guerrilla zones have to get a safe-conduct pass from us for their own safety. The CPP-NPA will not answer for those without it." A guerrilla leader in Quezon Province, interviewed by Agence-France Presse, confirmed NPA taxation of candidates, affirming that the money would be used to "advance the revolution." It is said that such "election passes" were sold for between 10,000 and 30,000 pesos ($500-$1,500) apiece. The Army claimed that about 10 percent of all candidates (say 15,000 people) were paying for such passes. See *The Philippine Daily Inquirer*, 18 January 1988.

96. *Malaya*, 21 January 1988.

97. *The Manila Bulletin*, 21 January 1988.

98. The government claimed that the elections were quite exceptionally peaceful: only 124 deaths all told, compared to 204 deaths in the 11 May 1987 congressional elections, 296 in the 1986 presidential elections, 178 in the 1981 presidential elections, 411 in the 1980 local elections, and 534 in the 1971 (pre-Martial Law) congressional campaign. *Malaya*, 19 January 1988. But as the *Philippine Daily Globe*, 20 January 1988, rightly pointed out, in both the 1986 and 1981 campaigns only four *candidates* had been murdered—the huge bulk of the victims being "small fry." What was new about January 1988 was that a full third of the dead were actual contenders.

99. In the summer of 1987 the liberal part of the Manila press was every day reporting with alarm on the growth of a nation-wide, coordinated system of extremist anti-Communist vigilante groups, financed by the oligarchy, the CIA and the gonzo American ex-General Singlaub. In January 1988, during the election campaign, this broad fascist front virtually disappeared from print. Needless to say, the groups had not themselves disbanded. It had become apparent that by then most had abandoned Singlaubian mufti and gone back to duty as local gangs of thugs, each recruited to promote the local power, especially in elections, of particular, contentious local dynasties. There is no question but that these gangs are instruments of class oppression and frequently cooperate closely with local military and police personnel. They play an important part in the ongoing civil war. But their very dispersion and localism show how confident the caciques are, and how little they feel the need to crawl together under the apron of the military.

100. *The Philippine Daily Inquirer*, 23 January 1988. The end of the final sentence is clearly garbled, and probably should read "anything to eat," or "any meat."

Part 2

Technologies of Colonial Rule

TWO

Cholera and the Origins of the American
Sanitary Order in the Philippines

REYNALDO C. ILETO

EVEN NATIONALIST WRITERS IN THE PHILIPPINES FIND IT IMPOSSIBLE TO INTER-
rogate the established notion that among the blessings of American
colonial rule was a sanitary regime which saved countless Filipino lives.
Take the historians Teodoro A. Agoncillo and Milagros C. Guerrero.
In their influential textbook they narrate in some detail the Philippine-
American war of 1899-1902, highlighting the Filipino struggle to defend
their independence 'through blood and tears.' In marked contrast to
colonial historians, they stress that although the republican commander-
in-chief Emilio Aguinaldo had been captured in mid-1901, guerrilla
warfare continued under the leadership of General Miguel Malvar until
relentless American campaigns forced him to surrender on 16 April
1902.

Agoncillo and Guerrero uphold their anti-colonial stance in the
discussion, several chapters later, of the educational system ("originally
established as an instrument of pacification"). But upon reaching the
topic of health and welfare, they seem to switch to another register:

Before 1900, ravages of cholera, smallpox, dysentery, malaria, tuberculosis, and other deadly diseases plagued the people . . . When the Americans came, they immediately set to work to minimize the spread of diseases and to improve, on the other hand, the health of the people. Epidemics that used to migrate to the Philippines were either prevented or minimized by the establishment of the Quarantine Service supervised by competent American doctors and public health officers.

The distinction between nationalist and colonial writing collapses. The task of educating the people in the "elementary principles of hygiene and sanitation" was difficult, continue Agoncillo and Guerrero, because the Filipinos

were superstition-ridden and ignorant of the strange power of the minute germs to cause deadly diseases, and were not easily convinced by the efficacy of medical methods in combating the cause of death from various sickness. The early Americans, then, were up against a formidable wall of ignorance and superstition.[1]

The 1899-1902 war of resistance and the 1902-4 cholera epidemic belong to two distinct series in Philippine historiography. The former is a moment in the epic struggle for independence from colonial rule, the latter a Philippine chapter in the saga of scientific progress. Like their nineteenth-century forebear Jose Rizal—the 'father' of nationalist historiography *and* doctor of medicine—Agoncillo and Guerrero as well as most others of the Filipino intelligentsia order the past in terms of the triumph of reason and science over superstition and backwardness. The apparent victory over the cholera in 1902-3 is thus assimilated into the universal history of medical progress, torn from its original moorings in a colonial war and pacification campaign.

Much of this disjunction stems from the fact that the most accessible accounts of cholera epidemics during the first decade of American rule are authored by the very architects of the anti-cholera measures: the Secretary of the Interior, Dean Worcester, and the Commissioner of Public Health, Dr. Victor Heiser.[2] The epidemic, says Worcester, "came soon after the close of a long continued war," hence not a few "evil-intentioned persons" took the opportunity to make trouble.[3] Worcester knew that the rumor-mongering and the popular resistance to his cholera campaign formed some continuity with the recent war (which was, in fact, still raging at the time the epidemic struck). However, since the health campaign is represented in purely medico-sanitary terms, and resistance to it conflated with superstition and backwardness, the issue of colonial domination simply fades away.

It is instructive to juxtapose Worcester's representation of the war against cholera, which he himself led, with his eyewitness account of a famous battle between American and Filipino forces in 1899, in which even the American commander praised the courage of the outgunned Filipino soldiers. Worcester could only perceive, and describe, the "gallant advance" and "intrepidity" of American troops. He turned the Filipinos, his biographer R. J. Sullivan notes, into "almost impersonal props in a drama whose theme was American heroism and military skill; if 'not retreating in great disorder,' or fleeing 'in confusion towards Imus' they were presented pictorially, impersonal beings whose very anonymity highlighted American individuality and military skill."[4]

The fight against the cholera of 1902-4 has been represented, even by nationalist writers, in similar fashion: as a drama whose theme is American heroism and medico-sanitary skill, where Filipino participants— the victims from the poorer classes in particular—function as the anonymous backdrop for the saga of progress. This study attempts to put such claims into question by exploring those months of turmoil in 1902 when the war against the cholera and the "pacification" of Filipinos were barely differentiated, when medico-sanitary measures and popular resistance to such, were continuing acts of war.

On 14 March 1902, a vessel from Hong Kong arrived in Manila with cholera on its bill of health. Despite strict quarantine inspections and prohibitions on such incoming vessels, shortly afterwards the first cases of cholera were discovered in a barrio called Farola near the mouth of the Pasig river where many stevedores, fishermen, and petty smugglers lived.[5] From here spread the epidemic which devastated the country up to November 1902, lingered on till early February 1904, and ultimately claimed a total—conservatively estimated—of 109,461 deaths, 4,386 of which were in Manila.

Upon confirmation of the existence of cholera Secretary Worcester mobilized both civilian and military personnel to contain its spread. The Farola district was razed and its inhabitants moved to a detention camp. The attempt to contain the epidemic in Manila proved fruitless, however, as people managed to "escape" by night or even by day through the ricefields. Small native canoes carried the infection to the towns around Manila bay. Worcester compared the situation to the U.S. Army's attempt, several years earlier, to cordon off Manila from republican forces surrounding it: "What General Otis could not accomplish with thousands of soldiers was an impossibility for the board of health, aided by the city police and a few hundred men from the insular constabulary."[6]

The cholera was certainly impossible to contain, for even American troop movements contributed to its spread. A military transport vessel carried it to the city of Nueva Caceres, in the southeastern part of Luzon, "from which source it was transmitted to a large number of pueblos in that section."[7] The first cases of Pagsanjan and Majayjay in Laguna province were among two batches of soldiers sent up from Camp Wallace in Manila on 24 April 1902.[8] Cholera was introduced into the Mariquina valley east of Manila by troops sent to guard against infection of the Manila water supply.[9] The board of health in that province warned constabulary detachments to keep out of the towns because they had infected one already.[10]

The cholera swiftly spread up the Pasig river arteries leading to the Mariquina valley and the coastal towns of (lake) Laguna de Bay, until it arrived upon the terrain of guerrilla resistance to American occupation: the provinces of Laguna, Batangas and Tayabas. In fact, it was the exigencies of war that caused a delay of about a month before the lake towns of Laguna were infected. On 10 December of the previous year all ports had been closed as part of General J. Franklin Bell's all-out effort to force Malvar's capitulation. The cessation of native traffic in the lake severely restricted the flow of supplies to the guerrilla camps, and held back the cholera as well. On 19 April, three days after Malvar's surrender, all restrictions to trade and travel in the region were to be lifted, but the cholera forced the ports to remain closed in order to give time for local health boards to organize and take the required precautions.[11]

As long as the ports remained closed, no cholera appeared, "but immediately on opening them [on the first of May] the disease attacked first the ports and thence spread back into the country." The coastal quarantine proved useless as infected Filipinos and "occasional Americans" managed to land surreptitiously, usually at night between ports. The shallow waters of the lake made it possible for some to wade ashore from quarantined boats up to half a kilometer distant. "The disease once landed made universal progress, especially through the barrios."[12]

Cholera claimed its victims from all levels of society, including American soldiers and residents, prominent Filipinos, Chinese, and Spaniards. The distribution of victims among the races and social classes was, however, unequal.[13] Americans, Spaniards, and Chinese had well-equipped hospitals catering specially for them. At the Santiago cholera hospital, on the other hand, the vast majority of patients belonged to the "unintelligent" class, among whom the rate of recovery was as low as 5.32 percent. This was attributed to bad sanitary conditions and "poor food in their everyday lives" which produced "such a low state of vitality that the system was unable to react from effects of the toxin produced by the cholera organisms."[14] Overcrowding, poor sanitation, and poor diet in certain districts of Manila were the primary causes of the malignancy of the cholera among the lower classes.

In the provinces south and east of Manila where guerrilla resistance had been intense, the epidemic was "especially severe."[15] The chief army surgeon noted in mid-June that "in Laguna, Batangas, and the adjacent part of the province of Tayabas, cholera [had] spread in virulent epidemic form, hundreds of cases probably having occurred without report."[16] The "sad and impressive" mortality figures—a recent study put the death toll for Batangas alone at 20,000—were attributed to the fact that "both troops and natives had, especially in Batangas and Laguna, been recently subjected to the demoralizing and debilitating influences of war."[17]

War, the cholera, and famine conditions came together, at least in southwestern Luzon. Such connections would be obscured if we relied on reports emanating from Manila. All we have, really, is this note by the Commissioner of Public Health in his report for August: "In one or two instances it has been necessary to send food, the scarcity of rice existing in some of the towns being so great as to become an important factor in the cholera situation."[18] Poverty and malnutrition, together with poor sanitation, are mentioned as some of the causes of the 'malignancy' of the epidemic among the lower classes. But any connection with the war is muted. When the concentration camps are mentioned, as in the Surgeon General's report for 1902, it is claimed that people in them had never experienced better living conditions and thus survived the epidemic better.[19]

Let us re-examine those critical months of March to May 1902. According to Malvar, his decision to surrender on 16 April was forced by

> the reconcentration in zones, the extinction of food supplies in the country . . . If I had not known what was passing with the people who petitioned my surrender that their deaths were very certain in the coming year, 1903, unless they could plant the rice in the month of May, I should not have surrendered.[20]

Malvar must have known, too, that the cholera, then ravaging Manila, was already present in his northernmost zone of operations, Laguna province. The official date of the cholera's first appearance in Laguna is 7 April. Five days later, the U.S. commander at Calamba, the provincial capital, reported a suspected case in a native barge that had arrived from Manila. The following day, a nipa hut was burned in a barrio at the edge of town after its owner's wife had died of cholera.[21] With the horrors of the 1882 and 1889 epidemics still fresh in many people's minds, there can be no doubt that rumors of the cholera in Manila added to the local elite's demand for an end to guerrilla resistance.

The surrender was supposed to lead to the break-up of the zones of reconcentration, the re-dispersal of peasants in their villages, the preparation of the ricefields, and the reopening of the rice-trade networks. General Bell, having asserted that there was "absolutely no hunger within the territorial limits of the brigade, and no suffering on that account," admitted that rice was being imported into the region. He was counting on the fact that with the war over "all land [could] be properly prepared before the planting season."[22] This was absolutely crucial. The glowing official report on the Tanauan and Santo Tomas "concentration camps" notes that there was enough rice, including reserves, to last only until 30 April and 1 May, respectively.[23] Search-and-destroy operation by the U.S. Cavalry had destroyed rice stocks which could not be transferred into the zones. Rice aid would enable the people to eat until the September harvest, but the region would only get back on its feet with the normalization of rice production. Unfortunately, Bell's optimism was soured by complicating factors such as the rinderpest, locusts, and cholera.

The case of Calamba and its adjacent towns illustrates the connection between the food problem and the new round of restrictions occasioned by the cholera. Calamba had been the headquarters of the republican Division of Southern Luzon, commanded by General Juan Cailles. In 1899 there had been fierce battles between U.S. forces and various defense perimeters around Calamba resulting in the destruction of the irrigation works. Thus, no rice had been planted around that town since 1900. When the populace were herded into the town center in March 1902, work teams were given permission, initially under guard, to repair several dams. It was hoped that rice would be planted that year. In the meantime, the town was rice-dependent on neighboring Cabuyao and Biñan. In February, the American commander of Biñan could still inform his Calamba counterpart: "If it becomes necessary for you to purchase rice for indigent or starving natives, I have a superabundance harvested which the natives are anxious to sell."[24]

Even before Malvar's surrender, rice had been allowed to enter from neighboring towns at regular market prices. This, however, was "suddenly cut off by unexpected quarantine regulations made necessary by the appearance of cholera." The border between Calamba and rice-rich Biñan, in particular, was "assiduously guarded." The only rice available was from the U.S. commissary, which was sold to wealthier Filipinos or distributed free to the poor as required. Not surprisingly, frequent attempts were made to run the guard lines. People traversed back lots and rice paddies at night. The situation was aggravated by the fact that May is the month of local feasts honoring patron saints. Apparently, infected food from Manila brought to a feast "materially assisted" in the infection of Biñan.[25]

There are numerous accounts of how quarantine lines disrupted the flow of food from surplus to dependent towns in the provinces of Rizal, Laguna, and Batangas. There are equally numerous accounts of how, particularly from July, as the rice reserves became depleted in some towns, there was a considerable movement of people seeking to buy or sell rice, fish, and other food products.[26] The quarantine was "absolutely useless," noted Chief Quarantine Officer J. C. Perry, owing to the smuggling of food. He attributed this to "ignorance" and wished he was dealing with "intelligent Americans or Europeans instead."[27] For the inhabitants of the war-torn areas, however, it was ultimately a choice between dying of hunger or dying of cholera. After a period of intense quarantines and house-to-house inspections, the Army had to content itself with isolating or "protecting" its soldiers from the native populace, or even withdrawing its garrisons.[28]

Even with the ineffectiveness and eventual lifting of the quarantine, the agricultural situation in 1902 was hopeless. Rinderpest, which first appeared on the eve of the 1888 cholera epidemic, had destroyed more than ninety percent of the work animals. Hand labor, aided in places by hoes provided by the U.S. garrisons, could only work a limited area. The work force was reduced by the ravages of the cholera, not to mention concurrent malarial fever and beriberi.[29] With the cholera sweeping through the region less than a month after the break up of the concentration camps in late April, and with reserve rice running out at the end of that month, southern Tagalog peasants would certainly have been "debilitated" and "demoralized." Only continued rice aid, which Malvar himself petitioned for in August, prevented "suffering" from turning into a demographic disaster.[30] "We have cases of cholera in this town," the mayor of San Juan, Batangas, urgently telegraphed Bell in mid-June. "A lot of people are dying of starvation than of the cholera, in view of which I beg you to give us protection."[31]

It may appear that Malvar's surrender and the increasing dependence of the peasants on American food aid effectively ended the war.

It can be argued, however, that the war was simply transposed from the battlefields to the towns, that the struggle continued over the control, no longer of territorial sovereignty, but of people's bodies, beliefs, and social practices. American military surgeons, the standard bearers of scientific medicine in the colonial world, merely supplanted the officers and combat troops of the initial period of conquest. It was, in a sense, the old war in a new, more complex setting—complex, since who can argue against the saving of human lives through proper disinfection, isolation, treatment, and disposal of the dead?

Sanitary work came in on the heels of General Bell's military offensive beginning in December 1901. As Heiser candidly admits, because they had to protect their troops, they decided that "something must be done about cholera." Having made this decision, the Americans were not disposed to tolerate obstacles to health measures.[32] Cholera, in fact, was the lesser problem compared to, as one veteran surgeon wrote, "an ignorant and suspicious people, impoverished by war, locusts, and rinderpest and embittered by conquest," making sanitation work "an extremely difficult task, calling for much patience, tact and firmness, the brunt of which fell on the Army."[33]

The rationale for the Army's interventions was to cleanse the regions, to eradicate the dual scourge of killer germ and popular stubbornness. The discourse matches that which framed General Bell's program for the December military offensive:

> I expect to first *clean out* the Looboo Peninsula. I shall then move command to the vicinity of Lake Taal, and *sweep* the country westward to the ocean and south of Cavite, returning through Lipa. I shall *scour and clean up* the Lipa Mountains. Swinging northward, the country . . . will be *scoured*. . . . Swinging back to the right, the same *treatment* will be given all the country, etc.[34]

Developments in nineteenth-century medicine contributed to the convergence of colonial warfare and disease control. American physicians by 1902 almost universally subscribed to the germ theory, or more generally the doctrine of specific etiology of disease. Pasteur's writings on the subject appeared at about the same time as Darwin's theory of evolution. At a time when relationships between living beings were being set in a context of a struggle for survival, where one was either friend or foe, the germ theory gave rise to a kind of aggressive warfare against disease-causing microbes, which had to be eliminated from the stricken individual and from the community. When specific pathogenic micro-organisms were discovered after 1870, they were viewed as *the* cause of specific diseases. It was then easy to think of disease as an entity incarnate in the germs and loose in the community. Towards the end of the nineteenth century, medical thinking that recognized the importance of a patient's state of mind, that attributed disease to a lack of harmony between man and his environment, had given way in Europe and America to the search for the specific germ and the specific weapon against it.[35]

Between 1875 and 1900, French and German bacteriologists identified the organisms involved in many of the serious infections like cholera, typhoid, and tuberculosis. As is well known, the German doctor Robert Koch discovered the cholera bacillus in the 1880s through investigations conducted in the British colonies of Egypt and India. Although few cures were to be found until half a century later, implications for preventive measures were apparent. In the United States, sanitary reform proceeded in earnest from the 1870s, spurred on by the public's fears of a recurrence of the cholera visitations of the 1830s and 1850s. By about 1905, control of water or food supplies and of insect vectors had checked typhoid, cholera, yellow fever, and malaria.[36]

American surgeons and sanitation personnel, then, had just witnessed the glimmer of victory over disease in their own country when they confronted the cholera in the Philippines. They were armed with the knowledge of Koch's and others' discoveries, of the processes of taming the disease in Europe, America, and the colonies; of its causes, means of prevention, and the treatments available at that time. Their feeling that nothing could hinder them or the march of science is captured by this passage from Inspector General's report of 1902:

The epidemics among men and beasts have been remarkable since our advent into the Far East. But they come and go like waves, making but little impression upon the national conscious-

ness; for science has seized the recurrent waves and almost obliter-
ated them. Even the bubonic plague has passed, scarce noted.
And the struggle goes on. A single sentinel of science remiss may
let many suffer.[37]

The tropical environment, the war, and the obdurate populace in
particular, were regarded as petty obstacles to the implementation of an
unsullied knowledge backed up by science and history. Not surprisingly
accounts of operations during the epidemic are suffused with a sense of
mission and righteous victory. The following episode is typical: "[In
Calatagan, Batangas] most of the natives, being ignorant and superstitious, the latter involving fatalism, had no faith in the efficacy of these
measures and were much opposed to the restrictions involved." Thus,
between 21 June and 3 July, 650 died of cholera before the native authorities decided to report the situation to the Americans. Within a week
"the surgeons and soldiers sent there had stopped the ravages of the
cholera."[38]

The cholera war proceeded along familiar military lines. Army
surgeons, for one, were armed with trial 'magic bullets' with which to
shoot down the bacillus. One widely used drug was benzozone, the
ingestion of which was found to burn the mouth and stomach linings. It
eventually was diluted and mixed in with solutions used to irrigate the
bowels and small intestines. Routine treatments involved the use of
benzoyl-acetyl-peroxide, guiacol carbonate, calomel, potassium perman-
ganate, two percent tannic acid, and dilute sulphuric acid. These treatments were really experimental in nature, based on the assumption that
some drug ought to be able to attack and destroy the cholera vibrio
within the patient. The American doctors' use of such and other, unfa-
miliar, methods of treatment only brought about an aversion in Filipino
cholera patients "so marked in many instances as to necessitate the use
of force in the administering of medicine."[39] In the end none of the
medicine, at least in Heiser's experience in the Philippines, proved of
any value.[40]

Of utmost importance in the war was the ability to conduct search
and surveillance operations. For this purpose Worcester organized platoons of inspectors led by surgeons from the Army Volunteer brigades.

Initially, most of the inspectors were Filipinos. But they were soon re-
lieved owing to their inability to understand that "these measures, to be
. effective, must be enforced upon the rich as well as the poor, and the
strong as well as the weak."[41] Americans of all kinds were enlisted: clerks,
schoolteachers, policemen and ex-soldiers. Among them were some
"who had slight regard for the natives and who enforced the already
distasteful regulation in an unwarranted manner, increasing the popular
opposition." Several of them were killed as a result.[42] In the southwestern Luzon towns, native inspectors and guards continued in service, but
they were supervised by patrols, often mounted, of white soldiers. Filipino scouts, a ruthless elite force consisting mostly of non-Tagalogs,
stood guard over quarantined houses.[43]

The cholera introduced the stern figure of the American army
surgeon, less open than the regular military officers to compromise with
the local elite. Detailed to most local health boards, army surgeons had
little regard for their Filipino colleagues and generally ignored local
knowledge gained from previous epidemics. As Captain C. de Mey put
it, their job was ideally "to rule with a rod of steel." A health officer
"should be the commanding officer of a city when that city is threatened
with or has an epidemic, and must be left free to act according to his
judgment."[44] In the context of an epidemic, therefore, the surgeon dis-
places the military commander. Heiser, though never detailed with the
army, speaks for the army surgeon as well in commenting that "whatever the relative importance of the medical man in other parts of the
world, he, and the profession he represented, *stood first* in the Philippines."[45]

Various "combat zones" can be identified in the cholera war. Prominent among them was the issue of confinement. We have seen how
quarantine lines crumbled before the more pressing need to obtain or
sell food. Quarantine formed part of the broader objective of containing the disease. When the epidemic was first discovered in the Farola
district, Worcester's platoons attempted to completely cordon off the
area in order to isolate the stricken and whoever had had contact with
them. However, "the disease spread rapidly among the imprisoned
people and a continuation of the quarantine would have been inhu-

man," so the inhabitants were transferred to a detention camp.[46] Several such camps were soon put up in Manila and provincial towns.

Heiser describes how "uniformed men clattered up with ambulances and without ceremony lifted the sick from their mats and carted them away from their wailing families." Families could not understand why they were forbidden to follow. "Four times out of five this was the last they ever saw of their loved ones until shortly they received a curt notice to come to the hospital and claim their dead."[47] Confinement in hospitals for patients, and in detention camps for contacts, was almost as feared as the cholera itself. For one thing, hospitals during the Spanish regime were regarded as places "where people so unfortunate as to have no homes to die in might go to end their days. It was almost impossible to get any other class of persons into them." Thus cholera victims "sometimes had to be taken to the hospital by force."[48] Compounding the traditional aversion were some terrifying rumors, current from Manila to Cebu, "of horrible abuses in the detention camps, and of deliberate murder of patients at the cholera hospitals." It was said that on arrival, patients were given poisoned vino (a cheap Spanish wine) and instantly dropped dead. There were also tales of strychnine poisoning, occasioned by its necessary use as a heart stimulant.[49]

Strict confinement was premised on the then-prevailing notion in American medicine of disease as a purely biological and physical entity, a foreign agent, which must be excised from the healthy parts of society. The Filipino public, however, largely refused to dissociate the disease from the network of social relationships in which it appeared. Rumors, concealments and evasions were various modes of resistance to an imposed definition of sickness and treatment. The conflict became so intense that a concession had to be made to the "ignorant classes": tents were pitched on the grounds of cholera hospitals to accommodate relatives or friends of patients. Once or twice daily they were allowed to visit the wards.[50] Filipino doctors were also allowed in to practice their "mixed treatments" which involved keeping the patient in a familiar and reassuring environment, where his morale as well as body was attended to.[51]

Sometime in mid-May, the removal of contacts to detention camps was finally stopped in Manila since this measure only made concealment of cases the rule. On 1 July, even detention in houses was scrapped. In Batangas and Laguna, General Bell abolished forcible detention on 23 May. Henceforth, people were to be isolated in their houses, over which municipal authorities were to place guards.[52]

During the first few weeks of the epidemic in Manila, not only were members of a stricken household sent off to detention camp, but their house itself was burned down if it happened to be a nipa-palm construction. The cholera germ lay in the filth and vermin associated with infected "native dwellings," which had to be destroyed, germs and all. Many books on Philippine health and sanitation display that famous photograph of the burning of houses in the Farola district.

The problems with such an efficient means of destroying cholera germs is obvious. An American teacher in Cebu put it this way:

> Many of the poor people see absolutely no way of replacing their houses. It's all very well to tell that they will be paid the value of the buildings destroyed. They have had too much experience to put much faith in such stories. They would also have to wait six months in order that the usual amount of red tape may be gone through. Where are they to live in the meantime? Better let father or brother die and say nothing about it.[53]

Resistance to burnings took the form of rumors, "widely circulated," that houses of the poor were burned in order to make room for the "future dwellings and warehouses of rich Americans." Because it "provoked great hostility among the poorer people," house burning was quickly abandoned in Manila in favor of thorough disinfection.[54]

In the provinces, Government Order 66 was implemented, which stipulated, among other things, that nipa houses of cholera cases were to be burned, while houses constructed of wood were to be disinfected.[55] The local elite was thus spared. We have only one actual report of a burning in southwestern Luzon—that of a nipa house in a barrio of Calamba valued at $15 (Mexican).[56] But there must have been a lot more. The Philippine Commission government awarded $4624.39 as payment for claims of owners of houses burned down by medical officers in the town of Lumbang.[57] If, say, each of the burned nipa huts at

Lumbang cost $15, then up to 308 houses could have been destroyed in that town. This is possible. An American teacher in Cebu could not bring himself to implement the order because "when a fire once starts in one of these towns, it sweeps over acres and acres before it can be stopped." He burned only "one or two crazy old shacks."[58]

In the towns of southwestern Luzon under General Bell's control, there must have been quite a few medical officers like the one who wrote, "I went next to Cavite, where cases had occurred in a populous market place. The market was burned down. Result, no more cholera for more than two months." Before this, Captain de Mey had burned down a house in Malolos, north of Manila.[59] In any case, since the burning of whole barrios outside the zones during General Bell's military offensive had already created mass resentment against the U.S. Army, well-meaning measures during the epidemic cannot have been accepted passively. There can be no doubt that the threat of burnings figured largely in the concealment of more than fifty percent of cholera cases in the region.[60] On 23 May, Bell finally sent out orders that no more houses were to be burned when there were only a few cases involved or where the cholera had already disappeared.[61]

Infected houses were not as much of a problem as the infected cadavers that piled up during a cholera epidemic. In 1882, when Manila experienced an estimated death toll ranging from 13,000 to 34,000, bodies remained unburied for days. San Lazaro district, site of the cholera hospital, was so filled with "gasses of putrefying flesh" that one could hardly go through it. The government finally intervened with a battalion of engineers to help bury the dead *en masse* in a common pit. The approaches to the Manila cemeteries "were blocked with vehicles of every description loaded with corpses."[62]

The same problem arose in 1902. By the end of July, the grounds of Tondo cemetery were filled with cadavers and further burials were banned. As in the past, new cemetery grounds were opened up in the suburbs, but the American government still worried that underground water tables would be infected. Certainly, no mass graves would be dug this time. The government instead preferred a more efficient solution: cremation. But this was not directly imposed. Rather, the Insular board of health decreed that cadavers must be placed in hermetically sealed metallic coffins before being buried in seven-foot deep graves. Otherwise, off to the crematories they would be sent, at government cost.[63] Now how many could afford metal coffins? Again, it was the poor that took the blow.

No Filipino in his right mind approved of cremation. An American teacher, convinced that the "ideal way" of disposing of bodies was "to burn them," discovered that "the very mention of such a thing aroused a storm of superstitious opposition":

> The Filipino and Spaniards both informed me that it would be a tremendous mistake even to attempt burning any bodies. The natives had such a horror of it that they would rather scoop out a trench under a house in which to bury the dead, or throw the body in the nearest swamp. I pointed out that in neither case would they be burying their dead in consecrated ground. Even so—that was a good deal better than having the bodies burned.[64]

In Manila hospitals, corpses left unclaimed after twenty-four hours were cremated. In the crowded conditions of the city slums it was possible during an epidemic's peak for cholera victims to be so regarded with fear and horror as to be abandoned. At least this is what happened in 1888, when victims were "not infrequently" carried out while in a state of coma and buried alive. Not a few survived and returned to terrorize their friends! It became necessary to issue orders to deposit bodies in shelters and leave them there for a few hours before burial.[65] In 1902, fear of cremation combined with fear of house burnings and fear of detention, forced poorer families to bury bodies in backyards, under woodpiles, or out in the ricefields at night, or even to throw them into the Pasig river.

On 1 July the board of health backed down on its strict burial regulations. "Owing to the religious prejudices of the people against cremation," and the consequent concealment of cases, families, and friends of persons dying of cholera in Manila could henceforth bury their dead in simple wooden coffins placed in lime-filled graves seven feet deep. On the 29th, the board conceded even more: the graves could be as deep as the condition of the ground permitted, but not less than three feet in any case. However, only two adult members or friends of the family could accompany the body. And no services, funeral processions or bands were to be allowed.[66]

Although the Insular board of health did not recommend cremation for the provinces, this did take place. There were times when the board had to order it to be stopped because none of the provinces had the proper facilities for it. The result of all cremation attempts had been "to arouse the horror of the people, and their passive, and in some instances active, resistance to such measures and to all general sanitary measures."[67]

In comparison to Manila's poor districts where overcrowding and intense government surveillance imposed additional pressures and fears on the inhabitants, there were fewer horror stories in provincial towns. The fact that American troops kept to their garrisons in the town centers, was a contributing factor. Army surgeons and their inspectors policed the center, while in the outlying villages either a vigorous local-led campaign was carried out, or the epidemic was simply allowed to run its course. In neither circumstance could there have been much American interference in the practices surrounding sickness and death.

In the town of Pila, Laguna, for example, the leading citizens were ordered to supervise the digging of about twenty graves daily, ten for grown persons and ten for children. In addition, they had to obtain burial permits from the American commanders and see to it that no excess people accompanied the corpses to the cemetery.[68] But if the people of Pila wished it, the rules could be broken. In the barrios, concealment was a simple matter. Relatives, neighbors and children visited the sick or the dead without constraints. Some came to pay their respects, to join in the feast called *katapusan*; others just wanted to see what the dying and the dead looked like—and cholera victims were a horrible sight. The same utter disregard for prohibitions was reported in towns all over the Philippines. "They have no fear of anything," sighed a frustrated teacher in the Visayas.[69] At Ibaan, Batangas, infected houses were required to display a red flag, "but the natives gave no heed to this warning and to them the presence of the flag was seemingly only a kind of joke."[70] Observers saw this as a sign of fatalism and ignorance. On the other hand, it can be read as an insistence that death and dying remain a social event.

The towns were the scene of conflicts between army surgeons and native officials. Such were the local tensions that Worcester, in touring the provinces, had to discipline some abusive American health officials.[71] Trouble usually erupted when local officials were accused of being incompetent or uncooperative. Provincial and municipal boards of health, composed of Filipinos, were regarded as "entirely incompetent to meet the emergency of dealing with an epidemic." In one Laguna town, members of the local health board were imprisoned for 'criminal laxity, that is, not reporting cases to the army surgeon. Uncertainty of diagnosis was the proffered excuse.[72] In the few provinces and towns where success in stamping out the cholera was reported, credit was given to army surgeons on detail with the local boards.

It is hard to accept such charges at face value when we take into account the fact that municipal health commissions, or *juntas sanitarias*, had functioned under similar guidelines during the 1882 and 1888 epidemics.[73] What is missing in American accounts of local bungling or intransigence is precisely the war context or, to put it another way, the local interpretations—shaped by recent memories—of the colonial enterprise of saving human lives from disease.

A brief report from San Pablo, Laguna, states that the army surgeon, Major Isaac Brewer, was engaged in a bitter fight with the mayor over the handling of the epidemic. The mayor was accused of being "too slow," while Brewer was allegedly "insulting and impatient."[74] Was this another one of those ubiquitous cases of native ignorance or stubbornness? In placing this incident in context we discover that just six months earlier the town church had been occupied by U.S. troops and the parish priest detained. The following month, the mayor had been unceremoniously dismissed, presumably for aiding the guerrillas. At the height of reconcentration, the door of the sacristy, where religious objects had been stored under guarantee of safety by the American commanding officer, had been forced open and several gold and silver chalices, ciboriums, albs, and plates stolen. Occupation troops only abandoned the church on around 17 May, the day the parish priest was freed.[75]

We do not know if the parish priest, Father Alcantara, was a party to the local opposition to interference by American health authorities. It is difficult to picture him bowing to an army surgeon after what the troops had done. He could very well have been one of those native priests who were telling people in the confessional that the Americans were making the anti-cholera campaign "a pretext for harassing them." This opposition or "interference" was great enough to provoke the government to warn the highest church authorities.[76] Priests had always taken charge in past epidemics, parading the host around town, leading novenas and processions, dispensing the last sacraments, at times even heading the local sanitation boards. They represented the notion, antithetical to the army surgeons', that sickness was both a moral as well as a physical state.[77]

San Pablo suffered much during the reconcentration and this the townspeople could not be expected to forget so quickly. The town center was transformed into one of the three largest concentration camps in southwestern Luzon. Yet, when it was found impossible to "protect" the people scattered along the main roads, the zone was further decreased in size.[78] People were packed even closer together, making a mockery of sanitation and vastly increasing the chances of infection. None were left outside to attend to the ricefields. Even in pre-war years, San Pablo's normal crop was only one-twentieth of demand. Its income from the copra trade enabled nearly all its rice to be bought from neighboring towns.[79] This revenue was severely cut back by the reconcentration. The copra trade recommenced in late April only to be hampered by the quarantine, the prohibition of lake traffic in June, and other cholera measures. For a while the townspeople survived on rice aid.

Even before the cholera the mortality from dysentery and malarial fever had been enormous in the San Pablo zone, with 362 deaths being reported in March alone. The army surgeon attributed this to the reconcentration, which gave rise to "crowded conditions and limited facilities" that prevented sanitation and curative measures from being enforced so as to significantly lessen the mortality. He recommended that the natives be permitted to return to their barrios as soon as conditions permitted. If not, "owing to the generally unhealthy conditions prevailing, an outbreak of cholera would jeopardize the life of every one in the town, both soldier and native." When the cholera did arrive, the town was still packed with people, now prevented by quarantine from moving out. However, as in several other garrisoned towns, the American troops were able to flee.[80]

Given such circumstances, it is not hard to imagine why the mayor of San Pablo and the American army surgeon were locked in a bitter squabble at the height of the epidemic. We can hardly doubt that Major Brewer was acting in good faith, but his stress on the "correctness" of his methods ignored the local context. From the townspeople's point of view, the American presence was as much a problem as the cholera. The mayor's irritating "slowness" was but another form of resistance. Representations of the event as an epic struggle against disease and ignorance only divert attention from the wider, all-encompassing colonial intervention which Filipino participants could not easily forget.

In towns where the overseer of epidemic control was the American garrison commander rather than an army surgeon, the tensions were much reduced. For example at Pila, only some twenty kilometers north of San Pablo, the commanding officer simply instructed the mayor to divide up the town into cholera districts under the headship of prominent citizens many of whom had fought in the resistance. A former guerrilla hero, Colonel Ruperto Relova, was put in charge of two barrios. All dealings with the people such as explaining health measures, reporting cases, and arranging burials, were made through men like him.

Militarily, Pila was of little consequence to the Americans. In July, at the height of the epidemic, the whole garrison was moved out. Furthermore, with a population only a quarter that of San Pablo, and being a traditional rice-surplus area, Pila was able to escape food supply problems. In this case, then, the principales were in control and the U.S. presence was weak. There was no need for a "poor fund," no dependence on rice aid, no threat of the traditional social order being upset by arrogant army surgeons. No fuss was made about concealment of cases and the like, because none were discovered.[81]

The example of Pila shows how a different tactic by the Americans could lead to mutual accommodation—a truce perhaps—within a combat zone. In fact, it seems to have been the norm that colonial health and sanitation control provoked popular resistance which, in turn, forced concessions to be made such as the elimination of detention, burnings and cremation, and, most crucial of all, the gradual turning over of disease control to Filipino doctors and local authorities.[82] The other side of apparent local victories in such adjustments, compromises, and accommodation of local customs, was that Filipinos were given the space within which to come to terms with colonial state power. In a sense, it was the Spanish conquista all over again.

As the local elites put their towns into line with at least the broader outlines of the colonial sanitation scheme, the government increasingly found itself confronting the traditional "other" of the Hispanized town-center. The new colonial order, in fact, merely reproduced the classic Philippine pattern of principalia-dominated, sanitary, towns whose outskirts faded into a world of "uncontrollable," "disorderly," or "subversive" elements. After Malvar's surrender, all forms of armed resistance to the regime were labeled "ladronism" (from the Spanish word *ladron*, "bandit" or "highwayman"). A particular form of this which incorporated religious beliefs and rituals was labeled "religious fanaticism."

In the Mariquina valley, the Filipino provincial medical officer and his American counterpart appealed at the end of July for an easing of quarantine restrictions for the following reasons: past harvest had been poor, war conditions had hindered planting in the past three years, the previous crop had been destroyed by locusts, and now the quarantine was preventing peasants from tilling their fields. Yet tenants were being forced to pay their annual rent, "crop or no crop." As a result "many of them, and many of the field labors [were] taking to the mountains and joining the ladrones as a means of earning a living."[83] Were these "bandits" among those who joined up with the revived Katipunan revolutionary government which began to appear in parts of Cavite, Laguna, Tayabas, and Rizal provinces beginning, not surprisingly, in mid-1902?[84]

The foothills of Mount Banahaw, straddling the provinces of Laguna, Tayabas and Batangas, were in a state of unrest in late 1902, to the extent that some Tayabas towns had to be reconcentrated again. Various post-Malvar guerrilla leaders like "Pope" Ruperto Rios and the Katipunan chief Macario Sakay, roamed these hills in late 1902 and 1903. A 1903 report on the religio-political movements based on these hills states that "independence" had become a religion among them. "The magical condition of independencia" was their goal.[85] In Tagalog, the word "independence" is *kalayaan*, one of whose meanings is derived from *kaginhawaan*: "relief from pain," "a life of ease."[86] "Relief from the cholera" would certainly have registered in 1902-3. Notably, the "password" among members of such movements was, and still is, *Ave Maria purissima . . . sin pecada concebida*—the first line of a prayer, posted on doors during the cholera epidemic, imploring the Virgin Mary and Jesus Christ for deliverance from the pestilence.[87]

Banahaw and its foot-hills were the base of operations of *curanderos*, curers who, rather than licensed physicians, were the first recourse of peasants in the region.[88] An American doctor described them as men and women "who do not constitute a class or caste like the medicine men of savage tribes, but are somewhat akin to the barber surgeons of villages in continental Europe in which doctors are not located." *Curanderos* commonly prescribed a cholera medicine extracted from the *manungal* tree (*Samadera Indica*) grown in Tayabas province.[89] A particularly gifted curer combined medical treatment with rituals involving the intervention of a guiding spirit. A condition of treatment was for the patient to undertake some form of pilgrimage to Mount Banahaw in fulfillment of a *panata*, or pledge, to supernatural beings. Cholera epidemics clearly offered ideal conditions for the appearance of healers who attracted villagers away from town-centers and to their fold.[90]

It was common for colonial authorities in 1902 and subsequent cholera years to forcibly disperse people gathered in places considered to be sources of infection: sacred springs, pilgrimage sites, even churches and cockpits. At times, a proscribed healer was the center of attention and promptly suppressed; in other cases, the normal ritual life of the people was disrupted. In accounts emanating from garrison commanders, health officers, teachers, and the like, such interventions are justified in the light of problems posed by ignorance and superstition.

But why did such "problems" persist? As late as 1914, Worcester continued to lament the "unending supply" of healers such as the "Queen of Taytay," discovered during another cholera outbreak in 1905, whose hundreds of followers threatened violent confrontation with the state should harm befall their leader.[91] What were the contours of the knowledge that such healers possessed? What lay behind pilgrimages to Antipolo and Banahaw besides "fanaticism"? The sources are silent. Little emerges from the world of the native inhabitants that is not mediated and distorted by the medico-sanitary discourse of the period. Whatever their real nature, such phenomena spelled danger for the representatives—Filipino and American alike—of the new colonial order. Crowds were being dispersed from sources of infection, they argued, but one suspects that such ritual gatherings were equally suppressed for what they forbode of alternative social orderings or sources of disorder.

Cholera cases and deaths in southwestern Luzon declined in September and October. Strong typhoons were lashing the islands then and, as army surgeons themselves noted, the resulting volume of water flushed the streams and banks. The virulence of the 1902 cholera strain had also expended itself by that time; the population gained increasing immunity. In fact, the cholera seemed to follow the course of the great visitation of 1882. But Worcester and other health officials disagreed, attributing the decline of cases to American health and sanitation measures. In terms of preventing further serious outbreaks, such measures, adapted to local conditions, were probably effective. But in 1902 their actual role was to close a chapter of the Philippine-American war.

NOTES

An earlier version of this chapter was presented at the conference "Death, disease and drugs in Southeast Asian history," held at the Australian National University. My thanks to all those who commented on the draft, especially Ben Anderson, Ben Kerkvliet, Norman Owen, and Rod Sullivan. A grant from the Ford Foundation Southeast Asian Fellowship Program enabled me to conduct the U.S. archival work on which this essay is based.

1. Teodoro A. Agoncillo and Milagros C. Guerrero, *History of the Filipino People*, Quezon City, 1977, pp. 262, 340, 423-25 (on education), 425-26 (on health and welfare).

2. Dean C. Worcester, *Asiatic Cholera in the Philippine Islands*, Manila, 1908; Dean C. Worcester, *The Philippines Past and Present*, New York, 1914; Victor Heiser, *An American Doctor's Odyssey*, New York, 1936

3. *Asiatic Cholera*, p. 18.

4. "Exemplar of Americanism: the Philippine career of Dean C. Worcester," Ph.D. thesis, James Cook University of North Queensland, 1987, p. 146.

5. Maj. C. Lynch, "Asiatic Cholera," Circular 24, Headquarters Division of the Philippines, Manila, 11 April 1902, in file 4981-5, United States National Archives, Bureau of Insular Affairs, Record Group 350 (henceforth cited as U.S.N.A. BIA/file number). An account of the spread of the epidemic to Asia and ultimately the Philippines is found in J. C. Perry, Chief Quarantine Officer, *Public Health Reports*, 17 (henceforth cited as Perry Reports), 26 September 1902, pp. 2240 ff., BIA/4981-9.

6. Annual Report of the Secretary of the Interior to 31 August 1902, in *Reports of the Philippine Commission*, 1902, Washington, 1903, p. 273.

7. Col. L. M. Maus, Commissioner of Public Health, *Report*, 31 July 1902; Appendix A to Worcester, *Annual Report*, pp. 342-43.

8. Chief Surgeon's Report, in "Annual report of the Third Separate Brigade to 1 July 1902," typescript, file 2354, United States National Archives, Records of U.S. Army Overseas Operations and Commands, Record Group 395 (henceforth cited as U.S.N.A. RG395/file number).

9. Lt. Col. P. Harvey, Chief Surgeon, Div. of North Phil., to Adjutant General, 13 May 1902, U.S.N.A. RG395/2635.

10. Dr. S. de los Angeles and Capt. F. W. Dudley, "Joint recommendations for Mariquina, San Mateo, Montalban," 31 July 1902, U.S.N.A. RG395/E2635-13845.

11. Davis, Adjutant, Third Separate Brigade, to commanding officer, Calamba, 19 April 1902, and to commanding officers of all seaport towns 26 April 1902, U.S.N.A. RG395/3287.

12. Surgeon General's Report in *Reports of the U.S. War Department*, 1902, House Documents IV, 57th Congress, 2nd session, 1902-3, p. 613, Chief Surgeon's Report, Third Separate Brigade.

13. An American surgeon assured the public that "the well-to-do in the Philippines, including most of the Americans and Europeans, are protected . . . by the better sanitary conditions under which they live." They merely had to remain vigilant, particularly against the "carelessness or ignorance of native or Chinese cooks"; Lynch, p. 8.

14. H. A. Lindley, Report of the Santiago Cholera Hospital, 17 June to 31 July 1902, exhibit F to Maus Report.

15. Chief Surgeon's Report, Division of the North Phil., Manila, 30 June 1902, U.S.N.A. RG395/2635-11535.

16. Pangasinan, north of Manila, is the only other province where the exceptional 'virulence' of the cholera is noted; Surgeon General's Report, 1902, pp. 613-14.

17. Chief Surgeon's Report, Third Separate Brigade. The complex causes of the massive decline in the Batangas population are analyzed in Glenn A. May, "150,000 missing Filipinos: a demographic crisis in Batangas, 1887-1903," *Annales de Demographie Historique*, 1985, pp. 215-43.

18. Dr. F. Bourns, Commissioner of Public Health, Report, August 1902, appendix B to Worcester, *Annual Report*, p. 393.

19. In a recent study of the zones of concentration in Batangas, Glenn A. May suggests that, in fact, conditions in the camps contributed to the spread of cholera; "The 'zones' of Batangas," *Philippine Studies* 29, 1981, p. 102.

20. M. Malvar, "Testimony," Lucena, 16-19 June 1902, U.S.N.A., Records of the Adjutant General's Office, Record Group 94, file 421607 (henceforth cited as U.S.N.A. RG94/file number).

21. Commanding Officer (henceforth C. O.) Calamba to C. O. Santa Cruz, 12 April and 20 April 1902, U.S.N.A. RG395/3284; Post Surgeon, Calamba, to Adjutant, 13 April 1902, U.S.N.A. RG395/3287. Dates of the first appearance of cholera in the provinces, with statistics, to 1 September 1902 are in exhibit A to the Bourns Report.

22. Cited in Maj. Gen. L. Wheaton (Commanding, Div. of North. Phil.), Report, 6 May 1902, in U.S. War Dept., *Annual Reports*, 1903, 9, pp. 232-23.

23. Col. A. L. Wagner, "Report on the zones of Tanauan and Santo Tomas," 22 March 1902, U.S.N.A. RG395/2635-7788. Wagner admits that the purpose of the report is to combat U.S. public opinion against "concentration."

24. C. O. Calamba to Adj. Gen. Third Separate Brigade, 14 March 1902, U.S.N.A. RG395/3284; C. O. Biñan to C. O. Calamba, 5 February 1902, U.S.N.A. RG395/3287.

25. Adjutant, Calamba, to Commissary, 1 June 1902, U.S.N.A. RG395/3284; Chief Surgeon's report, Third Separate Brigade.

26. On Rizal, S. de los Angeles to C. O., Mariquina river guard, 19 August 1902, RG395/2635; Harvey to Adj. Gen. Third Separate Brigade. On Laguna: C. O. Pila to Adj. Gen. Third Separate Brigade, 1 March 1902, RG395/4747; C. O. Santo Tomas to Adj. Gen. Third Separate Brigade, 7 August 1902, RG395/2354. On Batangas: C. O. San Jose to Bell, July 1902, RG395/2354; L. Gasser to Adj. Gen Third Separate Brigade, 1 August 1902, RG395/2354. (All U.S.N.A.)

27. Perry Reports, 2 August 1902.

28. Enlisted men at San Jose (Batangas) were prohibited from leaving the plaza unless sent on duty, "not on account of the cholera but because it prevents any possible friction or unpleasantness between the soldiers and natives"; C. O. San Jose to Bell. The last entry in the Pila record book is 12 July 1902, U.S.N.A. RG395/4747. On the withdrawal from Alaminos (Laguna), C. O. Alaminos to Adjutant at San Pablo, 13 June 1902, U.S.N.A. RG395/5101.

29. Lt. L. Gasser to Adj. Gen. Third Separate Brigade, 28 July and 1 August 1902, U.S.N.A. RG395/2354; W. Freer, *The Philippine Experiences of an American Teacher*, New York, 1906, pp. 140-41.

30. C. O. Santo Tomas to Adj. Gen. Third Separate Brigade, 7 August 1902.

31. Guzman to Bell, 15 June 1902, U.S.N.A. RG395/5058.

32. Heiser, pp. 39, 104. A typical case: the commanding officer to Pila requested large amounts of chemicals from the Chief Surgeon in order to "disinfect the infected sections of the town and thus save the troops from infection"; C. O. Pila to Chief Surgeon, Division of the Philippines, 24 May 1902, U.S.N.A. RG395/4747.

33. George de Shon, M.D., "Medical highlights of the Philippine-American war," *Bulletin of the American Historical Collection*, 12, 1984, p. 69.

34. Circular Order no. 22, 25 December 1901, cited in Charles B. Elliot, *The Philippines to the End of the Commission Government*, New York, p. 28; my italics.

35. R. Dubos, *Mirage of Health: Utopias, Progress, and Biological Change*, New York, 1959, p. 72; R. H. Shryock, *Medicine in America: Historical Essays*, Baltimore, 1966, pp. 98, 324.

36. Shryock, pp. 23-24, 174-75. The extensive historical literature on the cholera need not be listed here. For a comprehensive study of cholera in the context of nineteenth-century British colonialism, see David Arnold, "Cholera and colonialism in British India," *Past and Present*, 113, 1986, pp. 118-51.

37. U.S. War Department Reports, 1902, vol. 1, p. 437.

38. Bell to Adj. Gen. Div. of the Philippines, 2 September 1902, U.S.N.A. RG94/453824.

39. Lindley, pp. 389-90; Lynch, p. 13, 17-18.

40. Heiser, p. 101. In a report from the Santa Mesa cholera hospital, Capt. T. Marshall admitted that "the definite lines of treatment advocated from time to time have never proved of material service in true cholera"; "Report of Santiago cholera hospital, 27 April to 17 June 1902," exhibit B to Maus Report, p. 363. Lynch (p. 18) mentions the replacement of fluids with normal salt solution through intravenous or interstitial injection—probably the only treatment of real benefit. However, this does not appear to have been widely practiced in the treatment of Filipinos, at least in 1902.

41. Worcester, *Annual Report*, pp. 271, 275.

42. James A. Le Roy, "The Philippines health problem," *The Outlook*, 71, 13, 26 July 1902, p. 780; Worcester, *The Philippines*, p. 442; Sullivan, pp. 214-15.

43. Chief Surgeon's Report, Third Separate Brigade.

44. C. F. de Mey, "Cholera Report," 30 May 1902, appended to Worcester, *Annual Report*, pp. 412-13.

45. Heiser, p. 38; my italics.

46. Worcester, *Annual Report*, p. 268.

47. Heiser, p. 106. See also Sullivan, p. 215.

48. Worcester, *The Philippines*, p. 442.

49. Worcester, *The Philippines*, p. 416; Worcester, *Annual Report*, p. 271; Perry Reports, 13 August 1902; Heiser, p. 106. Le Roy (p. 781) says that abuses were, indeed, committed but does not give details.

50. Maus Report, p. 344.

51. Lindley, p. 390; Bourns, p. 392. Filipino doctors retained elements of the "traditional" treatment practiced since the 1840s, which is described in J. P. Bantug. *Short History of Medicine in the Philippines during the Spanish Regime, 1565-1898*, Manila, 1952, pp. 36-37.

52. Adjutant, Santa Cruz, to C. O. Pila, 23 May 1902, U.S.N.A. RG395/4748; Maus Report, p. 326.

53. "Teachers and cholera in the Philippines," *The Nation*, 77, 8 October and 15 October 1903.

54. Worcester, *Annual Report*, pp. 269, 271.

55. General Order 66, Headquarters, Div. of the Philippines, 25 March 1902, U.S.N.A. RG395/E3287.

56. C. O. Calamba to Adjutant, 13 April 1902, U.S.N.A. RG395/3287; C. O. Calamba to C. O. Santa Cruz, 20 April 1902, U.S.N.A. RG395/3284.

57. Acts of the Philippine Commission, no. 490, in *Report of the Philippine Commission for 1903*, Washington, 1904, pt. 2, 1149.

58. "Teachers and cholera." At Dagupan, sanitary inspectors set fire to several houses but the fire could not be controlled and the city itself was threatened with

destruction; *Manila Times*, 9 July 1902, cited in Sullivan, pp. 209-10.

59. de Mey, p. 412.

60. Fifty percent is, in fact, a conservative estimate. In the Chief Surgeon's report for the month ending 15 July, he states that "it is probable that in the whole archipelago not more than one-fourth or one-fifth of the cholera cases are now being reported"; cited in Surgeon General's Report, 1902, pp. 613-14.

61. Bell's instructions mentioned by the Adjutant at Santa Cruz, in a letter to C. O. Pila, 23 May 1902.

62. Bantug, p. 31, Worcester, *The Philippines*, p. 410.

63. Maus Report, pp. 327, 332.

64. "Teachers and cholera."

65. Worcester, *Annual Report*, p. 269; Worcester, *The Philippines*, p. 410.

66. Maus Report, pp. 326-27.

67. Bourns Report, p. 393. An account of a "macabre" cremation in Nueva Caceres, seat of the archbishopric of southern Luzon, is given in Sullivan, p. 210.

68. C. O. Pila to presidente of the town, 4 June 1902, U.S.N.A. RG395/4747.

69. T. Marshall, Chief Health Inspector, "Asiatic Cholera in the Philippine Islands," (Health Bulletin 2, 1 August 1902), Manila, 1904, U.S.N.A. BIA/4981-20, p. 11, "Teachers and cholera"; Bantug, p. 36.

70. Report of Capt. L. B. Sandall, cited in Surgeon General's Report, p. 613.

71. Le Roy, p. 781.

72. Perry Report, 2 August 1902; Chief Surgeon's Report, Third Separate Brigade.

73. An American doctor opposed to the imperial take-over pointed out that Americans were simply ignorant of the state of Spanish-Filipino medicine; D. Doherty, "Medicine and disease in the Philippines," *Journal of the American Medical Association*, 16 June 1900 (reprint), p. 16.

74. Report from post, San Pablo, June 1902, U.S.N.A. RG395/2635-12066.

75. Fr. F. Alcantara to Sr. Archbishop of Manila, 20 May 1902, U.S.N.A. RG359/ 2635-12912.

76. Le Roy, p. 781.

77. Freer, p. 146; "Teachers and cholera." The crucial role of priests in earlier epidemics is amply documented in the eight *colera* bundles located in the Philippine National Archives.

78. Wheaton Report, p. 233.

79. C. O. Santo Tomas to Adj. Gen., Third Separate Brigade, 7 August 1902.

80. Surgeon, San Pablo Military Hospital, to Post Adjutant, 14 April 1902, U.S.N.A. RG359/5099. This was the situation, as well, in the concentration camps of Batangas province; see May, "Zones," pp. 99-100.

81. C. O. Pila to presidente, 4 June 1902, RG359/4747; C. O. Santa Cruz to C. O. Pila, 13 February 1902, RG359/E4748; C. O. Pila to Adj. Gen., Third Separate Brigade, 1 March 1902. (All U.S.N.A.)

82. Worcester, *Annual Report*, pp. 271-72; Bourns Report, p. 392; Perry Reports, 31 July 1902.

83. Angeles and Dudley, "Joint recommendations."

84. See Reynaldo C. Ileto, *Pasyon and Revolution; Popular Movements in the Philippines, 1840-1910*, Quezon City, 1979, chapter 5.

85. Ileto, pp. 229, 233-34; Freer, pp. 136-38.

86. Ileto, pp. 107-8, 234-35.

87. Freer, p. 144. The full text, translated from the Spanish, is: "Hail Mary, most pure, who conceived without sin./ Holy God, Holy Strength, Holy Immortal,/ Deliver us, Lord from the pestilence and from all evil./ By thy wounds, by thy cross,/ Deliver us from the pestilence,/ thou divine Jesus."

88. Hence the saying, "le curo el tonto y le mato el sabio" (the stupid man cures while the learned man kills); Bantug, p. 35. Figures for as late as 1912 show that the towns around the mountain harbored an abnormally high proportion, in relation to trained medical personnel, of curanderos; *Infant Mortality in the Philippine Islands*, Manila, 1914, p. 439.

89. Dohery, p. 16; Fr. Joaquin Martinez de Zuñiga, *Status of the Philippine Islands in 1800*, orig. pub. 1893, Manila, 1973, p. 417; Bantug, p. 27.

90. From interviews with Dr. Consolacion Alaras, University of the Philippines. In 1902, old Visayans who eschewed American medicine reminisced about "a famous old native medicine-woman from Cebu who wrought miracles with her 'santas medicinas' during the 1888 cholera visitation"; "Teachers and cholera." On the unrest in Samar occasioned by pilgrimages after the cholera of 1882-3, see Bruce Cruickshank, *Samar: 1768-1898*, Manila, 1985, chapter 8.

91. Worcester, *The Philippines*, p. 437. Heiser (pp. 122-23) gives a more detailed version of the story.

THREE

"Where Every Prospect Pleases and Only Man is Vile": Laboratory Medicine as Colonial Discourse

WARWICK ANDERSON

WHEN ANDREW BALFOUR SPOKE TO THE LONDON SOCIETY OF TROPICAL MEDI-cine and Hygiene in 1914, his subject was "Tropical Problems in the New World," and he had some recent information from the Philippines that would surprise some of his audience and reassure others. Balfour announced that Weston Chamberlain, working in the Manila Bureau of Science, had recently reported on his investigations of the "physiological activity of Americans in these islands and the influence of tropical residence on the blood." It seemed probable that the tropical climate itself exercised no harmful influence on the new colonizers. "By far the larger part of the morbidity and mortality in the Philippines is due to nostalgia, isolation, tedium, venereal disease, alcoholic excess, and especially to infections with various parasites." Chamberlain's laboratory investigations thus challenged the long-held medical theories of inevitable white degeneration in the tropics.[1]

The economic and political aspects of American colonialism in the Philippines had rapidly been translated into the language of medical science. Even before Emilio Aguinaldo, the leader of the nationalist resistance, was captured in 1901, government laboratories had begun to operate out of a temporary building in Manila. By the following year, as a brutal American military campaign suppressed the last of the resistance, the laboratories had moved into permanent quarters from which they surveyed the Islands, collected information on the climate and tropical diseases, and conducted experiments on Filipinos and on blond and brunette soldiers.[2] The apparently technical literature of laboratory medicine would play an important role in constituting colonial social realities. The work of both the Manila Bureau of Science and the Army Board for the Study of Tropical Diseases on the acclimatization or adaptation of Filipinos and Americans to the tropics engaged its readers in a vivid spectacle of Western physical and cultural authority. At the same time as this discourse defined and multiplied physical difference, its assumption of universal explanatory power was an attempted erasure of Filipino authority in knowledge production.

My concern here is with the way a new American medical discourse in the Philippines fabricated and rationalized images of the bodies of the colonized and the subordinate colonizers. I intend to read the reports of biological (and in particular physiological) experiments as discursive constructions of the American colonial project, as attempts to naturalize the power of foreign bodies to appropriate and command the Islands.[3] The origin of the American colonial enterprise at a time when science gave a novel force and legitimacy to public policy permitted scientists and doctors to construct a new physiology of colonialism. The medical laboratory thus became a social space for the interaction of rediscovered American and Filipino bodies.[4] The Filipino emerged in this period as a potentially dangerous part of the zoological realm, while the American colonizer became a resilient racial type, no longer inevitably susceptible to the tropical climate but vulnerable instead to the crowd of invisible, alien parasites now associated with native bodies. This new medical discourse in the tropics is a local instance of a broad shift in the language and practices of medical science occurring at the end of the nineteenth century. Generally, the medical concern with constitutions and climate gave way to a greater interest in the specific microbial causation

of individual disease. At the same time, the colonial doctor's anec-
dotes and clinical impressions seemed less convincing, and increasingly the laboratory was called on to authenticate knowledge.

During this transitional period, the laboratory recast the constitutional dangers of tropical climates into a form that stressed the hazards of a parasitic environment, a biological and social terrain in which
the salients were Filipino bodies containing invisible microbes. The
alien blonds and brunettes now had more to fear from contact with a
variety of diseased native fauna than from exposure to the rays of the
tropical sun. The colonial scientific paper created both the "resistance"
of the American body to the tropical climate itself and the "natural"
differences in disease carriage and susceptibility between Americans
and Filipinos in this increasingly neutral climatic region. This medical
discourse determined settlement patterns, housing, clothing, and working conditions in the Philippines: together with the more popular texts
that it informed and reinforced, it served to consolidate racial hierarchies and to define possible colonial categories of experience.

Medical articles, geographical and political texts, administrative
reports, novels, and popular travel accounts were all more or less
predicated on the extraction and appropriation of the speech and
bodies of both the colonized and the laboring colonizers. Many of
these colonial genres have recently received scholarly attention.[5] But
in order to convey the heterogeneity of colonial discourse, a further
enlargement of "the disciplinary enclave" of the critique of colonialism may be necessary.[6] A recognition that even the most formally
structured technical knowledge could constitute a form of colonial
appropriation is long overdue. As yet, the technical contemporary
laboratory literature, a genre similar in form to the rationalist and
seemingly value-neutral accounts of modern tropical medicine, has
evaded the scrutiny of critics of colonialism. But recent social studies
of the laboratory and its inscriptions suggest that we should not continue to ignore these texts which comprise one of the more pervasive
and lasting of colonial discourses.[7] Historians of science are no longer
content simply to chronicle the progressive enlightenment that turns
one generation's "eternal verities" into lessons in fallibility for the next.
Increasingly, attention has been directed at local and contextual aspects of scientists' representational practices—though few scholars have

yet looked beyond the domestic laboratories of Europe and the United States. Paradoxically perhaps, this inquiry into the textual economy of the laboratory still permits us to describe the shift in the understanding of the body that occurred in the Philippines as a scientific advance, though now only in the sense that it indicates an expansion of the power of the laboratory to represent and, in so doing, to shape and to regulate colonial social life.

The insertion of colonial bodies into a metropolitan discourse provides sanction for the politics of colonialism at the same time as it reproduces them. The experimenters themselves take on the power to order and exploit subject bodies as they intervene repressively in the social world of the experiment. This procedural colonialism makes the scientific investigation of tropical medicine one of the more vivid and representative colonial discourses, not just in structure, style and content, but also in the obliteration of any record of resistance to its actual intrusions on the body. This textual despotism of the laboratory confirms, perhaps better than any other genre, Said's suggestion that colonial discourse can be possessed entirely by the colonizer.[8] That medical science emphasizes this should not surprise us. What we have here, of course, is a colonial instance of the more general "colonial" relationship that holds between all medical investigators and those whose diffident bodies they disassemble. What is perhaps more surprising is that a technical vocabulary has for so long disguised the contribution of this genre to the colonial project.

II

The Philippine commissioners, as they sat in a stuffy room of the Mania *audencia* early in July, 1899, kept returning to the same question. They had recently been appointed to report on conditions in the archipelago. "We would like to know particularly," the commissioners asked Simon Flexner and L. F. Barker, "what effect the climate and maladies would have on Americans coming here, whether they could endure the climate or not. . . ."[9] Neither of these professors of pathology was optimistic. "The climate," lamented Barker, "seems to affect Americans especially with regard to their assimilation. People who have lived here a long time grow gradually pale . . . Women, especially, grow pale, and the European children we have seen have a tendency to anemia." While Americans might live in the tropics for a few years, they could never labor there. "I think a great many men would sicken, and if they tried it for two or three generations without replenishment from home, to use a slang expression, they would 'peter out.'" Barker had himself endured the climate for some two months before giving his testimony, and so could speak with conviction. "Someone had said that here the sun is always dangerous, and I am inclined to think so. I have felt it very much."[10]

Nor was he alone. In its unspecified fear of the tropical climate and its reliance on anecdote, Barker's assessment represented medical opinion on acclimatization as it existed in the 1890s.[11] Most physicians still believed that human beings and their environments had no pre-destined harmony: all life forms strived constantly to maintain an equable physiology and temperament in the face of changed circumstances.[12] Until the end of the century, medical experts on the tropics argued that the European's struggle to adapt to the humid, equatorial regions, so unlike those in which the race had evolved, was an impossible one. The "white man's grave" was at least as real as the "white man's burden."[13] The high death rates in many of the more torrid colonial outposts could scarcely be denied. "Under the circumstances of ordinary life," warned Davidson's *Hygiene and Diseases of Warm Climates* in 1892, "a tropical climate . . . is inimical to the European constitution."[14] A continued high temperature seemed to produce in the white body "an excessive cutaneous action, alternating with internal congestions." Although "the effort of nature is to accommodate the constitution to the newly established physiological requirements" there were inherent racial limits to the extent of this accomplishment.[15] Indeed, it had long been common knowledge among "old hands" that while Europeans could supervise and instruct a native population (at least so long as they retired regularly to the hills and sent their children home at an early age) the settlement of a working white race in the tropics was out of the question. Benjamin Kidd, the American social Darwinist, did not doubt that "the attempt to acclimatize the white man in the tropics must be recognized to be a blunder of the first magnitude. All experiments based on the idea are foredoomed to failure."[16]

On the eve of the United States sending a white army to live and work indefinitely in the Philippines, Kidd pointed out that "in climatic conditions which are a burden to him; in the midst of races in a different and lower stage of development; divorced from the influences which have produced him, from the moral and political environment from which he sprang, the white man . . . tends himself to sink slowly to the level around him." For in the tropics, "the white man lives and works only as a diver lives and works under water."[17] Comparisons of the tropical climate with the depths of the ocean, the mountain summit and the foul atmosphere of the mines abound in the scientific and the lay press of the late nineteenth century. People of all races were incorporated into his natural world. Man was compared to the horse, ass and zebra, according to racial distribution;[18] or, when he wandered, to the exotic plants so vulnerable to a foreign environment. Since racial degeneration, brought about by climatic conditions alone, would decide the fate of even the best organized empire, the authors of these essays could claim that climatic conditions and their effect on Europeans should be fundamental factors in colonial policy making. Thus, in an influential review of the medical and geographical literature in 1898, the American economist W. Z. Ripley stated explicitly that "the almost universal opinion seems to be that true colonization in the tropics by a white race is impossible."[19]

At the end of the century these fears of racial degeneration in the torrid zone persisted, and indeed were expressed with ever more precision, as the disciplines of climatology and physiology professionalized. While most people loosely associated the "tropics" with a land of impenetrable jungle, heat, swamp and fever, a number of scientists began to define the climate more carefully in terms of its effects upon Europeans. Measures of heat and humidity—namely the readings of the dry and wet bulb thermometers—were used during the early twentieth century to construct a discomfort scale for the white race.[20] Griffith Taylor, a geographer at the University of Chicago, introduced a graphic representation of relative humidity and wet bulb readings, termed a climograph. From the average figures for towns situated in temperate regions where his experience told him that "human energy is at its best" he compiled a climograph that represented the ideal conditions for the white race.[21] The tropics were redefined as that region which deviated most from this "white race climograph." Thus one part of the colonial world became enclosed physiologically, not just politically or economically.

The effect of sunlight on living organisms was the subject of many of the nineteenth-century case reports relevant to the emerging empires. Colonel Charles Woodruff of the United States Army wrote an extensive monograph on the impact of tropical light on the white man, and his conclusions were widely quoted. He contended that the ultraviolet rays of the tropical sun are inimical to white settlement; thus a blond race could never live closer to the equator than 50 degrees and "even in New Zealand and Australia the native white families are already dying out or kept alive by constant new importation from home."[22] Christian Eijkman, in nearby Batavia, interrupted his studies of beriberi in order to elucidate the protective role played by pigment. He covered the bulbs of two thermometers with pieces of white and colored skin and left them in the sun to see which caused a higher rise in the mercury.[23]

This, then, is the rather anecdotal scientific fieldwork that was challenged by the laboratory workers of the Manila Bureau of Science. Two features of this old style of investigation are especially significant. First, the prevailing discourse had redefined colonial geography in terms of the discomfort of European bodies; secondly, this redefinition presupposed an essential racial constitution potentially in harmony only with the particular ancestral environment, or climate, in which a race had evolved. For the "old-guard" tropical specialists, the very idea of acclimatization, of the adaptation of a temperate race to a torrid region, implied a need to correct a disturbance of normal body function: but in many cases the disease or disequilibrium would be so severe as to lead to degeneration and death before the balance could be restored by returning to one's native climate. This process seemed to underlie the constitutional decay that medical men had observed in Europeans long resident in the tropical colonies, and it incorporated all races into their own particular ecology, subject to zoological law. Thus, despite the contemporary advances of bacteriology, many colonial physicians were still arguing, until well into the twentieth century, that disease in the equatorial region could arise directly from physical imbalances caused by a mismatch between race and environment, and not from a specific invasive entity.[24]

III

Increasingly though, during the first decade of the twentieth century, the ecological theory from which acclimatization drew its strength met resistance from experts in the emerging discipline of tropical medicine. These men, trained in the recently established European and American schools of tropical hygiene, expected to find a specific microbe or an isolated toxin for every disease.[25] Sir Ronald Ross, the discoverer of the role of *Anopheles* in the transmission of malaria, was among their leaders. In his opinion the causes of the degeneration of whites in the tropics were parasitism, alcohol, diet, and "intestinal intoxication."[26] Most of this younger generation of doctors, whose careers often lay in the laboratory, believed that acclimatization could be understood in terms of the character and behavior of infectious agents of disease and their pathogenic activity. As the role of environmental conditions appeared to diminish, attention shifted to the specific interaction of the microbial parasite and its host. The climate accordingly would influence the condition of Europeans in the tropics only to the extent it gave rise to street filth, poor disposal of animal and human waste, dubious milk and water quality, and (most importantly) to a heavier burden of parasitic disease. "It is not the mere influence of climate which opposes colonization in tropical lands," advised Luigi Sambon, "but the competition of other living organisms—from man, wild beasts, and snakes to protozoa and bacteria—with which we have to struggle for existence."[27] According to this new medicine, developing apace with the American involvement in the tropics, sunlight and humidity alone did not sap one's racial integrity. The white race's germ plasm (to use a term that Weissman had recently made popular) was more resilient than hitherto supposed.[28]

It is thus possible to discern a shift from a passive to a more interventionist approach to the tropical environment; from a notion of vulnerable, refined European constitutions to a confidence in the continuity of racial type; from an emphasis on the medical ecology of colonialism to a concern with the medical meaning of interpersonal relations. The constitutional pathology within the individual colonial body became less important than the biological exchanges occurring in the space between stable, typical bodies. The new microbial tropical medicine asserted the importance of controlling contact with the "natives," any of whom might be silent carriers of disease. A native race that has evolved with tropical microbes must, unlike the otherwise more robust and energetic European types, have developed some *modus vivendi* with them, rendering members of the race more likely the asymptomatic transporters of microbes than their victims. Thus it seemed now that disease manifestation and susceptibility depended more on racial character, and personal habits in acquiring microbes, than on climate.[29]

Until the late 1900s, in every picture of Philippine progress there was " . . . a somber background of a baneful climate making it impossible for the American or the European to live in health and strength in the Islands for any length of time."[30] Yet more and more it seemed, in the words of the president of Philippine Medical Association, "that of all the ills particularly among women, from real bodily ailments to a poor complexion, for which the climate is usually blamed, the great majority are hereditary or acquired, were brought here by the patient and often aggravated by careless or unhygienic living."[31] Acclimatization was thus becoming either unnecessary or at least possible to achieve through enforcement of a strict medical regimen. It was no longer unnatural for a European to thrive in the tropics, if sanitary precautions were observed—that is, if one avoided (or controlled at a distance) the native "reservoirs" of disease, and the insect vectors. There was "the vast amount of clinical material under the control of the Bureau of Science" to prove it. And proof was desirable, for "if the United States is to continue its governmental relations indefinitely, the fact that Americans can lead healthful lives in the Philippines is important of itself."[32]

The very existence of a Bureau of Science in the Philippines, and the success of its publications such as the *Philippine Journal of Science*, was taken to be evidence of superior American rationality and modernity.[33] As Joseph Hayden, vice-governor-general of the islands in the 1930s, recalled "it was one of the great achievements of the period that within the Philippine government an essentially scientific attitude should have been substituted for unscientific ways."[34] And nowhere did this scientific attitude prevail more than in the Bureau of Science. Created in 1905 from a reorganization of the Bureau of Government Laboratories, it provided a haven for those medical officers of the U.S. armed forces who sought a career in research.[35] From 1906, the Bureau's laboratories also housed the military medical officers of the Army Board of Study for the investigation of "tropical diseases as they exist in the Philippine Islands."[36] The Board undertook diagnostic work for the Army, collected specimens for the Army Medical School, and conducted experiments on the U.S. forces and Filipino scouts, investigating unknown fevers, dengue, the microbial carriage of healthy men, and the acclimatization of blond and brunette recruits. Between 1906 and 1914, the Board took advantage of "the vast field for original research which has been opened to our medical officers by service in the tropics."[37]

Many of the scientists of the Bureau and the Board eventually converted this stint in the field into a more distinguished academic post: P. R. Strong later became the first professor of tropical medicine at Harvard; Charles Craig was a professor of tropical medicine at Tulane; Edward Vedder, a professor of experimental medicine at George Washington University; and Weston Chamberlain was later a commandant at the Army Medical School. In the Philippines, the Bureau of Science was a staging post for the emissaries of high scientific culture, allowing them to work in the field before resuming their metropolitan careers. From their quarters in Manila they undertook the rigorous and systematic inscription of the Philippines, producing volumes of ethnographies, laboratory reports, environmental descriptions, discussions of hygienic engineering and architecture, as well as a number of physiological investigations, carefully reinforced with statistics. For the next forty or more years whenever a textbook of tropical medicine dealt with human acclimatization—if only to discredit the problem—it cited the investigations of the Manila Bureau of Science and the Army Board of Study.

IV

The scientific paper was as authoritative a genre in the colonies as elsewhere.[38] Several features of the texts give them special coherence and distinguish them from other, often less defensible, colonial documents. Each paper conforms to the same sequence of argument, with an introduction, methods section, results (often tabulated), and a conclusion (usually in point form). In each case, this logic is stabilized and reinforced with copious references and statistics; publication dates and volume numbers are prominent; the authors are listed, along with their qualifications and institutional affiliation; and the information is conveyed in the third person, located in the present or immediate past. The assemblies of physical signs and test results have no obvious history. Where Filipinos were concerned, an investigator admitted privately that "it was impossible, even with the good interpreters available, to obtain histories, for the men were sullen, stupid and often purposefully deceptive."[39] In the final published form, the documents reveal the transforming, contemporary medical spectacle: temperatures are *taken* and specimens are *extracted* from apparently submissive bodies; blood counts are *performed*. It has become a peculiarly disembodied and ahistorical drama: within the paper, the scientific actor, too, becomes conventionally effaced, invisible, innocently acquiescing in the "reality" of laboratory technique.

The frequent statement of genre within the text confers a sense of the distinction of the work, and implied what Spivak has called the rules of recognition.[40] The introduction makes it clear that we are reading "scientific investigations," or "medical examinations," not mere travelers' tales, or administrative reports. "The large number of independent observers minimizes as far as possible the influence of the personal equation in this work." Usually a list follows of all the "army medical officers" engaged in the "experiment." The scale of the proceedings is also emphasized. "The number of men observed is so large that the element of chance is eliminated."[41] The text thus appears orderly and systematic, distinct from any local disarray that gave rise to it. The sense of place that the papers evoke is a rarefied one: Filipinos do not belong to a village or even an island, though the soldiers may be attached to a military unit—in these texts everyone becomes a resident of the idealized, reconstituted tropical region.[42]

Much of the plausibility of the acclimatization research derives from a laborious description of methods, a detailing of techniques, and from the statistical marshalling of crowds. The scientific inscription devices permit the "virtual witnessing" of these medical parades.[43] Colonial bodies in general are reduced to figures, sorted out, and then aggregated in tabular societies. The visibility and simplicity of the composition gives a rhetorical force to the scientists' arguments, and undermines the claims of anyone who would, without a laboratory, attempt to challenge this concentration of marshalled data. The colonial scientific paper so convincingly conveys to an elite Western audience the impression of veracity that it assumes the power to determine the language of debate.

As part of an intertextual series, the separate papers on blood pressure, hemoglobin, white cell count, complexion, and clothing, become complementary accounts of the innocuousness of climate. When the anecdotal claims of earlier observers, such as Woodruff, are cited, it is only to undermine the old, competing paradigm. Without a modern laboratory, the fears of these earlier writers appear unsupported and untenable. In addition, recurrent references in the Manila experimental records to parallel scientific work in the Dutch East Indies, Indochina and India, confirm the legitimacy of the literature at the same time as they imply an emerging consensus on the nature of the white man in the tropics. Common to all these modern papers is an emphasis on the intercolonial and international deployment of scientific reputation.

Securely located in the contemporary scientific categories, the texts were treated accordingly with respect by their audience of colonial administrators and medical scientists. As resources for apprehending the Philippines, they meant that Filipinos could be taken as collectives, unclean, subject to zoological laws and part of the ecology, akin to parasites; while Europeans appeared singularly in case studies, and even as groups would stand apart from the tropical fauna, having evolved in a different environment. The most complete and separate case study was conducted on a single enlisted man of the Medical Department of the U.S. Army; the comparable studies of Filipinos averaged the results of a collective.[44] But even individual Americans are described in passive constructions in these texts: while these subordinate colonizers have been allowed some independence from the tropical environment, they are obviously not the authors of the documents that insist on their limited freedom. The autonomy of all the objects of investigation—especially of Filipinos, but also of Americans—is restricted and controlled (though in significantly different ways) by an emphasis on community responsibility and medical direction.

The investigation of human acclimatization represents the extraction and appropriation of the bodies of both the colonized and the laboring colonizers. In a sense, then, the scientific papers force a dialogue between white and colored bodies. The taking of specimens and the measuring of the body in various ways can be seen as rituals of speech extortion.[45] The objects of investigation are excluded from the full meaning of this "utterance." And, furthermore, the structure of colonial inequality required for this extortion—the imbalance of power required for a scientist to generate such texts—is carefully disguised. The scientific paper thus amplifies this forced, but misrecognized, dialogue—the coerced, reduced, translated speech of apparently docile bodies—beyond the social and historical situation in which it was created. Science thus produces subjects without a history or a culture, situating them in a temporally indeterminant, yet spatially redifferentiating, experimental project.

V

The extensive observations of medical men in the Philippines first contributed to a dissolution of the sense of tropical peril that had accumulated over the previous century. Aron concluded that "the spectrum of the sun's rays does not extend much, if any, further into the ultraviolet in Manila than in Northern climates."[46] Gibbs expressed a similar opinion, and was unable to believe that "when the normal intensities are compared, the light of the tropics is different from the sunlight of any other region."[47] This clearly represented a challenge to Woodruff, who had attributed the deterioration of the white organism to the influence of ultraviolet rays only. Shaklee found that his experimental monkeys, exposed to the sun in Manila, died from heat stroke after varying periods depending more on local conditions, such as the proximity of a fan, than on any quality of the sun's rays. Evidently, exposure to the direct sun's rays caused such an increase in body temperature that the animals finally succumbed to hyperpyrexia, just as they might in more temperate climates. In every case, Shaklee noted, animals of dark color died more quickly than those with light fur, on account of the greater absorption of heat.[48] Thus the "white organism" should not necessarily be regarded as a transgressor against nature in the tropical colonies.

One of the more striking demonstrations of the supposed advantages of a *lack* of pigmentation in the tropics was the influential test of colored underwear. In 1907, Lt. Colonel W. T. Wood, the Inspector-general of the Army, Philippine Division, ordered the Board of Study to conduct a long-term study of orange-red clothing to see whether Americans could artificially adapt themselves to the tropics.[49] Over the next three years, J. M. Phalen and his co-investigators supplied 500 soldiers with orange-red underwear, and compared their well-being in the course of a year with another group wearing white underwear. Records were kept on cards, detailing age, height, nativity, color of hair, color of eyes, complexion and length of tropical service. Weight, pulse, and respiratory rate were measured regularly—and some recruits were also studied more closely with blood pressure readings, "for the effect of short exposures to the sun." Interestingly, the men attired in orange-red underwear—far from being protected—showed changes due to heat, such as loss in body weight and hemoglobin and decreased blood pressure, more marked than the control group. Phalen concluded from his experiments that the colored garments were more receptive to heat rays than the white, since wearers complained persistently of greater heat, greater weight, and increased perspiration, and he expressed the opinion that conventional khaki clothing afforded enough protection from the sun's chemical rays, without the ill-effects of the special underwear.[50] In this case, though, to have color had actually been disabling in the tropics.

Until the Manila laboratory began recording temperatures in a systematic way, it was widely believed that the metabolism of Europeans increased in the tropics. John Davy, in 1839, had published a number of observations made upon the mouth temperature of seven healthy young men during a voyage from England to Ceylon, and he concluded that the temperature of a European increased when passing from a temperate to a torrid zone, and that, in addition, the body temperature of residents in the tropics is raised slightly above normal.[51] Many others during the nineteenth century, including Rattray, Brown-Sequard, Jousset, and Maurel, confirmed this slight rise.[52] Yet Chamberlain, after recording 3,000 mouth temperatures taken at quarterly intervals from 600 healthy American soldiers living in the Philippines, concluded that body temperature showed no appreciable variation with season or complexion. The average differed little, if at all, from the mean normal temperature of white men living in the United States.[53]

The effect of the Philippine climate on blood pressure was, however, somewhat more ambiguous. The blood pressure was frequently referred to as the organism's "tension," which diminished with a fall in peripheral resistance. It was important for the white man to maintain his tension in the tropical environment. "If loss of physical or mental tone is measurable in objective terms it has seemed to us that blood pressure readings should show it."[54] In 1910, Musgrave and Sison examined 97 Americans, 10 sisters of charity, and 40 Filipinos, all residents in Manila. They concluded that a decided decrease in the blood pressure had occurred after long residence in the tropical climate—with the lowest tensions recorded among Filipinos—perhaps as a result of a lowered peripheral resistance, brought about either by a reduction in vasomotor tone or by splanchnic influences.[55] But despite these findings, Chamberlain argued in 1911 that a permanent change in the blood pressure should not be anticipated. He took the pressures of 992 American soldiers and made 5,368 observations, concluding that "the average blood pressure of 115 to 118 millimeters found in these large bodies of men differed little, if any, from the accepted standard among males of the same age in a temperate zone."[56] Only temporary variations might occur, such as a rise on exertion or a lowering due to venous hyperemia of the skin, similar to that produced by a hot bath in a temperate region, but both would be evanescent and certainly not peculiar to tropical life.

In order to construct a more resilient white body in a less menacing climate, attention also had to be paid to the supposedly poor

quality of the blood of Europeans long resident in a tropical possession. The existence of a tropical anemia for a long time had been
regarded as an established fact. Visitors to the colonial outposts often
observed that the skin of healthy Europeans inhabiting a tropical climate appeared pale and sallow. This gave rise to the notion that "thin-
ness and poorness" of blood was a natural consequence of inappropriate residence in the tropics, and an incontrovertible sign of racial
degeneration.[57] Yet it was not until the early 1900s that microscopical
techniques made the constituents of blood visible in the tropics. The
results were rather surprising. The ever-vigorous Chamberlain performed 1,718 red cell counts and 1,433 hemoglobin estimations of 702
soldiers, and concluded that the figures "do not differ from the normal at present recognized for healthy young men in a temperate
zone."[58] In most cases of anemia in the tropics, hookworm or malaria,
not the climate, could now be identified as the cause—and these pathogens could be avoided according to a strict sanitary regimen.

Yet Chamberlain and Vedder did detect some "abnormalities"
in the blood of both soldiers and Filipinos.[59] In each group—but especially among the Filipinos—the total number of leukocytes, the white
cells, was less than expected, while the numbers of eosinophils, yellow-staining cells, were increased. Furthermore, the Arneth blood picture of the expatriate soldiers showed a slight "shift to the left," that of
the Filipinos a much more marked shift, which meant that the "less-
mature" polymorph fraction of the total white cell count was higher
than that of healthy Europeans living in a temperate climate. Chamberlain was convinced that this "disturbance of the normal proportions of different varieties of leukocytes is probably common to most
primitive and semi-civilized peoples in the tropics." He concluded:
"We may therefore look upon Igorots (and probably most Filipinos)
as having a chronically increased percentage of eosinophiles and small
lymphocytes . . ."[60] The isomorphism of blood and supposed racial
features is marked: Filipinos had an abundance of yellow-staining cells,
and a scarcity of white cells, which were in any case small and imma-
ture. But this blood picture was not regarded as a primary racial characteristic, but rather interpreted as a feature secondary to disease carriage—which had become a characteristic more closely related to racial habits. Breinl and Young thought the results indicated "a greater

activity of the bone marrow, but [did] not necessarily imply that the resistance of the organism is lowered."[61] In other words, here was evidence not of degenerative change, but of an effort to cope with the increased load of specific pathogens, the germs and parasites that had been revealed in the tropics, which were particularly associated with the "unsanitary habits" of Filipinos. Thus the similarities in the blood pictures merely indicated that Americans long-resident in the tropics had begun to behave more like the locals, and mix with them more frequently—not that the white race was degenerating under the influence of climate.

Tropical science thus managed to convert the dirty, humid, teeming, complex environment into controllable specimens and measurements, which were further consolidated as figures in the scientific paper. Latour, writing about Pasteur, has observed that "in this succession of displacements, no one can say where the laboratory is and where the society is."[62] Colonial society and environment were given meaning in the laboratory, and colonial bodies were there reduced to the categories of medical science.

VI

The apparently fixed tropical space into which America expanded was in the process of being reconstructed by American science. An important trend in the Philippines research was toward the domestication of the tropical climate, with the result that only the alien pathogenic fauna, a biological community that potentially included the native inhabitants, made the tropics different from temperate zones. The murky and diffusely pathogenic atmosphere had cleared to reveal parasites whose life cycle included residence in native bodies. Disease surveys had confirmed the hitherto hidden threat: 92.5% of Igorots showed parasites in their stools,[63] while 95.9% out of 1,000 Filipinos were infected, though usually asymptomatic. Malarial organisms "commonly" were found in the blood of lowland Filipinos, especially children.[64] The islands acquired by America had been "left foul and insanitary by generations of hygienically ignorant peoples."[65] Just when the European germ plasm appeared insulated from the atmosphere, it faced destruction from the peculiar tropical infections that the microscope had recently made visible. Safety might be achieved not by the avoidance of the climate, but by the restriction of contact with tropical fauna—a fauna that included Filipino bodies.

The colonized were construed as a collection of hygienically degenerate types, requiring constant surveillance, instruction, and sometimes isolation. Victor Heiser, the commissioner of health in the Philippines and a keen advocate of the local scientific investigations, initially suspected that "the Oriental could not be sanitated; he always had lived in filth and squalor . . ."[66] But he soon came to believe that, with unceasing American medical intervention and control, some improvement in native disease carriage might be achieved, despite "Oriental guile" and the "innate Filipino predisposition to take life easy."[67] For Heiser was convinced that "as long as the Oriental was allowed to remain disease-ridden, he was a constant threat to the occidental who clung to the idea that he could keep himself healthy in a small, disease-ringed circle."[68] In his extraordinary popular autobiography, Heiser described Filipinos in the following terms: grown-up children, dirty, unsanitary, diseased, ignorant, unscrupulous, superstitious, born actors, resigned to death, untrustworthy, cowards, a nation of invalids, incubators of leprosy, unhygienic. If left to themselves, Filipinos would inevitably reassert these characteristics, victims of an unsanitary atavism. The fear of these "innately unhygienic" people justified Heiser's "almost military power," his "sanitary squads" that conducted house-to-house inspections, and separated the sick from their communities.[69] "Necessarily," Heiser recalled, "we had to invade the rights of homes, commerce, and parliaments."[70] He believed that by 1914, as a result of such relentless, and continuing, disciplinary action, "the great pestilence had been brought under control, and the archipelago had become a healthful place for the white man to live in."[71]

The developing medical knowledge thus gave the ramifications of social relationships a novel significance. The body, reconstituted in the colonies as an object of the medical laboratory, was to be moved around, sometimes isolated, always investigated. Although domestic medical science and public health work had called for rigorous surveillance in America itself, their empowerment in a colonial situation was distinctive. In the Philippines, the scientific texts articulated a more extreme sense of threat and the consequent need for containment in a foreign environment: the regulation of society had to be more secure than at home, less slippage was allowed. Furthermore, medical science in the Philippines worked more explicitly and completely to consolidate specifically racial hierarchies and to secure an economy of racial privilege, developing the Manichean dichotomy that Fanon has identified as a characteristic psychopathology of colonial governance.[72] Thus the distinctive trope of the native as a potentially dangerous part of the zoological realm, and the subordinate American colonizer as a resilient racial type vulnerable only to alien parasites, emerged in an especially colonial medical discourse.

JanMohamed has recently reminded us that the ideological functions of colonial discourse should be understood in terms of the exigencies of a metropolitan culture and politics.[73] The object of representation, especially in this case, has virtually no access to the texts. In this "allegory of the general epistemic violence of imperialism,"[74] Filipinos are assigned no position of enunciation: their bodies are inscribed in the language of scientists. This discourse was addressed toward two distinct audiences whose anticipated responses shaped the earliest formulation of the texts. The scientists addressed issues that their peers deemed creditable: the application of zoological laws to man, the relationship of disease and climate, the physiology of temperature regulation, and the description of a microbial ecology. But they did so in a way that, while legitimate scientifically, also promoted the colonial enterprise and so attracted the sponsorship of the American and Philippine administrations.

The construction of the "white American in the tropics" as an object of knowledge meant that colonial and medical interests had, in effect, to accommodate the laboratory in order to pursue their goals.[75] As Heiser observed, from 1898 a new order developed in the Philippines, and "the microscope supplanted the sword, the martial spirit gave place to the research habit."[76] By invoking parasites and native carriers as agents of disease, and discounting the effects of a climate that was never amenable to change, the new colonial doctors held out the possibility that expert social and environmental intervention might yet naturalize Americans in the tropics. Parasitology thus gave many colonizers a sense of purpose and a practical program. Yet the physiological studies, which demonstrated the harmlessness of the climate, had also required the scientific decomposition of the subordinate colonizers' body into pigment, eye-color, blood pressure, hemoglobin, white cell count and lung capacity. The white bodies that American soldiers were told did not degenerate could, in this sense, scarcely have appeared to be their own. They had become the objects of expert opinion and professional dispute, ever in need of surveillance and control, to be kept apart from the crowd of invisible, dangerous forces that the scientists had uncovered.

The dehumanization of the Filipinos, their disappearance into the general ecology, derived from a discourse that reciprocally bound the Americans to an alien image of their own bodies. As Sartre has observed, in a similar context: "The impossible dehumanization of the oppressed, on the other side of the coin, becomes the alienation of the oppressor. . . . [T]he colonizer must assume the opaque rigidity and imperviousness of stone. In short, he must dehumanize himself as well."[77]

The subordinate American colonizers and the colonized Filipinos are both degraded, though in significantly different ways, in order to secure an economy of racial privilege and to consolidate the political boundaries of the colonial order. In defining the white laboring colonizer as an object of study, the colonized merges into the surroundings, into the local fauna, at best as a contrasting absence of individuality. But even the subordinate colonizer, reduced to a scientific body in the New World, ultimately is disarmed by the peculiar, alienating construction of his presence in a reinscribed place.[78]

VII

Andrew Balfour's talk to the Society of Tropical Medicine in London, on that evening in 1914, was well received. Sir Ronald Ross, probably the most distinguished member of the audience, stood at the end to endorse Balfour's report, and to confirm that the white races had nothing to fear from the tropical climate alone: the insanitary ways of the region's native inhabitants were far more menacing. But there was cause for optimism, since he understood that "there is in Mauritius a white population, which has remained there for some centuries and which is not degenerate in any way."[79] As Balfour had noted, it seemed that laboratory work in the Philippines demonstrated the truth of the couplet:

Where every prospect pleases
and only man is vile.[80]

NOTES

---

1. Andrew Balfour, "Tropical Problems in the New World," *Transactions of the Society of Tropical Medicine & Hygiene* 8 (Jan. 1915): 83. Balfour had recently returned from the Sudan, where he was director of the Wellcome Tropical Research Laboratories. He was later the director of the London School of Hygiene and Tropical Medicine.

2. Dean C. Worcester, "The coordination of scientific work," *The Philippines: A Past and present* (New York, 1914): 488-500; and WP Chamberlain, "The study of tropical diseases in the Philippine Islands: A summary of the work performed during the last two years by the United States Army Board," *JAMA* 58 (April 1912): 998-1002. On the U.S. in the Philippines, see William H. Taft and Theodore Roosevelt, *The Philippines* (New York, 1902); W. Cameron Forbes, *The Philippine Islands*, 2 vols. (Boston, 1928); Glenn A. May, *Social Engineering in the Philippines: The aims, execution and impact of American social policy 1900-1913* (Westport CT, 1980); and Peter W. Stanley, *A Nation in the Making: The Philippines and the United States, 1899-1921* (Camb MA, 1974).

3. Let me emphasize that I do not discuss in detail the more readily contested inscriptions of the medical fieldworkers, the sanitarians and public health officials, though these groups were frequently mobilizing laboratory inscriptions—among others—in their own work. [For more on the work of these groups, see Reynaldo C. Ileto, "Cholera and the origins of the American sanitary order in the Philippines," pp. 51-81 of this book and Rodney Sullivan, "Cholera and colonialism in the Philippines, 1899-1903," in Roy McLeod and Milton Lewis, eds., *Disease, Medicine and Empire: Perspectives on western medicine and the experience of European expansion* (London, 1988).] Aspects of medical theory and practice (not often laboratory based) have been studied in colonial contexts, but usually in terms of legitimation and assimilation, for instance: Frantz Fanon, "Medicine and colonialism," in *The Cultural Crisis of Modern Medicine*, John Ehrenreich, ed., (New York, 1978), pp. 229-51. On the other hand, laboratory medicine and epidemiology have been analyzed as forms of subject construction *within* Europe: see, for example, David Armstrong, *The Political Anatomy of the Body: Medical Knowledge in Britain in the Twentieth Century* (London, 1983).

4. More generally on the history of the body: Michel Foucault, *History of Sexuality*, vol. 1, trans. Robert Hurley (New York, 1978); Dorinda Outram, *The Body and the French Revolution: sex, class and political culture* (New Haven, 1989); and Armstrong, *Political Anatomy*.

5. In particular, see Homi Bhabha, "Difference, Discrimination and the discourse on colonialism," in *The Politics of Theory*, ed. Francis Barker, et al (Colchester, 1983) pp. 194-211; and Abdul R. JanMohamed, "The economy of Manichean allegory: the function of racialist difference in colonialist literature," *Critical Inquiry* 12 (Autumn 1985): 59-87. For a review of approaches to the study of colonial discourse, see Robert Young, *White Mythologies: Writing history and the West* (London, 1990).

6. On the "disciplinary enclave" see Angela McRobbie, "Strategies of vigilance, an interview with Gayatri Spivak," *Block* 10 (1985): 9.

7. In particular, see Bruno Latour and Steve Woolgar, *Laboratory Life: the construction of scientific facts* (Beverly Hills, CA, 1979); Bruno Latour, *The Pasteurization of France*, trans. Alan Sheridan and John Law (Camb MA, 1988); Charles Bazerman, *Shaping Written Knowledge: Essays in the Growth, Form, Function, and Implications of the Scientific Article* (Madison, 1988); Greg Myers, *Writing Biology: Texts in the Social Construction of Scientific Knowledge* (Madison, 1990); and Michael Lynch and Steve Woolgar, eds., *Representation in Scientific Practice* (Camb MA, 1990).

8. Edward W. Said, *Orientalism* (New York, 1978).

9. *Report of the Philippine Commission to the President*, 4 vols. in *Senate Journal*, 56th Congr., 1st Sess., 31 Jan. 1900, 2:231. President William McKinley appointed Jacob Gould Schurman, professor of philosophy and president of Cornell, Dean Worcester, professor of zoology at Michigan, and Charles Denby, former U.S. envoy to China, to the first Philippine Commission in early 1899. Simon Flexner, then professor of pathology at Pennsylvania, and L. F. Barker, professor of anatomical pathology at Johns Hopkins, were among the 60 witnesses they interviewed in Manila. Note that in all the literature on the subject in this period, the European and American constitutions were considered identical.

10. L. F. Barker, *ibid*, pp. 237, 238, 239. Elihu Root, Roosevelt's Secretary of War, typically observed that American soldiers became "enfeebled and sick from their long stay under a tropical sun and in tropical rains" ["The American soldier"] and referred to "the very great hardships of the climate" ["Events in the Philippines"], in his addresses and essays, collected in *The Military and Colonial Policy of the United States: Addresses and Reports* (Camb MA, 1916): 7, 227.

11. Very little has been written on human acclimatization: David N. Livingstone, "Human acclimatization: perspectives in a contested field of inquiry in science, medicine and geography," *History of Science* 25 (1987): 359-94, emphasizes the geographical literature.

12. Georges Canguilhem, *La connaissance de la vie* 2nd ed. (Paris, 1965).

13. See Philip D. Curtin, *Death by Migration: Europe's encounter with the tropical world in the nineteenth century* (Cambridge, 1989). Of course, Rudyard Kipling wrote "The white man's burden," *McClure's Magazine* 12 (Feb 1898): 290-91, in praise of U.S. expansion into the Philippines.

14. Edward A. Birch, "Influences on warm climates on the constitution," in Andrew Davidson, ed., *Hygiene and the Diseases of Warm Climates* (London, 1893), p. 4.

15. *Ibid*, p. 19.

16. Benjamin Kidd, *The Control of the Tropics* (New York, 1898), p. 48.

17. *Ibid*, pp. 50, 54.

18. E.g. Charles W. Daniels and E. Wilkinson, *Tropical Medicine and Hygiene* (London, 1912); and William Ridgeway, "The application of zoological laws to man," in *Report of the 78th Meeting of the British Association for the Advancement of Science*, Dublin, Sept. 1908 (London, 1909): 832-47. Ridgeway proposed "to touch briefly on the vast importance of such natural laws when dealing with the native races of our great dependencies and colonies, and in our own social legislation. I venture to think that the gravest mistakes which at present are being made in our administration and legislation are due to the total disregard of the natural laws, which not only modify and differentiate one race from another, but also are constantly producing variations within our own community," p. 843.

19. W. Z. Ripley, *The Races of Europe: A sociological analysis* (London, 1900), p. 584.

20. For example, see Anton Breinl and W. J. Young, "Tropical Australia and its Settlement," *American Tropical Medicine and Parasitology* 13 (1920): 351-411.

21. Griffith Taylor, *The Control of Settlement by Humidity and Temperature* (Melbourne, 1916), p. 18. See also his "The distribution of future white settlement, a world survey based on physiographic data," *Geogr Rev* 12 (1922): 375-402.

22. Charles E. Woodruff, *The Effects of Tropical Sunlight Upon the White Man* (New York, 1905), p. 278; see also his *Expansion of Races* (New York, 1909).

23. C. Eijkman, 1895, in Breinl & Young, "Tropical Australia," p. 367.

24. On the North American and European history of this ecological and constitutional medicine: Charles E. Rosenberg, "The therapeutic revolution: medicine, meaning and social change in nineteenth-century America," in *The Therapeutic Revolution: Essays in the History of American Medicine*, ed. Morris J. Vogel and Rosenberg (Philadelphia, 1979); John H. Warner, *The Therapeutic Perspective: Medical practice, knowledge and identity in America 1820-1885* (Camb MA, 1985).

25. The transition from medical geography to tropical medicine, which meant colonial medicine, is sketched in Erwin Ackerknecht, *The History and Geography of the Most Important Diseases* (New York, 1965). For histories of tropical medicine that focus on the progress of parasitology, see H. H. Scott, *A History of Tropical Medicine*, 2 vols. (London, 1939); Philip H. Manson-Bahr, *The History of the School of Tropical Medicine in London, 1899-1949* (London, 1956); Michael Worboys, "The emergence of tropical medicine: a study in the establishment of a scientific specialty," in *Perspectives in the Emergence of Scientific Disciplines*, ed. Gerard Lemaine, et al (The Hague, 1976), pp. 75-98; and "The emergence and early development of parasitology," in *Parasitology: A global perspective*, eds. Kenneth S. Warren and John Z. Bowers (New York, 1983), pp. 1-18. For the U.S., see Charles M. Wilson, *Ambassadors in White: The story of American tropical medicine* (New York, 1942); Victor G. Heiser, "Reminiscences on early tropical medicine," *Bull NY Acad Med* 44 (1968): 654-60.

26. Sir Ronald Ross, in discussion section, of R. Havelock Charles, "Neurasthenia and its bearing on the decay of northern peoples in India," *Trans Soc Trop Med & Hyg* 7 (Nov. 1913): 15.

27. Luigi Sambon, "Remarks on acclimatization in tropical regions," *British Medical Journal* i (Jan 9, 1897): 63.

28. The importance of new theories of heredity should not be underestimated: see George W. Stocking, Jr., *Race, Culture and Evolution: Essays in the history of anthropology* (New York, 1968); Nancy Stepan, *The Idea of Race in Science: Great Britain 1800-1960* (London, 1982). By 1910, the elite of medical practitioners (and certainly the scientists), even in the tropics, were emphasizing the relative stability of hereditary material, losing interest in processes of physiological adaptation, and urging a cultural protection from the physical and social environment.

29. On related issues of medical theory, racial segregation and urban design in Africa and India, see Philip D. Curtin, "Medical knowledge and urban planning in tropical Africa," *American Historical Review* 90 (1985): 594-613; and John W. Cell, "Anglo-Indian medical theory and the origins of segregation in West Africa,"

Am Hist Rev 91 (1986): 307-35; and Maynard W. Swanson, "The sanitation syndrome: the bubonic plague and urban native policy in the Cape Colony 1900-1909," *J Afr Hist* 18 (1977): 387-410.

30. William H. Taft, "Special report of the Secretary of War on the Philippines," in *Eighth Annual Report of the Philippine Commission to the President, 1907*, 3 vols. (Washington DC, 1908), 1:281.

31. John R. McDill, "Presidential address," March 1905, quoted *ibid*, p. 281.

32. *Ibid.*

33. One of the more vivid examples of a colonial discourse that is not only the medium of inscribing difference, but also a sign of difference. See also Homi Bhabha, "Signs taken for wonders: questions of ambivalence and authority under a tree outside Delhi, May 1817," *Critical Inquiry* 12 (Autumn 1985): 144-65; Henry Louis Gates, Jr., 'Writing 'race' and the difference it makes," *Critical Inquiry* 12 (Autumn 1985): 1-20; Michael Adas, *Machines as the Measure of Man: Science, Technology and Ideologies of Western Dominance* (Ithaca, 1989).

34. Joseph R. Hayden, *The Philippines: A study in national development* (New York, 1942), p. 644.

35. See record group 350, file 3966, U.S. National Archives, Washington, D.C. While this is not the place to go into the subject fully, it should be noted that the work of the Bureau should also be seen in the peculiar context of U.S. military medicine and southern medical theory and practices. See F. K. Mostofi, "Contributions of the military to tropical medicine," *Bull NY Acad of Med* 44 (1968): 702-20; John S. Haller, Jr., "The negro and the southern physician: a study of medical and racial attitudes 1800-1860," *Med Hist* 16 (1972): 238-53; Thomas S. Szasz, "The sane slave: an historical note on the use of medical diagnosis as justificatory rhetoric," *Am J Psychotherapy* (1971): 228-39.

36. See record group 112, file 68075, U.S. National Archives, Washington, D.C. [USNA]

37. Surgeon-general, U.S. Army, to Chief-surgeon, Philippine Division, June 23, 1906, record group 112, file 68075/25, USNA.

38. My analysis here is modelled on William Hank's examination of colonial Mayan texts in "Discourse genres in a theory of practice," *Am Ethnologist* 14 (1987): 668-92.

39. Capt. John R. Barber, "Report on fever as a cause of debility among Filipinos," Sept. 7, 1911, record group 112, file 68075/105, USNA.

40. Gayatri Chakravorty Spivak, 'Three women's texts and a critique of imperialism," *Critical Inquiry* 12 (Autumn 1985): 243-61.

41. Weston P. Chamberlain, "The red blood corpuscles and the hemoglobin of healthy adult American males residing in the Philippines," *Phil J Sci* 7 (1912): 484.

42. For other examples of the detachment of person and place in colonial texts, see: Mary Louise Pratt, "Scratches on the face of the country; or, what Mr. Barrow saw in the land of the Bushmen," *Critical Inquiry* 12 (Autumn 1985): 119-43.

43. On virtual witnessing in scientific texts: Steven Shapin and Simon Schaffer, *Leviathan and the Air-Pump: Hobbes, Boyle, and the Experimental Life* (Princeton, 1985).

44. See Albert Memmi, *The Colonizer and the Colonized* (New York, 1965), on the "mark of the plural." W. D. Fleming, "The basal metabolism of a normal young man as affected by a tropical residence of one year," *Phil J Sci* (1923): 283-90.

45. On coerced speech in Conrad's *Heart of Darkness*, see Aaron Fogel, "Coerced speech and the Oedipus dialogue complex," in Gary S. Morson and Caryl Emerson, eds., *Rethinking Bakhtin: Extensions and Challenges* (Evanston, IL, 1989), pp. 173-96.

46. Hans Aron, "Investigation on the action of the tropical sun on men and animals," *Phil J Sci* 6 (1911): 101-23, p. 102. "[T]he monkey does not live in the fields; his home is in the forest, into which only a small proportion of the direct rays of the sun can enter. The same is true of the native of the Tropics, if he is left to his own customs," p. 130.

47. H. D. Gibbs, "A study of the effect of tropical sunlight upon men, monkeys, and rabbits, and a discussion of the proper clothing for the tropical climate," *Phil J Sci* 7B (1912), p. 92.

48. Alfred O. Shaklee, "Experimental acclimatization to the tropical sun," *Phil J Sci* 12 (1917): 1-22.

49. James M. Phelan and H.J. Nichols, "Outline of an experiment for U.S. soldiers serving in the Philippines," 1909, record group 112, file 68075/68, USNA.

50. James M. Phelan, "An experiment with orange-red underwear," *Phil J Sci* 5 (1910): 525-46. The literature on scientific clothing, and housing, in the tropics is immense.

51. John Davy, *Researches, Physiological and Anatomical*, 2 vols. (London 1839), 1:161.

52. See M. S. Pembrey, "Animal heat," in *Textbook of Physiology*, ed. E. A. Schaeffer, 2 vols. (Edinburgh, 1898-1900), 1:812.

53. Weston P. Chamberlain, "Observations on the influence of the Philippine climate on white men of the blond and of the brunette type," *Phil J Sci* 6 (1911): 427-63. "The matter is of some practical importance," Chamberlain argued, "in the selecting of recruits and civil service employees for tropical countries," p. 429. See also "Some features of the physiological activity of white races in the Philippine Islands," *Am J Trop Dis & Prevent Med* 1 (1913): 12-32.

54. Phalen and Nichols, "Outline of an experiment."

55. W. E. Musgrave and A. G. Sison, "Blood pressure in the tropics: a preliminary report," *Phil J Sci* (1910): 325-29. The Filipinos were selected "from the student class and from the local police forces," p. 325.

56. Weston P. Chamberlain, "A study of the systolic blood pressure and the pulse rate of healthy adult males in the Philippines," *Phil J Sci* 6 (1911): 467-81. For comparison, 552 blood pressure readings and 200 pulse counts were made on 386 Filipinos. "The Filipinos examined were from various tribes. One hundred were soldiers of the Philippine scouts and an equal number were from the Philippine Constabulary. The remainder of the group were laborers, servants and convicts." The pressures for Filipinos and white men were "practically identical," pp. 468, 481.

57. See Daniels and Wilkinson, *Tropical Medicine and Hygiene*; and Davidson, *Hygiene and Diseases of Warm Climates*.

58. Chamberlain, "The red blood corpuscles," p. 488. See also: William A. Wickline, "Effects of tropical climate on the white race," *Mil Surgeon* 23 (1908): 283.

59. Weston P. Chamberlain and Edward B. Vedder, "A study of Arneth's nuclear classification of the neutrophils in healthy adult males and the influence thereon of race, complexion, and tropical residence," *Phil J Sci* 6 (1911): 405-19.

60. Weston P. Chamberlain, "Quarterly report of the U.S. Army Board of Study," June 30, 1910, record group 112, file 68075/81, USNA.

61. Breinl and Young, "Tropical Australia," p. 380.

62. Latour, "Give me a laboratory and I will raise the world." In Karin Knorr-Cetina and Michael Mulkay, eds., *Science Observed: Perspectives on the social study of science* (London, 1983). p. 154.

63. See Weston P. Chamberlain, H. D. Bloomberg, and E. D. Kilbourne, "Examinations of stools and blood among the Igorots at Baguio, Philippine Islands, *Phil J Sci* 5B (1910): 505-14.

64. Philip E. Garrison, Ricardo Leynes, and Rosendo Llamas, "Medical survey of the town of Taytay," *Phil J Sci* 4B (1909): 257-68.

65. Victor G. Heiser, "Unsolved health problems peculiar to the Philippines," *Phil J Sci* 5B (1910): 177-78.

66. Victor G. Heiser, *An American Doctor's Odyssey: Adventures in forty-five countries* (New York, 1936), p. 35.

67. *Ibid*: pp. 30, 236.

68. *Ibid*: p. 37.

69. *Ibid*: p. 62. See also Ileto, "Cholera and the origins of the American sanitary order."

70. *Ibid*: p. 151.

71. *Ibid*: p. 265.

72. See Frantz Fanon, *Wretched of the Earth*, trans. Constance Farrington (New York, 1968).

73. JanMohamed, "Economy of Manichean allegory." While I have stressed the exigencies of colonial administration and exploitation, it should not be forgotten that the language of tropical science was also inflected to promote scientific institution-building in America. The colonial medical laboratory in the Philippines, rather than a mere marginal adjunct to an established metropolitan scientific culture, is a strategic site for investigating the necessary complicity of the early twentieth-century American academy with the institutions of colonial power.

74. Spivak, "Three women's texts and a critique of imperialism," p. 251. Let me emphasize that this is not a characterization of all public health and sanitarian texts in the Philippines: a preliminary study indicates much more "play" in the field inscriptions than in the laboratory texts.

75. Latour, "Give me a laboratory," makes this point when describing the strategy of Pasteur.

76. Victor G. Heiser, "The progress of medicine in the Philippines," *JAMA* 47 (1906): 245.

77. Jean-Paul Sartre, "Introduction," in Memmi, *The Colonizer and the Colonized*, p. xxvii.

78. See Armstrong, *Political Anatomy of the Body*.

79. Ronald Ross, in Balfour, "Tropical problems," p. 110.

80. Balfour, *ibid*, p. 86. This is a minor misquotation of Bishop Heber's "Hymn":
> What though spicy breezes
> Blow soft o'er Ceylon's isle,
> Though every prospect pleases
> And only man is vile.

FOUR

"Nothing Without Labor": Penology, Discipline, and Independence in the Philippines Under United States Colonial Rule, 1898-1914

MICHAEL SALMAN

IN 1909 IGNACIO VILLAMOR BECAME THE FIRST FILIPINO TO HOLD THE POSI-
tion of Attorney General for the Philippines. A legal scholar, later
president of the University of the Philippines, Villamor used the techniques of social science in his reports and studies of criminality. As a
nationalist, Villamor was eager to portray Filipinos as law-abiding and
therefore civilized people, ready for independence.[1] In this context,
penology was yet another test for the qualities of "civilization." Thus it
was with some pride that Villamor wrote, in his report for 1910:

> The penitentiary system of the Philippines follows the lat-
> est reforms adopted by the most civilized countries of Europe
> and America, in the sense of "securing the protection of society
> by the correction as well as the reformation of the criminal";
> considering, therefore, a penal establishment as a "special com-
> munity of future free citizens, segregated temporarily, on account
> of certain weaknesses and placed under observation for treat-

ment and regeneration." The principle of such a system is summarized in the following words: "isolation, work, and education."[2]

Villamor's depiction of the purpose and methods of the Philippine penal system bears a striking resemblance to the rationalization of colonial rule. In this essay, I will discuss the colonial penal system in the early twentieth-century Philippines with three ends in view: to present an empirical and analytical narrative of colonial penal practices attentive to the reciprocal problems of agency and structure, to reflect on Michel Foucault's writings on the prison, and to make an evocative argument about the value of the prison as an interpretive metaphor for rethinking the history of United States colonial rule in the Philippines.[3]

I propose the prison not as a perfect analog for all of colonialism's forms, functions, and morphologies, but as an interpretive device which will direct our attention to colonialism's totalizing propensities, its boundaries (the walls) of classification and influence, and also to the possibility of resistance within even the most claustral social settings. The prison—an asylum to segregate "criminals" from their environment—highlights the alienating quality of colonialism as a project of cultural disparagement, rejection, and reformation. As a space of punishment and coercion, the prison shares with colonialism an explicit extra-societal legitimation of force and an implicit structural encouragement to even greater levels of brutality—all rationalized in discourses of justice, the protection of society against danger, and a mission to reform and rehabilitate.[4]

With the prison as a metaphor we can situate United States colonial rule in the Philippines within two historical contexts: the background of prison reform as a defining practice of benevolent humanitarianism from the late-eighteenth century to the present, and the currency of the reformative asylum (of which the prison is a type) as a model for the "civilization" of colonized peoples, such as Francis Amasa Walker's conception of the Indian Reservation as an asylum and U. B. Phillips's famous depiction of the slave plantation as a school of civilization.[5] The prison is an institution charged with both punitive and reformative tasks. It is the prototype of all total institutions; yet it ever fails to accomplish its objectives. Above all the prison is fraught with moral ambiguity—it is a site of brutality and humanitarianism, it is a widely acknowledged failure but it is maintained nevertheless. This pattern of moral and practical ambiguity should move us beyond instrumental historical analyses of successes or failures to reconsider the persistence and reproduction of the prison, on the one hand, and the culture and ideology of colonialism (and racism), on the other.

It is here that the work of Michel Foucault proves invaluable. In using the prison as a metaphor for United States colonial rule in the Philippines I would like to suggest that it is in the colonies of the late nineteenth and early twentieth centuries that we might find the most complete examples of the "carcereal continuum," the concept Foucault introduced to represent the circulation of disciplinary techniques throughout societal institutions and the human sciences. Discussing the "self-evidence" of the prison, the ease with which it became accepted as a "natural" feature of nineteenth century Euro-American society, Foucault asked:

> How could the prison not be immediately accepted when, by locking up, retraining, and rendering docile, it merely reproduces, with a little more emphasis, all the mechanisms that are to be found in the social body? The prison is like a rather disciplined barracks, a strict school, a dark workshop, but not qualitatively different. This double foundation—juridico-economic on the one hand, technico-disciplinary on the other—made the prison seem the most immediate and civilized form of all penalties. And it is this double functioning that immediately gave it its solidity.[6]

The prison persists, deeply rooted and enmeshed in Euro-American society, and as an instrument of the Philippine state. "Prison continues," writes Foucault, "on those who are entrusted to it, a work begun elsewhere, which the whole of society pursues on each individual through innumerable mechanisms of discipline. By means of a carcereal continuum, the authority that sentences infiltrates all those other authorities that supervise, transform, correct, improve . . . in its function, the power to punish is not essentially different from that of curing or educating."[7] If nineteenth century Euro-American societies approached a "carcereal continuum," then the carcereal continuum was all the more complete and explicit in colonies such as the Philippines, which were conceptualized in terms of reformative asylums. This is not to say that the colonial Philippines was a disciplined society, but only that we can find a pervasive disciplinary apparatus which did indeed prompt struggles over deployment, conflicts in implementation, resistances, escapes, and evasions. In Euro-American countries, the creators of the carcereal continuum consciously directed their efforts at correction and rehabilitation. With the exception of children who had to be disciplined for the first time, they aimed at the restoration of a norm which they assumed already existed.[8] These disciplinary techniques were extended to the Philippines and other colonies within the hierarchical structure of colonial rule, which explicitly classified the entire society in racial terms as unfit for independence, uncivilized, in short, undisciplined. Precisely to this extent the colonial regime classified Filipinos generally as subjects needing "tutelage"—a supervisory, reformative kind of incarceration under colonial rule.

I present the following brief vignettes about the colonial penal system as illustrative of the ways that structures, techniques, and discourses circulated beyond prison walls and throughout the colonial project. This is not a proof or even a full demonstration, but rather an evocation of the existence of a colonial carcereal continuum intended to raise questions and implications for future research.

Bilibid Prison in Manila was the hub of the colonial penal system. Constructed in 1865 by the Spanish regime, Bilibid's buildings were spokes emanating from a central observation tower. By 1904 Bilibid averaged a daily count of 4,400 inmates, 1,000 more than in its official capacity. The overcrowded conditions were hellish. Morbidity and mortality soared due to unsanitary conditions and epidemics. 256 prisoners died at the prison in fiscal year 1904, and 375 died in 1905.[9]

The colonial regime arranged to send Bilibid's prisoners out to labor on public construction projects. The most significant of these was road work in Albay Province, south of Manila on Luzon Island. The very prosperity of Albay, fueled by the high demand for hemp on the world market, had put the cost of day labor for road work beyond the province's budget. Convict labor would provide cheap, forced labor, and it would relieve crowding at Bilibid. More than other convict labor projects, the road work at Albay was expressly conceived as an experiment.[10]

On December 7, 1904, a full month before the first convicts departed for Albay, Bilibid exploded. Two hundred "detention" prisoners (i.e., awaiting trial or appeal) rioted. Guards restored order in seven minutes with the aid of the gatling gun on the observation tower. Nineteen prisoners were killed, forty wounded.[11]

Between January and March 1905, approximately 500 Bilibid inmates were transported to road camps in Albay. By the end of the calendar year, some 1,500 prisoners had been sent out of Bilibid to labor on various projects.[12] The official evaluations of convict labor in Albay were effusive. The Bureau of Public Works wrote, "This experiment with prison labor has shown that such labor is more effective in work accomplished than was anticipated."[13] In June 1905 the Director of Prisons exulted: "That the native can be, and has been, taught to perform good labor and enjoys doing so has been demonstrated beyond a doubt." He cited the "experiment" in Albay, but also the December 7 riot at Bilibid as "[a] very good proof of the wholesomeness of good, hard, interesting work for those in confinement." The detention prisoners who rioted were legally exempt from forced labor, while "some 3000 sentenced prisoners who are interested in working seven and a half hours each day quietly looked on and made not the slightest demonstration."[14]

Much like this almost cheery description of the riot at Bilibid, celebrations of the experiment with convict labor in Albay obscured a more complex and dirtier reality, which included a mortality rate even higher than Bilibid's and resistance by the convicts. On March 24, 1905, fifty-seven convicts rebelled and headed off through the hemp fields to escape. The Philippine Scout guards and local authorities killed thirteen of the fugitives, another forty-two were captured alive and returned to Bilibid. Two escapes remained unaccounted for.[15] According to the only source that purports to explain the cause of the rebellion, it was sparked by "some mix-up in regard to the feed of prisoners, they having been given too much canned salmon, which has had a bad effect." Indeed, the canned salmon was probably rancid or contaminated, inducing severe illness similar to cholera or dysentery.[16]

The convicts' resistance prompted a great reduction of the amount of canned salmon in the diet of prisoners in Albay and other penal camps. It also led to a change in the regime of work on the road. To tighten discipline, the prison authorities considered a "plan of working in a barbed wire fence" that could be moved down the road as the convicts moved. Rejecting this because of its appearance, they implemented a more subtle system of surveillance. The Scouts stationed guards in the thickly-planted hemp fields along the road. They told prisoners to work within "a deadline," beyond which they would be shot. The system worked much like Jeremy Bentham's fabled "Panopticon." Convicts could never know the location of guards, or even if guards were present at all. William Cameron Forbes, the colonial Secretary of Commerce and Police whose jurisdiction over the prison system united his interests in labor and surveillance, wrote of this measure, "The mysteriousness of not knowing where the guards are placed seems to help very much . . . to all appearances the prisoners are working without guard." The new disciplinary arrangement created the illusion of voluntary labor and a solution of the Philippines' "labor problem."[17]

In addition to being sent out of Bilibid as laborers, the collecting and classifying functions of Bilibid made it possible to send out objectified images of convicts as subjects for scientific study. For the 1904 Louisiana Purchase Exposition in St. Louis, the colonial government published an *Album of Philippine Types: Found in Bilibid Prison in 1903*, a book of photographs and anthropometric data to present North Americans with graphic representations of the variety of "physical types" indigenous to the Philippines. The photographs are in the form of mug shots—facing-straight and profile, from the neck up, against a light background that sometimes lends the effect of decapitation by obscuring the outlines of shirt-collars and shoulders. Closed mouths, expressionless faces, some scars, the glare of the flash, and identification numbers placed on collars distance the photographic images from lived familiarity, all the more so for a North American audience. Across the page from each set of photographs is a chart recording body dimensions, cephalic index and nasal index for each subject and for groups of their "type." Some "types" are named for provinces, some for ethnolinguistic groups, some by region (like the Visayas), sometimes by religion, some by race (Negritos), and some are identified by combinations of these classifications. The book's short introduction vouches for the representativeness of the sample and the "purity of type" of each province. The book's compiler simply excluded the large number of Spanish and Chinese mestizos, noting "the Manila contingent in the prison was so preponderatingly *(sic)* Chinese—three-fourths of the men admitting that they have mixed blood of one sort or another—that this group was rejected entire *(sic)* as unsuitable for a study of Philippine types."[18]

Much could be written about this and similar attempts of colonial anthropology to observe, map, and normalize Philippine peoples by examining them as social groups, individuals, and dissected bodies, figuratively by anthropometric measurements and photographs, and also quite literally with scalpels and bone cutters after death.[19] My immediate interest in the *Album of Philippine Types* lies in the special function of Bilibid Prison in producing objectified subjects for scientific study. On a practical level, Bilibid was the one place where so many different Philippine peoples could be seen, collected together from far-flung provinces by the colony's criminal justice system. In an era of virulent racism, still engrossed in debate over Lombroso's criminal anthropology of physical stigmata, the presentation of Bilibid inmates as "fairly typical, physically, of the populations from which they come," conflated the categories "Filipino" and "criminal" in distressingly meaningful ways.[20]

In 1904 the colonial regime also opened the Iwahig Penal Colony in Palawan, at the western edge of the central Philippines. For several years Iwahig suffered terribly from disease. There were mutinies, escapes, and also a vibrant inmate sub-culture—a kind of self-government—in shanty huts at the outskirts of the colony's settlement. By 1908 order and health stabilized at Iwahig. Within years the number of resident convicts rose above 1,000, and the colony was organized as originally intended—as a so-called self-governing republic of prisoners without guards, producing commodities, and staffed by only one or two colonial supervisors. Iwahig was modelled after the George Junior Republic, a reformatory school for delinquent and wayward children located in an upstate New York town with the improbable name of Freeville. Soon after the conquest of the Philippines, the renowned prison reformer Thomas Mott Osborne explained to another of the Junior Republic's trustees, "We who are trying to free the children from the application of the idea of a beneficial tyranny ought to be the first to recognize that Imperialism is only the reform school principle on a larger scale."[21]

The convicts of Iwahig—adult Filipinos convicted of all manner of offenses from murder to theft to the often political crime of banditry—lived under what a superintendent called "moral restraints" and "interior discipline maintained without guards."[22] Like the Junior Republic, Iwahig's inmates elected officials, staffed a colony police force, a judicial system, and participated in an internal economy. As the founder of the Junior Republic once put it, "Underneath the whole plan ran the economic system of the big Republic"—the motto of both institutions was "Nothing Without Labor."[23] Iwahig's system added the feature of allowing colonists of good standing to be joined by their families and it promised the opportunity to homestead on colony land upon conditional pardon.

The "self-government" of "Discipline and Work" was Iwahig's alternative to the externally imposed discipline of "fear and force" typical of most prisons. Iwahig's division of labor had a "double organization." Each "work division" had a "disciplinary section;" the supervision of work in quasi-military squads doubled as the surveillance of convicts.[24] Labor played such an enormous role in Iwahig's progressive penology that one observer saw in forced labor a more positive evocation of the colony than the prison-like appellation, "Iwahig Penal Colony." In 1912, the Secretary of Public Instruction, whose department then supervised the Bureau of Prisons along with the public schools, believed the label "Penal Colony" was "unfortunate." It "had no little retarding effect on the growth of this colony, which is really only a great plantation employing forced labor and which should be considered as such. There are neither stockades nor guards, and [therefore] a much clearer conception of the real status and purpose of this colony would be had if it were known either as the Iwahig Reservation or the Iwahig Plantation." Here prison reform was expressed in the historically resonant terms of the plantation and reservation, likening colonial benevolence to the structurally paternalistic institutions of slavery and Indian removal.[25]

Episcopal Bishop of the Philippines Charles Henry Brent, the director of a large missionary and educational enterprise among the "non-Christian" population of Northern Luzon, visited Iwahig as part of a tour of the Southern Philippines in 1914. He found the penal colony a place "where fourteen hundred prisoners by methods of self-government and instruction are taught the meaning of self-respect and industry." Iwahig, he told his home office, was the most "successful experiment in the treatment of criminals in the world, so far as I know. Any school we attempt ought to be built on the principles which make Iwahig what it is." In the same communique he described a copra plantation on Cagayan de Sulu, in the Sulu chain in the extreme South. The American planter was, Brent wrote, "an aid to the natives while promoting his own commercial interests. These people of Malay origin need above all else just leadership. In one way they are quite childlike, though in other respects full of guile." In Brent's colonial view of Philippine progress, framed by the valorization of labor and an infantilizing racism, the plantation, the mission school, and the penal colony worked to the same end.[26]

Iwahig was by all official accounts a striking success. Its program of privileges, incentives, disguised coercions, and self-cleansing of failures by returning recalcitrant prisoners to Bilibid produced order without armed guards and an exceptionally low rate of recidivism. In the context of colonialism, however, such "benevolent" prison reform lent itself to cruel twists. One North American newspaper report on Iwahig carried the title: "Doing the Filipino Good By Jailing Him." Lyman Beecher Stowe, a grandson of Harriet Beecher Stowe and a prison reformer associated with the George Junior Republic, wrote an article in which he called Iwahig "A Prison That Makes Men Free." He lauded Iwahig as proof that Junior Republic methods would succeed among adults. Stowe wrote, "Though the success of the colony as a maker of dollars is still to be demonstrated, the experiment of giving adult Filipinos, guilty of the worst crimes, a chance to develop the best that is in them under conditions approximating those under which they must live when released has proved a complete success."[27] The irony of Stowe's assessment was surely unintended. Did Iwahig resemble a Philippine village or a Philippine plantation? Did Iwahig approximate an exterior society of free citizens or did the exterior society, a colonized society where conquerors professed a mission of "political education" that disparaged Filipino society, approximate a penal reformatory? If Iwahig was "a prison that makes men free" among a people supposedly "unfit" for independence, then should not the entire population be incarcerated to make them free? This was the logic of the carcereal continuum in the colonial Philippines.

NOTES

1. Villamor, *Criminality in the Philippines* (Manila, 1909); "Annual Report of the Attorney General of the Philippine Islands for the year 1910," USNA, RG 350, File 6751-17.

2. Villamor, "Appendix A—Penology," in idem., "Annual Report of the Attorney General of the Philippine Islands for the Year 1910," USNA RG 350, File 6751-17, p. 53.

3. I see these themes as an integral whole. For good reasons some very insightful scholars have contrasted the approach of E. P. Thompson (*et al*) to the history of crime and punishment with that of Michel Foucault. For example, Michael Ignatieff writes, "[Douglas] Hay's and Thompson's works show up Foucault's tacit assumption that the only limits on public order policy were the mental assumptions of the authorities themselves and the structural weaknesses of the state apparatus. What is missing in his work is the idea that public order strategies were defined within limits marked out not only by the holders of power but also by those they were trying, often vainly, to persuade, subdue, cajole or repress. Foucault's account consistently portrays authority as having a clear field, able to carry out its strategies without let or hindrance from its own legal principles or from popular opposition. Power is always seen as a strategy, an instrumentality, never as a social relation between contending forces" (Ignatieff, "State, Civil Society and Total Institutions: A Critique of Recent Social Histories of Punishment," in Stanley Cohen and Andrew Scull, *Social Control and the State*, St. Martin's Press: New York, 1983, p. 86). I think Ignatieff is correct to highlight the respective schools' tendencies to focus on agency (Thompson) and structure (Foucault, who might prefer the word "technologies"), but I also think that he exaggerates the mutual exclusiveness of the two research strategies. Thompson finds agency, in good part, by reflecting on how the relative autonomy of the law (as a structure) allows it to be read, changed, and restored to serve different and complex interests while still following its own (legal) imperatives (Thompson, *Whigs and Hunters*, Allen Lane: London, 1975). Foucault finds structure by rethinking the prison's place in society, its persistent failure, unintended consequences (the creation of the criminal), and its seemingly perpetual incitement to rebellion—arguably the effects of agency, subjectivity, and action (*Discipline and Punish,* trans. by Alan Sheridan, Pantheon: New York, 1978). I think historians can profit by tacking back and forth between these modes of analysis. Foucault, in this sense, can provide starting points for detailed narratives attentive to ambiguity, agency, and contingency. Historians can treat power both as an intrinsic, reciprocal element of social

relations and as a technology or mode of those social relations, with an internal logic, to some degree manipulable by competing parties, but just the same, imposing the consequences of its logic. As Anand Yang has suggested, "in some respects . . . the theoretical orientations of Thompson and Foucault are not entirely incompatible" ("Issues and Themes in the Study of Historical Crime and Criminality: Passages to the Social History of British India," in Yang, ed., *Crime and Criminality in British India*, University of Arizona Press: Tucson, 1985, p. 5).

With regard to the history of United States colonial rule in the Philippines, my goal is to redirect and subvert the theme of colonial "benevolence" that still dominates the historiography produced in the United States. The "uniquely benign" nature of United States rule is the central theme of Stanley Karnow's Pulitzer Prize-winning *In Our Image: America's Empire in the Philippines* (Random House: New York: 1989), a book which reiterates interpretations from much of the secondary literature produced in the United States. Karnow's work and the histories on which it is based elide the violence of colonial rule by studiously ignoring relations of power and avoiding any serious depth of context. I think studies of the colonial prison system can resituate the issue of colonial "benevolence" in a historical context where power figures prominently.

4. The modern prison is a complex institution that has been charged with some shifting mixture of all these functions since its invention in the late-eighteenth and early-nineteenth centuries. See, for instructive discussions, Michael Ignatieff, *A Just Measure of Pain: The Penitentiary in the Industrial Revolution* (Macmillan: London, 1978); David Rothman, *The Discovery of the Asylum: Social Order and Disorder in the New Republic* (Little, Brown: Boston, 1971); Christopher Lasch's review of Rothman, "The Discovery of the Asylum," in Lasch, *The World of Nations: Reflections on American History, Politics and Culture* (New York, 1975). Foucault formulated this crucial problem in synchronic terms that I find persuasive and not necessarily unassimilable to a historian's more specific, diachronic point of view:

> Prison 'reform' is virtually contemporary with the prison itself: it constitutes, as it were, its programme.
>
> * * *
>
> Word for word, from one century to the other, the same fundamental propositions are repeated. They reappear in each new, hard won, finally accepted formulation of a reform that has hitherto always been lacking. The same sentences or almost the same could have been borrowed from other 'fruitful' periods of reform: the end of the nineteenth century and the 'movement of social defense'; or again, the last few years, with the prisoners' revolts.
>
> One must not, therefore, regard the prison, its 'failure' and its more or less successful reform as three successive stages (*Discipline and Punish*, pp. 234, 270-71).

5. On Walker and the asylum model for Indian Reservations, see Ronald Takaki, *Iron Cages: Race and Culture in Nineteenth Century America* (Alfred A. Knopf: New York, 1979) pp. 181-93. U. B. Phillips, *American Negro Slavery* (New York, 1918) pp. 342-43; Idem., "The Plantation as a School of Civilization," 1904.

6. *Discipline and Punish*, p. 233.

7. *Discipline and Punish*, p. 303.

8. Of course, Foucault is concerned with the creation of these norms in and by the disciplinary apparatus.

9. For statistics and descriptions of Bilibid, see M. L. Stewart, "Annual Report of the Bureau of Prisons for the Year Ending June 30, 1904," Manuscript Report of the Philippine Commission 1904 (MSS RPC 1904), United States National Archives (USNA), RG 350, Bureau of Insular Affairs Library, Vol. 3, Pt. 1, p. 1; Dr. William R. Moulden, "Report of the Resident Physician," 7/14/04, in *ibid.*; "Supplementary Report of Bilibid Prison From July 1 to August 31, 1904," in *ibid.*; Dr. Wm. R. Moulden, "Report of the Resident Physician," 6/30/05, in George N. Wolfe, "Annual Report of the Bureau of Prisons for the Year Ending June 30, 1905," MSS RPC 1905, Vol. 3, Pt. 2, Appendix E, p. 21.

10. For a history of hemp production in Albay and the whole of the Bikol Peninsula, see Norman G. Owen, *Prosperity Without Progress: Manila Hemp and Material Life in the Colonial Philippines* (University of California Press: Berkeley, 1984). Owen does not, however, discuss the use of convict labor. On the amount of labor needed to produce quality of hemp, see A. U. Betts, "Report of the Provincial Governor of Albay to the Insular Governor P. I., For the Year Ending December 31, 1902," USNA, RG 350, File 3022-16 1/2, pp. 8-9. Earlier that year, Betts reported "the greatest complaint from the interior of the province is the lack of labor to work the hemp fields" (Betts to Luke E. Wright, 5/12/02, USNA RG 350, File 3022-7) In his annual report for 1905, the year the Ligao-Tabaco road was under construction, the Filipino Governor of Albay warned "there will be the usual cry of shortage of hands" when the hemp crop reached its mature size. He saw the labor shortage as "a great and increasing detriment to the interests of the province." Consequently, he devoted a large section of his report to a sermon on want creation as a technique of labor control more "philanthropic" than the traditional practice of debt bondage (R. Santos, "Annual Report of the Governor of the Province of Albay," dated 7/1/1905, pp. 51-55, MSS-RPC 1905, USNA, RG 350). Day labor drew twice the wage common in other provinces, and to work on the roads it would have to be diverted from the lucrative production of hemp. Summarizing the results of the Tobaco-Ligao Road project, the Director of Public Works reckoned convict labor, with all the expenses of guard, transportation from Bilibid, etc., more costly than

"hired labor at P0.50 per day, but in the province of Albay, where labor is more than P1.00 per day, and difficult to secure, the work [was] economically accomplished" (Charles Kendall, "Annual Report of the Bureau of Public Works for the Fiscal Year Ending June 30, 1906," MSS RPC 1906, Vol. 2 Pt. 2, p. 14).

11. The first convicts arrived in Albay on January 7, 1905; see J. D. Fauntleroy, "Annual Report of the Bureau of Engineering for the Fiscal Year Ending June 30, 1905," MSS RPC 1905, Vol. 3, Pt. 1, p. 28. Descriptions of the Bilibid riot can be found in Wolfe, "Annual Report of the Bureau of Prisons for the Year Ending June 30, 1905," MSS RPC 1905, Vol. 3, Pt. 1, p. 4; and in Willian Cameron Forbes, "Annual Report of the Department of Commerce and Police for 1905," MSS RPC 1905, Vol. 3, Pt. 1, p. 40; Telegram, Fred W. Carpenter to Wright, 12/28/04, USNA RG 350, File 4340-5.

12. For details, see Forbes, "Annual Report of the Secretary of Commerce and Police," MSS RPC 1905, pp. 33-40; Wolfe,, "Annual Report of the Bureau of Prisons for the Year Ending June 30, 1905," MSS RPC 1905, p. 18; and Fauntleroy, "Annual Report of the Bureau of Engineering for the Fiscal Year Ending June 30, 1905," MSS RPC 1905, p. 28.

13. The quote is from Charles Kendall, "Annual Report of the Bureau of Public Works for the Fiscal Year Ending June 30, 1906," p. 14, MSS RPC 1906, Vol. 2, Pt. 2. For similar remarks, see Fauntleroy, "Annual Report of the Bureau of Engineering for the Fiscal Year Ending June 30, 1905," p. 29; and Forbes, "Annual Report of the Department of Commerce and Police [1905]," p. 35.

14. Wolfe, "Annual Report of the Bureau of Prisons 1905," MSS RPC 1905, pp. 2-3. As the Warden of Bilibid, Wolfe discussed the multiple intended functions of convict labor in some depth. His reflections are a richly meaningful comment on the relation of the prison to colonialism. The Warden gloated that ninety percent of the colony's prisoners, who "had neither advantages nor opportunities to lift themselves above a more or less clouded mentality that allowed them no consciousness of possessing a mind of their own that they could exercise independent of the will of others . . . [are] built up physically and mentally by the treatment they receive along reformatory lines." They "rapidly learn a trade; take up lines of independent thought; and in fact in a remarkably short time become fitted for citizenship to an extent that is more than gratifying." Upon release, he claimed, "they become good, industrious, law abiding citizens, and in many instances are pointed to with pride by their neighbors as men who can and do work like Americans." The warden attributed this success to the discipline of constant labor. (*Ibid.*).

15. For accounts of the rebellion, see the following: Ramon Santos, "Report of the Governor of Albay, 1905," *op. cit*, pp. 63-64; William Cameron Forbes, "Report of the Secretary of Commerce and Police," MSS RPC 1905, Vol. 3, Pt. 1,

pp. 34-35; H. H. Bandholtz, "Report of the Officer Commanding the Second District, Philippine Constabulary," in "Annual Report of the Chief of the Philippine Constabulary," MSS RPC 1905, Vol. 3, Pt. 1, pp. 4-6.

16. William Cameron Forbes to Luke Wright, 4/11/1905, Forbes Papers, Houghton Library, fMS Am 1366, Vol. 2.

Extensive information on prisoners' rations can be found in the "Report of the Bureau of Prisons," MSS RPC 1905, pp. 47-53. The rations were inexpensive, probably poorly canned, and then most likely over-aged in the course of shipping from North America to the Philippines. (So I have been advised by Professor Rico Azicate of the University of the Philippines Department of History. Similar problems were recorded with corned beef fed to Philippine exiles on Guam, including Apolinario Mabini.) Such a hypothesis is lent credence by reports on the health of the convicts in Albay. Morbidity and mortality were so high on convict labor construction projects that Forbes once mused "it does not seem to me humane to continue" unless conditions improve. Of the 500 convicts sent to Albay, reports list a total of eighty-six deaths in just over one year. One hundred and one were returned to Bilibid for medical reasons by June 30, 1905, just six months after they arrived in Albay. More than 100 cases of "dysentery" and "intestinal amebasis" are listed (some possibly from the salmon), as well as cases of malaria, beri beri, wounds, and tuberculosis. (Forbes to James F. Smith, 10/31/1905, Forbes Papers, Houghton Library, fMS Am 1366, Vol. 3. For medical statistics, see the "Medical Report From Road Camps in Albay" in "Report of the Bureau of Prisons," MSS RPC 1905 Vol. 3, Pt. 2, p. 69; "Annual Medical Report, 1905," in *ibid.*, p. 73; Wolfe, "Report of the Director of the Bureau of Prisons," in MSS RPC 1906, Vol. 3, Pt. 2, p. 18.)

17. Forbes to Leonard Wood, 4/22/1905, Forbes Papers, Houghton Library, fMS Am 1366, Vol. 2. On the principles of surveillance and discipline embodied in Bentham's panopticon, see Foucault, *Discipline and Punish*, pp. 195-228.

18. Daniel Folkmar, *Album of Philippine Types (Found in Bilibid Prison in 1903) Christians and Moros (Including a Few Non-Christians) Eighty Plates Representing Thirty-Seven Provinces and Islands* (Bureau of Public Printing: Manila, 1904). Folkmar's data remained influential in anthropological circles at least through the 1920s, as evidenced by Louis R. Sullivan, *Racial Types in the Philippine Islands*, in *Anthropological Papers of the American Museum of Natural History*, Vol. 23, Pt. 1, (New York, 1918); and A. L. Kroeber, *Peoples of the Philippines*, *American Museum of Natural History Handbook Series*, No. 8, 2nd revised edition, (New York, 1928).

19. Several projects of symbolic dissection were reported, with photographs of ears, noses, hair, etc., in the pages of *The Philippine Journal of Science*. One example is especially interesting, for it found an institutional source for a diversity

of bodies analogous to Bilibid: Robert Bennett Bean, "Filipino Types: Found in Malecon Morgue," *The Philippine Journal of Science* Vol. 4A, No. 4 (1909). Actual dissections were arranged in the United States as a consequence of the 1904 Louisiana Purchase Exposition. Anthropologists at the Smithsonian and Columbia University agreed, before the living Philippine exhibits arrived, on how they would literally divide up the corpses of tribal peoples they expected to die during their tenure in the exhibition. For this and a generally fascinating account of the Philippine exhibit at the 1904 fair, see Robert Rydell, *All the World's a Fair: Visions of Empire at American International Expositions, 1876-1916* (Chicago, 1984).

20. For a lively account of the debate over Lombroso's theories, see Stephen J. Gould, *The Mismeasure of Man* (W. W. Norton: New York, 1981) pp. 113-43. It seems remarkable, but there has been no full-length, critical, historical study of race, crime and punishment in the United States. Only South Africa rivals the United States for historical patterns of massive incarceration by race, yet the subject has received little attention in the United States. For some beginnings, see Edward J. Ayers, *Vengeance and Justice: Crime and Punishment in the 19th Century American South* (New York, 1984); Michael Hindus, *Prison and Plantation: Crime, Justice, and Authority in Massachusetts and South Carolina, 1767-1878* (University of North Carolina Press: Chapel Hill, 1980).

21. Osborne to V. Everit Macy, 8/1/1900, quoted in Holl, *Juvenile Reform in the Progressive Era: William R. George and the Junior Republic Movement* (Cornell University Press: Ithaca, 1971) p. 205.

22. John R. White to Carroll H. Lamb, 9/25/1908, John R. White Papers, University of Oregon Library, Box 6, File 300-9. 1b, p. 4.

23. George, *The Junior Republic*, pp. 63-64.

24. Carroll H. Lamb, "Annual Report of the Iwahig Penal Colony for Fiscal year 1909," MSS RPC 1909, Vol. 4, pp. 105, 120-25. Also see John R. White, "Annual Report of the Iwahig Penal Colony for Fiscal Year 1908," White Papers, Box 6, File 300-9. 1b, pp. 39-45.

25. Newton W. Gilbert, "Annual Report of the Secretary of Public Instruction for Fiscal Year 1912," MSS RPC 1912, Vol. 4 p. 56. With reference to "benevolence" and paternalism in slavery and Indian removal, see Eugene Genovese, *Roll, Jordan, Roll: The World the Slaves Made* (Vintage: New York, 1976); Michael Paul Rogin, *Fathers and Children: Andrew Jackson and the Subjugation of the American Indian* (Vintage: New York, 1975); and Bernard Sheehan, *Seeds of Extinction: Jeffersonian Philanthropy and the American Indian* (W. W. Norton: New York, 1973); and Takaki, *Iron Cages*, op. cit.

26. Brent to Reverand Hugh L. Burleson, 11/25/1914, Episcopal Church Archives, RG 76, Box 16, pp. 2, 5.

27. Stowe, "A Prison That Makes Men Free," *World's Work* (April 1914) pp. 626-28.

Part 3

Nationalism and Diaspora

FIVE

Nationalism, Imagery, and the Filipino Intelligentsia in the 19th Century

VICENTE L. RAFAEL

NATIONALISM AS ARTIFACT

Benedict Anderson has written perceptively on nationalism as a cultural artifact.[1] Like all artifacts, it is overdetermined, reducible neither to an ideological effect nor a pathological symptom of modernity. Instead, ideas of nationhood are informed by paradox and contradiction. For example, Anderson points out that despite their relatively recent invention, nations are thought to be quite archaic and timeless. In the same way that a nation is conceived to be both contingent and natural, it is also regarded as simultaneously universal—"in the modern world everyone can, should, will 'have' a nationality, as he or she 'has' a gender"—and particular—"such that, by definition, 'Greek' nationality is sui generis" (*IC,* p. 14).

To see nationalism as a cultural artifact is to argue against attempts at essentializing it. Anderson claims that nationalism can be better understood as obliquely analogous to such categories as religion and kinship. Membership in a nation draws on the vocabulary of filiation whereby one comes to understand oneself in relation to ancestors long gone and generations yet to be born. In addressing pasts and futures, nationalism resituates identity with reference to death, one's own as well as others.' Herein lies nationalism's affective appeal, that which makes it possible to sacrifice oneself for the "motherland." It lends to the accident of birth the sense of continuity and converts mortality into something that is meant for as much as it is realized by one. By placing one in a certain relationship to death and generativity, nationalist discourse therefore frames the arbitrariness of existence. "It is the magic of nationalism to turn chance into destiny" (*IC,* p. 19).

However, while nationalism tends to mime the idioms of kinship and religion, the historical conditions of its emergence undermine the logic and stability of these inherited categories. Thus Anderson defines nations as "imagined communities." Built on the rubble of traditional polities, the nation invokes a radically secular subjectivity that sets it apart from its predecessors. Dynastic states presumed power and privilege as functions of the purity of bloodlines guaranteed by a divine order. Colonial states as dynastic states in drag replicate the obsession with hierarchy by reorganizing social and epistemological categories according to a metaphysics of race and progress. By contrast, the nation envisions a more egalitarian community. "Regardless of the actual inequality and exploitation that may prevail in each, the nation is always conceived as a deep, horizontal comradeship" (*IC,* p. 16). It thus reveals the mutability of all sorts of hierarchies. Rather than take power for granted as natural and inherited, nationalism asks about "rights" and thereby opens up the problem of representation: who has the right to speak for whom, and under what circumstances?

To speak of nations as imagined communities is to posit national identities as explicitly fictional, though not in the sense of being "false" but in the sense of being constituted in and through a vernacular language. It is for this reason that nations are thought to be inclusive and open-ended, yet limited and bounded (thus the endless irony, as Anderson points out, of the category "naturalized citizen"). The vernacular matrix of national identity is, however, historically determined. Any language, given the right conditions, can serve as a vernacular insofar as it is able to produce the identity of its speakers in ways that feel both constructed and appropriate to them (see *IC,* p. 140). Because it is historical, a vernacular is never pure. It is rather the result of an indeterminate series of usages, translations and mistranslations, and interested codifications. If language localizes identity, to imagine a community in the vernacular would be to represent subjectivities in process: divided, fragmentary, and changeable. Indeed it is arguably such explicitly impure and unstable imaginings that lend nationalism its modernity.

One can also see the modernity of nationalism in the peculiar way that it posits a "community in anonymity." As Anderson points out, belonging to a nation need never entail face-to-face contact with its members. Instead, one's sense of belonging is mediated by a complex set of symbols and events that cohere with the temporal rhythm of clock and calendar. Nationalist consciousness thus presupposes the secularization of time—time as "transverse [and horizontal], cross-time, marked not by prefiguring and fulfillment, but by temporal coincidence"—as one of its conditions of possibility (*IC,* pp. 30, 28-40).

Time as coincidence rather than apocalyptic punctuation historically was made possible by, among other things, the rise of print capitalism, which promoted print vernaculars and the emergence of newspapers and novels as the dominant means for delineating and particularizing the social and cultural field of a nation. Unfolding in "homogenous, empty time" (*IC,* p. 30), novels and newspapers in the vernacular provided a space for the juxtaposition of previously unrelated events, people, and objects. As commodities, their circulation was dependent on the workings of the market while their production relied on the technology of print. In the sense that it was shaped by the exigencies of print capitalism and print vernacular, nationalist (like bourgeois) consciousness became mechanically reproducible. Hence while the vernacular provided the medium for imagining "continuity-in-discontinuity" where the nation was concerned, the technical and temporal context within which nationalism emerged suggests the presence of another moment in the imagination of nationhood, one that might escape the boundaries set by the vernacular. Rather than result in the consolidation of a particular, autonomous identity, such a moment would posit the possibility of the mechanical proliferation and indeterminate circulation of identities. It would then point not only to the workings of the imagination in bringing about a sense of community; it might also indicate the risk in such imaginings, including the failure of imagination itself.

I want to suggest that not only is nationalism inherently conflictual, caught between dynastic/colonial modes of apprehension on the one hand and the possibilities of an egalitarian, postcolonial existence on the other; but that the means for imagining nationhood may at times be at odds with the very nature of the images that are reproduced. I propose this not as a general theory about nationalism but as a conceptual hook for reflecting on the particular historical moment I am concerned with: the formative period of Filipino nationalism in the late nineteenth century. In what follows, I want to illustrate the tension between imagination and imagery by examining two sites of Filipino nationalist representation: the textualized embodiments of the motherland and the photographed bodies of male patriots. In both texts and photographs, the project of imagining a national community was alternately sustained and superseded by the figurative and mechanical means of their reproduction.

Engendering Nationhood

The early Filipino nationalists were a remarkable group. For the most part they were members of an emergent bourgeoisie educated in the universities of the colonial capital of Manila and European cities such as Madrid, Paris, and Berlin. They were well-traveled and multilingual, though Spanish was the preferred lingua franca. And they were all males who self-consciously referred to themselves as *ilustrados*, literally, "enlightened." From the 1880s to the middle of the 1890s they engaged in campaigns calling for the reform of the economic, political, and educational conditions in the Philippines. Because of the hazards of colonial censorship and threats of imprisonment, the site of their political activities eventually shifted to the more liberal Spanish cities of Madrid and Barcelona.

Known in Philippine historiography as the Propaganda Movement, their political efforts varied widely in scope. Among other things, they organized among Filipino expatriates and Europeans sympathetic to Philippine problems; wrote novels as well as philological, ethnological, and historical studies of the colony; and publicized nationalist causes in the liberal Spanish press and, from 1889-95, in their own propaganda newspaper, *La Solidaridad*. Such causes initially had an assimilationist nature: the granting of Spanish citizenship to Filipino colonial subjects by way of equal application of the Spanish civil law to the colony and Filipino representation to the Spanish parliament. But as assimilationist hopes dimmed by the mid-1890s the more prominent leaders of the Propaganda Movement began to favor Philippine independence from Spain.[2]

A crucial feature of the nationalist movement was the *ilustrado* critique of the Catholic church, a key institution in the history of Spanish colonialism.[3] Filipino nationalists were particularly antagonized by the enormous influence of the Spanish friars whom they held as chiefly accountable for the colony's backwardness. They saw the friars as forces of reaction, and with good reason, for the friars regarded Filipinos as inferior to Spaniards, liberalism and learning as threats to the power of the Church, and the *ilustrados* themselves as subversives. It would be difficult to overstate the political and symbolic import of the Spanish friars for the Filipino *ilustrados*. In nationalist writings, they were seen as figures of denial and agents of exclusion, hoarders of wealth and women, purveyors of religious fetishism, and merchants of ritual practices and devotional paraphernalia.[4]

The Jesuit historian John Schumacher rightly notes that without the Spanish clergy, Filipino nationalism would have taken a different course.[5] The friars occupied a near-totalizing significance in the minds of the ilustrados and came to represent the negative limit in the formation of nationalist consciousness in the late nineteenth century. In this sense we can think of them as mirror images of Filipino nationalists. Indeed, the intensely negative tenor of antifriar rhetoric among the ilustrados was a way of recognizing the Spanish clergy as the source of their own divided identity. For as the Filipinos repeatedly pointed out, the friars were themselves doubled, split between spiritual and material concerns. Despite their vows of celibacy, they were accused of using the confessional to prey on the gullibility of women and thus monopolize access to their bodies and minds.[6] As figurative fathers, they were invested with phallic authority, yet were often snidely referred to by the ilustrados as men "who wear skirts" and "soured nurses."[7] Representatives of Catholic monotheism, the friars nonetheless acted like pagan priests (*babaylan*), encouraging the substitution of faith with the fetishistic regard for an endless array of religious images among the populace. Though mortals, they behaved like gods (*diosdiosan*); and despite their vows of poverty, they lived lavish lives akin to that of oriental despots.[8]

The ilustrados thus saw the Spanish fathers not only as figures of denial but also of excess. They were imagined, that is, as going beyond their proper roles and traditional boundaries. Translating between languages and moving between cultures, the Spanish fathers seemed like retrograde versions of the youthful nationalists. The former were thought to monopolize the language of power and the circulation of money and women, thus threatening to cut the latter off from access to their own future. Given the oedipal texture of ilustrado anxieties, it is not surprising to see that the future they imagined and desired took on a specifically feminine shape.

Anderson writes, "*amor patriae* does not differ . . . from the other affections, in which there is always an element of fond imagining . . . . What the eye is to the lover, . . . language . . . is to the patriot. Through that language, encountered at mother's knee and parted with only at the grave, pasts are restored, fellowships are imagined, and futures dreamed" (*IC,* p. 140). In the context of nineteenth-century Philippine nationalism, the association of language with sight and mother with nation is highly suggestive. As we've seen, Spanish fathers figured the negative moment in the production of ilustrado consciousness. Mothers, however, tended to play a far more ambivalent role in nationalist thinking. To the extent that they were imagined to be the source of the vernacular with which to articulate nationhood, real mothers tended to be conflated with figurative mothers, such as "Mother Spain" or "Mother Philippines." Ilustrado sons expressed their relationship to the "motherland" (whether Spain in the early assimilationist phase of nationalist history, or the Philippines in the later more separatist period) in familial terms. Equating love of nation with love of mother idealized the former in terms of the latter. Thus could sacrifice and loss appear necessary and reasonable: by acting as their protectors, sons could reciprocate the affections of mothers, real or imagined.

The love of country was thus far from disinterested inasmuch as it engendered, in the double sense of the term, the idea of the nation. By doing so, nationalist discourse reflected as much as it re-fracted domestic politics. One way of getting a sense of the complex-ity of interests informing *amor patriae* is by taking a look at some of the writings of Jose Rizal (1861-96), undoubtedly the most prominent and articulate of the ilustrados and the national hero of the Republic of the Philippines.[9]

Writing to his mother from Berlin in 1886, Rizal tells her,

> "I continually dream of you and sometimes the dream re-peats itself in a single night. I would not like to be superstitious
> . . . but I like to believe that you are thinking constantly of me and this makes my mind reproduce what goes on in yours for after all my brain is a part of yours, and this is not strange be-cause while I am asleep here, you are awake there, etc. etc."[10]

"You're at the center of my thoughts," Rizal seems to be telling his mother so that her images return to him as if unwilled. Biogra-phers of Rizal have noted the close ties shared by mother and son. The letter above is one example of their intimacy. Yet Rizal accounts for the involuntary repetition of his dreams by attributing it to his mother's constant thoughts of him. His dreams are the "reproduc-tions" of her waking thoughts, which in turn are invariably about him. His mother thus comes across as a repository for images of himself. Dreaming of her is a way of reproducing those images but in dis-placed fashion so that they involve not only memories of her but images of her thinking about him as well. The involuntary nature of such imaging suggests the workings of a kind of mechanical memory—one that escapes conscious intentionality—that draws on the labor of the mother's thoughts.

The image of the mother as both the source of memories and as a mechanism for the reproduction of images about the self is in fact a recurrent motif in much of Rizal's writings. In an early autobiographical fragment entitled "My First Reminiscence," Rizal talks about his mother as his first teacher of Spanish, painstakingly correcting his pronunciation and grammar. She also translates stories for him from Spanish to Tagalog. The one he recalls in particular involved the story of an old moth telling its offspring not to fly too close to the flame of a lamp lest it burn its wings. The younger moth nonetheless is attracted to the light and disobeys the older one's counsel. Flying too close to the flame, it plunges to its death.

While his mother translates this story for him, Rizal recalls being distracted by the sight of moths flitting around the flame of a kerosene lamp. What is odd is that he fails to listen to the story, yet remembers its lesson:

> My mother continued her reading . . . [but] the fate of the two insects interested me intensely. The light agitated its golden tongue on one side, a singed moth in one of these movements fell into oil, clapped its wings for some time and then died. That assumed for me the proportions of a great event and as a strange phenomenon that I have always observed in me when something excites me. It seemed to me that the flame and the moths [in the story] were moving far away, very far, and that my mother's voice acquired a strange, sepulchral timbre.
>
> My mother finished the fable. I was not listening; all my attention, all my mind, and all my thoughts were concentrated on the fate of the moth, young, dead, and full of illusions.[11]

In this memory, Rizal's mother is less the origin of language than a figure who translates, as well as one who teaches the boy about the hazards of translation. The moral of the mother's fable lies in the passage from Spanish to Tagalog, from listening to obedience. The failure to translate from one to another brings up the possibility of death, figured in the fate of the errant moths. Yet Rizal learns these lessons not only despite, but because of the fact that he's distracted by the flickering light of the kerosene lamp. Hence, his first memory is split between two images: that of his mother and that of the light from the lamp. Each marks the significance of the other. For just as the light makes it possible for Rizal's mother to translate the story, the story illuminates, as it were, the dangers that the light poses to translation. Indeed, by fastening onto the light, Rizal fails to listen and so disobeys his mother. But disobedience still brings with it the knowledge of death, the very same knowledge that was already implied in the mother's fable.

Rizal's first memory is anything but innocent. Rather, it is about the difference between Spanish and Tagalog, story and experience, obedience and transgression. By bringing to surface two seemingly opposed images—mother and light—it also shows these images to be inherently divided. The mother is both a storyteller intent on imparting a lesson and a kind of machine for translation. The light from the lamp is both a metaphor for knowledge and its attendant risks as well as a mechanism that allows reading to take place at all. Small wonder then that Rizal ends his narrative on a note of ambivalence. On the one hand, he recalls the "sweet lessons" taught to him by his mother standing out amidst the "bitter lessons" learned in adult life. On the other hand, he continues with "the heart of a child . . . [to] believe that light is the most beautiful thing . . . and that it is worthy for a man to sacrifice his life for it."[12]

What are the effects of seeing the nation as either "mother" or "light"? What difference does it make to imagine nationhood either as a gendered metaphor or as an impersonal machine that generates memories of individual and collective images?

To address these questions, I want to turn to an essay Rizal wrote shortly after arriving in Europe. It is appropriately entitled "El Amor Patrio" ("The Love of Country"). Published in 1882 when Rizal was barely twenty-one years old, this essay established his notoriety among both Filipinos and Spanish colonial officials.[13] Much of the imagery and logic of his later writings are foreshadowed in this essay. And because Rizal's style of imagining nationhood was regarded as exemplary among his contemporaries and future nationalists, the essay is worth following at some length.

Rizal begins by invoking the timeless universality of nationhood.

From the cultured Europeans to the enslaved Africans, from the ancient to the modern peoples of the world, all have had and have an idol [*idolo*]—beautiful, brilliant, sublime, but implacable, fierce, and demanding—whom they have called Motherland [*Patria*] . . . she is in the thoughts of everyone, and like the light enclosed in clear crystal, she goes forth in the most vivid splendor. ["AP," p. 12]

Rizal sees nationhood as transhistorical; thus he regards the motherland as both idol and light, an image that unifies opposed terms and the means for producing such images. For the patriot, however, the ideality of the *patria* comes through in direct relationship to her absence. The motherland is "ever more idolized in proportion to one's . . . distance from her" ("AP" p. 13). One imagines the *patria* only in missing her. And missing her is, in turn, indissociable from recalling one's first memories of childhood:

> . . . there in our country are our first memories [*recuerdos*] of childhood, a happy ode, known only in childhood, from whose traces spring forth the flower of innocence and happiness; because there slumbers a whole past and a future to be hoped; because in her forests and in her meadows, on every tree on every blade, on every flower, you see engraved [*grabado*] the memory of a being you love, as her breath in perfumed breeze, her song in murmur of the fountains, her smile in the rainbow of the sky, or her sighs in the confused moans of the night wind. ["AP," p. 13]

Here, the love one feels for the *patria* is conveyed by what we might call a rhetoric of mourning. Mourning implies a process of working through, then setting apart one's memories of a lost object or person from one's experience of them while still alive. In doing so one is able to reconcile oneself to the fact of loss. Such a reconciliation is accomplished through the idealization of the person or object. Put another way, mourning succeeds when what one remembers is an image of what was lost, no longer the lost object itself.[14] Mourning thus entails the reproduction of stereotypical images of the lost object. In such a context, memory attaches itself not to direct experience but to its mediated versions.

The distance between the patriot and the *patria* enables the former to establish the latter as an image of loss as well as the space for locating loss as such. Worth noting is the specific way by which such imaging takes place. The "memory of a being you love" is said by Rizal to be "engraved" [*grabado*] on the motherland's body. The engraving of these images on the *patria*, like the imprinting of the vernacular in a novel or newspaper, brings to mind the mechanical process of standardization and reproduction of a vernacular that precipitates nationalist consciousness. Hence, the sense of loss that occasions the imagination of nationhood is localized by a certain style and process of imaging. As in Rizal's dream about his mother, the patriot misses the motherland and so constitutes her absence as that which brings about the presence of a self who remembers others who remember him: "It is because you see there with the eyes of your imagination under the tranquil roof of your old home, a family who remembers you and awaits you . . . whatever her name . . . we love her always, as the child loves his mother" ("AP," p. 13). Nationalism as a kind of mourning is built on remembering as a reciprocal act. This is why Rizal thinks of the recollection of the *patria* as a form of return, both in the sense of a giving and a journeying back. The circulation of memory between patriot and motherland binds together the living with the dead, culture with nature, innocence with mortality. Hence, to the question, "why is it that people are compelled to return to their country," Rizal responds, "is it gratitude; is it affection for everything that reminds us of something of the first days of our own life, the land where our ancestors are sleeping?" ["AP," p. 14].

Yet the latter section of this passage seems to suggest that his response was not merely the rhetorical reiteration of the sense of mourning and the process of reciprocity informing the love of nation. Rizal intimates that there also seem to be nonreciprocal, profoundly nonhuman and nondivine elements that "attract, captivate, and seduce us" into returning to the *patria*. These include "the raging storm that lashes and knocks down with its terrible force everything it finds in its way; the lightning which, escaping from the hands of the Almighty, annihilates everything; . . . the avalanche or the cascade, matters of perpetual motion and endless menace" ("AP," p. 14).

It is almost as if undecipherable violence underwrites—or at least subtends—the clarity and availability of the motherland's body to the patriot's memory traces. The land described above is one that resists all attempts at human and divine inscription. Instead it is thought to be the site of a series of actions freed from intentions, of images that exceed the localizing pull of the vernacular. Depersonalized and degendered, it becomes sheer automaticity, "the avalanche or the cascade, matters of perpetual motion and endless menace." The nation can therefore be imagined as that which threatens the very workings of the imagination. It is perhaps this possibility that seizes Rizal when he speaks about the *patria* not only as the storehouse of fond memories but also as the source of a certain disease:

> Probably these beauties or tender remembrances fortify the bond that unites us to the land of our birth, endangering sweet feelings of well-being when we are in our country, or profound melancholia when we are far away from it, the origin of a cruel disease called nostalgia.
>
> Oh! Never sadden the stranger who arrives at your shores; do not awaken in him vivid memories of his country, of the comfort (*delicias*) of his home, because then, unfortunately, you will evoke in him this disease, a tenacious phantom [*tenaz fantasma*] that will not abandon him until he sees his native soil or the borders of his tomb. ["AP," p. 14]

The love of country brings with it both pleasure and dread. In imagining a community, one also risks contracting nostalgia, a "disease" provoked by the emergence of unbounded images. Such images threaten to run rampant like phantoms, simultaneously inhabiting the realm of the living and the dead, moving between the boundaries of absence and presence. They thus signal the failure of mourning. To be gripped by nostalgia is to see loss converted neither to memory nor reciprocity. Instead loss comes across as the unsublatable experience of being haunted. Hence, while the nation can be thought of as an absence reconstituted in the vernacular of mourning, it could also exist, as in the highly charged passage above, as a ghostly presence. In the latter case, the nation suggests intimacy as it escapes localization. As a phantom it is neither mother nor machine but a restless image that remains eccentric and heterogeneous to native imaginings.

In Rizal, therefore, the compulsion to return to the motherland takes on an added complexity. Not only is it an expression of love and gratitude, a memorialization of innocence sanctifying mortality; it can also be the result of sporadic haunting which drives the patriot to "his native soil or the borders of his tomb." Laying to rest these ghostly images unleashed by the disease of nostalgia brings up the question of death and hence the possibility of putting an end to the work of imagination. This latter possibility for Rizal remains unthinkable. Towards the latter portion of his essay, he draws back from conjuring further apparitions of the nation and instead returns to those familiar and "pious sentiments" [*piadosos sentimientos*]. As we have seen, such sentiments hinge on reciprocity and mourning:

> Some have sacrificed for her their youth, their pleasures, others have dedicated to her the splendors of their genius; others shed their blood; all have died, bequeathing to their motherland an immense future: liberty and glory. And what has she done for them? She mourns them, and proudly presents them to the world, to posterity and to her children to serve as examples. ["AP," pp. 16-17]

Once more, the nation is gendered and domesticated within the circle of sacrifice and the idealization of loss that binds the child-patriot to his motherland. By doing so, the patriot not only expresses his love but also reverses the relationship of dependency between mother and child. He posits his future authority over her, imagining himself and others like him as potential patrons, "bequeathing" to the *patria* the legacy of freedom. In this way, the motherland inherits from her sons an "immense fortune"—a surplus of symbolic wealth with which to nurture future sons. Offspring and lover, the patriot is now also father to the nation. It is thus wholly without irony that Filipinos have regarded Rizal as the "father" of Philippine nationalism and that one of his biographers has referred to him as the "first Filipino."

This dialectic of filiation, however, doesn't always work in the way I've described above because the familial discourse for engendering nationhood runs up against the conditions of mechanical reproduction—those conditions stressed by Anderson that allow for the vernacularization of images. In Rizal, such images draw their power from their inherent instability. Maternal and mechanical images can slide into as much as stand against one another. And the entire process of sorting out such images could, at certain moments, enter into a crisis of imaging when the "disease" of nostalgia hits the patriot, unleashing the proliferation of ghostly images. To return to the motherland thus incurs the risk of being stranded in a zone of images that drift away from the text of nationalist imagination. It is the risk of seeing the products of one's work assume an existence unmoored to and unrecognizable from one's original intentions. Rizal's attempt to reimagine community in terms of mourning and reciprocity not only allows him to repress such ghostly images; it also enables him to posit a patriarchal basis for nationhood. Yet such a move is provisional. In the history of Philippine nationalism, the ghosts would keep coming back.

Patriots and Photographs

The tension between imagination and imagery is dispersed over the field of nationalist writings.[15] It recurs, however, in a somewhat puzzling way in a medium related to but distinct from print vernacular, that of photography. Whereas nationalist texts articulate national identity with reference to the absent figure of the motherland, photographs bring forth the image of the nation with reference to the absent bodies of patriots. Yet texts and photographs differ in their ways of imaging. Whereas one involves the setting forth and working through of the contradictions and divisions of national identity, the other entails rendering such contradictions obvious, that is, visible and therefore tangential to conceptualization. In what follows, I offer a preliminary discussion of the curious role of photography in nationalist discourse.

I want to begin by turning again to Rizal. His letters and diaries give us a sense of how photographs had become commonplace among late nineteenth-century Filipino bourgeoisie.[16] He routinely mentions the exchange of photographs as tokens of affection among friends and family. Rizal himself kept at least two large photo albums and regularly had his portraits taken in Europe for the benefit of his family and acquaintances.[17]

Pictures were gifts by which the recipient could remember the giver in his or her absence. In this sense, they supplemented the work of mourning, providing one with a memory trace of the other. "My father and my mother should have their pictures taken and sent to me," Rizal writes from Madrid in 1883, "at least in that way I shall always have their figure before me and [they] would not be erased from my memory" (17 Jan. 1883, *OHL*, p. 67) His older brother informs him in another letter, "I picked up in Manila your five photographs delivering each one to its owner."[18] Rizal's mother, Doña Teodora, writes to her son, "We three had our group picture taken to send to you so that you will not get sad. We happen to talk about your great desire to see our pictures."[19] Consider as well Rizal's letter to his fellow ilustrado Mariano Ponce from London—"At present I cannot send you yet my photograph because I have none; the only one I have was taken sometime ago and I wish to present you with a new one—"[20] and to a German friend in Berlin—"I take the liberty of sending you now my picture and I beg you to send me yours."[21] Leonor Rivera, Rizal's cousin and one-time fiancée writes an inscription on the back of her photograph: "To my unforgettable and most beloved lover, this photograph is dedicated. Your devoted Leonor."[22] And Rizal in his Madrid diary of January 1883 writes of refusing another ilustrado's request to show his collection of photographs "because these were gifts and had dedications," even though a couple of weeks later he "merrily" engages two sisters in conversation over the same pictures.[23] And years later while exiled in Dapitan, he writes to his sisters somewhat impatiently, "You have not sent me the album of my pictures" (12 Feb. 1896, *OHL*, p.487).

What's interesting about these passages is how flat and unremarkable they are. Among Filipinos photographs seemed to elicit at most formulaic inscriptions of affection, passing remarks, and marginal notes in letters and diaries rather than sustained disquisitions on their aesthetic value or political significance as had been the case among nineteenth-century European and American writers on photography. This is perhaps one reason why a history of photography in the Philippines is yet to be written. Photographs have seemed so obvious to those who took and exchanged them that they have become barely visible to historians of Philippine nationalism. The photographs of ilustrados persist as perhaps the most concrete evidence of their existence; yet they also seem to be the most troublesome of documents. While they permit the tracing and enumeration of their details, photographic images discourage the generalization of their meanings. Silent and elusive, they also appear unchanging. Meant for private consumption, these photographs nevertheless attracted public interest because of the history of their referents. How then to understand images of bodies that seem to demand as they evade historical interpretation?

When I started thinking about photography and nationalism, I thought it might be possible to find a link between pictorial and textual images—that perhaps one could be made to illuminate the other. It is possible to do so, but only to a point. Take for example the photograph of Rizal with two other ilustrado propagandists in Madrid, Mariano Ponce and Marcelo H. del Pilar (fig. 1). One could think of this photograph as part of a larger attempt at nationalist self-fashioning. By posing in European clothes they appear tendentiously out of context. Their photographed bodies take visible exception to Spanish racial stereotypes such as were current in the latter nineteenth century. These stereotypes amounted to the infantilization of native Filipinos. The women were regarded as gullible and excessively accommodating to foreigners, and the men were said to be "lacking even the beard which is the sign of virility in a race. . . 'Bodies without clothes, brains without ideas...an inanimate heap of human entities.'"[24] By contrast, this photograph shows the seriousness of expression on the ilustrados' faces that makes one think of collected interiors in command of their exterior representations, of rational minds holding together bodies in studied repose. The photograph specifies with remarkable precision the boundaries of those bodies, fixing their limits and proportions in ways that other forms of representation would be incapable of doing.

Fig. 1. Jose Rizal, Marcelo H. del Pilar, and Mariano Ponce. Madrid, 1890.

We might also read a similar process of self-fashioning at work in another photograph of Rizal, this time with the Filipino painter Juan Luna and ilustrado Valentin Ventura posing in Paris between their fencing exercises (fig. 2). While attending the Paris Exposition of 1889, Rizal and his fellow Filipinos saw a Wild West show featuring Native Americans performing various skills on horseback. Impressed not only by their daring but also by the enthusiastic applause they received from the crowd, the Filipinos decided to form a mutual-aid association and call it *Los Indios Bravos*. Rizal himself had suggested the name, thinking to subvert the racist designation *indio* used by the Spaniards to refer to native Filipinos. Referring to themselves as "brave Indians" coincided with their interest in fencing, gymnastics, martial arts, and weightlifting—again, ways of marking their bodies apart from colonial categories. Posing with their swords planted firmly between their legs, the Indios Bravos display a masculine alternative to what they conceived to be the menacingly androgynous and corrupt regime of the Spanish friars. That image of masculine solidarity is further suggested by the barely visible figure of a woman—Paz Pardo de Tavera, Luna's wife—situated in the background, at the margins of the frame, as if to signal the sexual hierarchy that patriotism reinstitutes. Considered along with the first photograph, this picture has the effect of remapping the body of the colonized subject in ways that peel away from the grid of colonial assumptions.

Fig. 2. "Los Indios Bravos": Juan Luna, Rizal, and Valentin Ventura. Seated on extreme left, Paz Pardo de Tavera. Paris, 1890.

Both photographs reproduce alternative identities in the precise manner by which they trace the physical differences between Filipinos and Spaniards even as they evoke the translation and transvaluation of clothing and sensibility from one to the other. These pictures and others like them could be understood as continuing the project of articulating a nationalist identity predicated on demarcating the boundaries of the imagined body—whether those of the motherland or the patriot. Exchanged and circulated among friends and family, such photographs were ways of intimating a community built on the absence of their members. It would therefore seem appropriate to read these photographs historically and politically as images that promote a radical estrangement between colonizer and colonized that would in time become the basis for Philippine independence.

Yet such readings do not exhaust the contents of these and other pictures. Again, it is worth recalling that Filipinos did not write about photography as such or about particular photographs except to register their receipt and delivery. There is therefore no textual evidence by which we can verify our readings of these pictures just as there is no definitive context into which we can enclose the photographic images that would make them the product of the intentions of their referent. There is instead an irreducible *there-ness* to these images that remains unaltered from the particular moment they were taken. While they exist as residues of prior imaginings, both public and private, they also resist conversion to other images, allowing only for their mechanical duplication. Captions and commentaries may alter their significance within the discursive field of colonialism and nationalism, but these do not alter their appearance. In this sense, photographs are typical of mechanically reproducible imagery. They lead a life linked to yet radically attenuated from the objects they represent. They are the "afterlife" of these objects, but only in the sense of being their dematerialized repetition rather than their material transformation. Such images forge bonds of intimacy without yielding their autonomy. Photographs of patriots thus seem both appropriate and anomalous. Whereas nationalist writings imagined a new community through a vernacular history of love and the reconciliatory labor of sacrifice, photographs of nationalists hover over their texts, instantly imaging, with no more work than the click of the shutter, identities that can circulate and reproduce but that cannot translate.

We can see the peculiar nature of photographic images in the portraits of Rizal. Shortly before and long after his death by firing squad on charges of fomenting the Philippine revolution of 1896, Rizal's pictures took on an iconic value among many Filipinos. One in particular taken in Madrid in 1890 became widely reproduced (fig. 3). Numerous smaller copies were circulated with the outbreak of the revolution, carrying the following legend on the reverse:

> Doctor Jose Rizal! Shot in Manila, 30 December 1896. Tyranny snatched you away from us! . . . But what she will never do is to erase you from the hearts of your countrymen. When the Philippines is able to decide its own destiny, she will know how to erect an altar to your memory in the temple of immortality and to put your name in letters of gold in the eternal pages of history. For now, you must satisfy yourself with the ardent worship [*culto fervoroso*] that each Filipino devotes to you from the depths of their souls.[26]

Fig. 3. The last studio portrait of Rizal.
Madrid, 1890.

For many Filipinos at the turn of the century, the portrait of Rizal could be made to function in much the same way as images of the motherland did in Rizal's writings. It memorialized loss and converted it into a potent basis for visualizing a new history for the country. Indeed, Rizal's portraits—probably copies of the one above—hung on the walls of the Katipunan headquarters, the Filipino revolutionary forces that initiated the armed struggle against Spain.[27] With Rizal's death, his photographic likeness could be made to stand for the as yet to be realized nation. As the passage above indicates, his images were invested with a certain archaism, as if they had been freed from the vagaries of time. For this reason, they could become cult objects, pointing to an alternative realm of power and redemption.

Yet there is also a sense in which the process of imaging the nation through Rizal's photographs differed from that of imaging it through his writings. Precisely because of their conflictual nature, his writings leave something hidden and potentially unknown. For this reason, one can engage them dialectically in terms of the ways they enact the history of nationalist imagination. Or one can treat them, as most biographers of Rizal have done often with the sponsorship of the Philippine state, as sacred texts whose meaning has always been prefigured and whose significance current history confirms.

His photographs, however, expose him as an image on a flat surface that is seen rather than read. Unlike his writings, Rizal's photographic images do not entail the expenditure of work over time that would lend itself to the metaphorics of sacrifice and loss. Instead, they are reproduced automatically so that their dissemination becomes difficult if not impossible to control. Consequently, Rizal's images could cross boundaries of class, gender, and language to become a national symbol by the turn of the century despite, indeed because of, the fact that they remained autonomous and unassimilated. His photographs served as the basis for the Rizal monument built in Manila in 1912 (under the auspices of the U.S. colonial state) and other similar monuments that have since been erected in virtually all Philippine towns. These, along with nearly all representations of Rizal, show him in the European clothes that he wore in his pictures so that he appears consistently out of place in a tropical setting. Just as interesting is the fact that such an anomaly has remained largely uncommented on by Filipinos.

The oddness of his images lies in this: they project him as the "father" of the nation but in ways that lead in time to the flattening of his legacy. Since Rizal's death, his photographic likeness has adorned everything from stamps to currency notes, matchboxes to amulets, book covers to postcards. Like "tenacious phantoms," his images have clung to the national consciousness. However, unlike the uncontrollable imaging induced by nostalgia for the motherland, Rizal's images do not seem to produce anxiety or even pathos. That is, they mark the boundaries of an imagined community but do so without the labor of mourning. Again, this has to do with the way such images drastically abbreviate the work of memory and imagination. Rizal's photographs conjure up the nation by circumventing the history of its imaging. They seem familiar to the extent that they remain alien—so alien as to become unremarkable. They thus suggest something of the way photographic imagery resists the hermeneutic pull of nationalist imagination. Existing on the border of colonial and national history, such photographs recall the difference between imagination and imagery, between a "community in anonymity" and the anonymity that persistently, even if mechanically, haunts community.

NOTES

1. Benedict Anderson, *Imagined Communities: Reflections on the Origin and Spread of Nationalism* (London, 1983), pp. 11-15; hereafter abbreviated *IC*.

2. Some of the ilustrados would join the revolution against Spain by 1897 while others rejected armed struggle altogether. Nonetheless, most of the ilustrados sought to control the short-lived Philippine Republic in Malolos in 1898, but when war against the United States broke out in 1899, some of them fought while others collaborated with the U.S. With war's end in 1902, nearly all the ilustrados and their descendants would eagerly participate in the expanded American colonial bureaucracy. And when Japanese forces occupied the Philippines between 1942 and 1945, most of the second-generation ilustrados collaborated with the Occupation government in varying degrees of willingness. With independence in 1946, they faced a peasant-led, Communist-supported uprising known as the Huk revolt and with massive aid from the United States quashed the revolt and consolidated their hold over the economy and politics of the new Republic. Indeed, the ancestors of former president Ferdinand Marcos and current president Corazon Aquino were both part of the ilustrado tradition.

For a concise but incisive overview of ilustrado history, see Anderson, "Cacique Democracy in the Philippines: Origins and Dreams," Chapter 1 of this book, pages 3-48. The most comprehensive account of the early stages of ilustrado nationalism can be found in John N. Schumacher, *The Propaganda Movement 1880-1895: The Creators of a Filipino Consciousness, the Makers of Revolution* (Manila, 1973). See also Renato Constantino, *The Philippines: A Past Revisited* (Quezon City, 1975).

3. See John Phelan, *The Hispanization of the Philippines: Spanish Aims and Filipino Responses, 1565-1700* (Madison, Wis., 1959), and Vicente L. Rafael, *Contracting Colonialism: Translation and Christian Conversion in Tagalog Society under Early Spanish Rule* (Durham: Duke University Press. 1993).

4. For some of the more representative antifriar polemics, see Graciano Lopez-Jaena, "Fray Botod," *Discursos y articulos varios* (Barcelona, 1891), pp. 203-27; the pamphlets of Marcelo H. del Pilar, *La soberania monacal en Filipinas* (Barcelona, 1888), and *La frailocracia filipina por M.H. Plaridel* (Barcelona, 1889); and in many of the writings of Jose Rizal, especially the two novels, *Noli me tangere* (Berlin, 1887), and *El Filibusterismo* (Ghent, 1891). See also Schumacher, *The Propaganda Movement*, pp. 271-77.

5. See Schumacher, *The Propaganda Movement*, pp. 272-78.

6. See, for example, Rizal, "Sa mga kababayang dalaga sa Malolos," *Escritos politicos e historicos*, vol. 7 of *Escritos de Jose Rizal* (Manila, 1961), pp. 55-65, and Lopez-Jaena, "Fray Botod."

7. Quoted in Leon Ma. Guerrero, *The First Filipino: A Biography of Jose Rizal* (Manila, 1963), pp. 82, 115.

8. Again, see Rizal, "Sa mga kababayang dalaga sa Malolos," and Lopez-Jaena, "Fray Botod."

9. The standard biographies of Rizal include W. E. Retana, *Vida y escritos del Dr. Jose Rizal* (Madrid, 1907); Carlos Quirino, *The Great Malayan* (Manila, 1940); Rafael Palma, *Biografia de Rizal* (Manila, 1949); and Guerrero, *The First Filipino*.

10. Rizal to Doña Teodora Alonso y Quintos, 25 Dec. 1886, *One Hundred Letters of Jose Rizal to His Parents, Brother, Sisters, Relatives* (Manila, 1959), p. 312; hereafter abbreviated *OHL*. Rizal's mother (1825-1911) was born to a family of *principales*—the Filipino colonial elite. Rizal describes her as "a woman of more than average education," having been schooled at the convent-run Colegio de Santa Rosa in Manila at a time when literacy among men, much less women, was rather low in the colony. The son's relationship with his mother was such that when her eyesight began to deteriorate in the early 1880s, he decided to study ophthalmology in order to cure her. In his novels and journalistic writings, Rizal often alludes to his mother's influence on his political education. Curiously and for reasons that remain unclear to me, Rizal rarely ever spoke of, much less communicated with, his father, Don Francisco Mercado (Guerrero, *The First Filipino*, pp. 18, 30-32).

11. Rizal, "My First Reminiscence," *Reminiscences and Travels of Jose Rizal*, trans. Encarnacion Alzona (Manila, 1961), pp. 36-37; I have been unable to find the Spanish original of this text.

12. Ibid., p. 37.

13. Rizal, "El Amor Patrio," *Prosa por Jose Rizal* (Manila, 1961), pp. 12-17; hereafter abbreviated "AP"; my translation. See Rizal, *Rizal's Prose*, trans. Alzona (Manila, 1962), pp. 15-21.

14. The classic formulation of mourning is found in Sigmund Freud, "Mourning and Melancholia," *The Standard Edition of the Complete Psychological Works of Sigmund Freud*, trans. and ed. James Strachey, 24 vols. (London, 1953-74), 14:239-60. See also the useful explication by J. Laplanche and J. B. Pontalis,

"Work of Mourning," *The Language of Psycho-analysis*, trans. Donald Nicholson-Smith (New York, 1973). pp.485-86.

15. See, for example, Rafael, "Language, Identity, and Gender in Rizal's *Noli*," *Review of Indonesian and Malaysian Affairs* 18 (Winter 1984): 110-40.

16. The earliest mention of photography in the Philippines occurs in 1841 when a Spanish offical named Sinibaldo de Mas began to photograph members of the Spanish community to supplement his income. Stereoscopic photos of a Philippine tribal group, the Tinguianes, taken about 1860 by an unknown French traveler are the earliest known surviving photographs in the archipelago. By the late 1860s, several photo studios had been established in the capital city of Manila as well as in few provincial capitals where Filipino principales had their portraits taken. See John Silva, *Colonial Philippines: Photographs, 1860-1910* (exhibition catalog, Lowie Museum of Anthropology, University of California, Berkeley, 9 May-11 July 1987). As I indicate below, a history of photography in the Philippines is yet to be written.

17. Two of Rizal's photo albums can be found at the Rizaliana section of the Lopez Memorial Museum in Manila.

18. Paciano Rizal to Jose Rizal, 26 May 1883, *Letters between Rizal and Family Members*, vol. 2. bk. 1 of *The Centennial Edition*, trans. and ed. National Heroes Commission (Manila, 1964), p. 97.

19. Doña Teodora to Rizal, 27 Nov. 1883, ibid., p. 134

20. Rizal to Mariano Ponce, 27 July 1888, *Reminiscences and Travels*. p. 301.

21. Rizal to Pastor Ullmer, 10 May 1887, trans. Alzona, vol. 2, bk. 4 of *The Centennial Edition*, ed. National Heroes Commission (Manila, 1963), p. 91.

22. Rizal, *Epistolario Rizalino*, ed. Teodoro M. Kalaw, 2 vols. (Manila, 1930-31), 2:50-51.

23. Rizal, *Reminiscences and Travels*, pp. 88-89, 91.

24. This passage comes from one of the best-known racists of the latter nineteenth century: see Quioquiap [Pablo Feced], "Ellos y nosotros," *El Liberal*, 13 Feb. 1887; cited in Schumacher, *The Propaganda Movement*, p. 56 n.7.

25. See Schumacher, *The Propaganda Movement*, pp. 213-14, and Guerrero, *The First Filipino*, p. 120.

26. Quoted in Retana, *Vida y escritos del Dr. Jose Rizal*, pl. 13.

27. Guerrero, *The First Filipino*, pp. 421-22.

SIX

Filipinos in the United States and their Literature of Exile

OSCAR V. CAMPOMANES

IS THERE A "FILIPINO AMERICAN" LITERATURE? CURRENT AND INCLUSIVE NO-tions of Asian American literature assume the existence of this sub-stratum without really delineating its contours. There is no sustained discussion of how "Filipino American" literature, if shaped as such a substructure, problematizes some of the claims of Asian American literature as a constitutive paradigm. Although developed unevenly as a category and distinctive body of writing,[1] "Asian American Literature" now commands a significant presence in the American acad-emy and the movement to revise the national literary canon. The imperative, then, is to test the descriptive and explanatory powers of this general paradigm in light of its as yet undetermined but nomi-nally acknowledged tributary formation of "Filipino American writ-ing." To leave this area unmapped is to create exclusion, internal hierarchy, and misrepresentation in the supposedly heterogeneous field of Asian American cultural production.[2]

The informal but long-standing directive to align "Filipino American" literature with the Chinese and Japanese American mainstream of Asian American literature has had its own consequences. When asked to construct "a literary background of Filipino-American works" for a founding Asian American anthology, the writers Oscar Peñaranda, Serafin Syquia, and Sam Tagatac declared: "We cannot write any literary background because there isn't any. No history. No published literature. No nothing. (49)" Their statement proved not only to be quite precipitate but also uncritical of the limiting assumptions foisted on their project by the anthologists.[3] Already implicit in this view was their disconnection from the exilic literature created by N.V.M. Gonzalez and Bienvenido Santos, or in more recent times, by Ninotchka Rosca and Linda Ty-Casper. Perhaps, rather than the veracity of its claim, what remains compelling is how this declaration expresses the incommensurable sense of non-being that stalks many Filipinos in the United States and many Americans of Filipino descent.

Without Names: Who Are We?

Indeed, one cannot discuss the (non-)existence of "Filipino American" literature without interrogating the more decisive issues of self- and peoplehood, of invisibility. This combined problematic certainly shapes the available expressions. For example, the Bay Area Pilipino American Writers titled their first collection of poetry after Jeff Tagami's historically textured piece, "Without Names" (Ancheta et al. 1985). "Who are we? / What are we?" asks public historian Fred Cordova in his picture book and oral history on Filipino Americans (230). In a 1989 essay, the journalist Cielo Fuentebella pointedly observes that even with the group nearing the two-million mark, "our numbers don't add up to visibility in business, media, and the cultural field. And all these at a time in history that is being dubbed as the Asian/Pacific Century" (17).

From these various expressions, one detects some hesitance to claim the name "Filipino American" unproblematically. The term "Filipino American" itself seems inadequate, if oxymoronic. "The Filipino American cannot be defined without elucidating what the problematic relationship is between the two terms which dictates the condition of possibility for each—the hyphen which spells a relation of subordination and domination" (San Juan, "Boundaries" 125). There is some recognition, in other words, of the irreducible specificity of the Filipino predicament in the United States, and corollarily, of the literary and cultural expressions that it has generated. Although one finds many self-identified Filipino Americans and Filipino American texts (the preferred term is "Pilipino American"), their relationship to this provisional term seems to be ambivalent and indeterminate, shored up only by its roots in 1960s ethnic identity politics.[4] Hence, I choose the formulation "Filipinos in the United States" for this discussion while also tactically deploying the conditional but meaningful category "Filipino American."

The task of my essay is to characterize the available writings by Filipinos in the United States and Filipino Americans in light of community-formation and Philippine-American (neo)colonial relations. I seek to describe a literary tradition of Filipino exilic writing and an exilic sensibility that informs both the identity politics and the cultural production of this "community-in-the-making" (San Juan, "Exile" 36).

As does any preliminary account, this essay has several limitations. Because of the urgency of the task and space considerations, the survey of some of the available writings is only suggestive, if incomplete, and the arguments or propositions (along with the bases) for constituting them as a tradition are abbreviated. That the writings and the history of the group codify their own theoretical claims is a question to which I pay the most attention, for "each literary tradition, at least implicitly, contains within it an argument for how it can be read" (Gates xix-xx). I concentrate on the older writers whose works have reached a certain consolidation, and then suggest some beginning orientations with which to steer future readings of the work of the younger writers who are in several stages of emergence.

Motifs of departure, nostalgia, incompletion, rootlessness, leave-taking, and dispossession recur with force in most writing produced by Filipinos in the United States and Filipino Americans, with the Philippines as always either the original or terminal reference point. Rather than the United States as the locus of claims or "the promised land" that Werner Sollors argues is the typological trope of "ethnic"

American writing (40-50), the Filipino case represents a reverse telos, an opposite movement. It is on this basis that I argue for a literature of exile and emergence rather than a literature of immigration and settlement whereby life in the U.S. serves as the space for displacement, suspension, and perspective. "Exile" becomes a necessary, if inescapable, state for Filipinos in the United States—at once susceptible to the vagaries of the (neo)colonial U.S.-Philippine relationship and redeemable only by its radical restructuring.

The intergenerational experience will certainly dim this literary/historical connection to the Philippines for many Filipino Americans. But the signifiers "Filipino" and "Philippines" evoke colonialist meanings and cultural redactions which possess inordinate power to shape the fates of the writers and of Filipino peoples everywhere. These considerations overdetermine their dominant sense of non-belonging in the United States, the Philippines, and other places. The word "overdetermine" adequately describes the complex of historical inscriptions, developments, processes, interventions, and accidents in which their present predicament is embedded.

For Filipinos in the United States and their history of community-formation, it is not enough to examine immigration policies (symptomatic of a U.S.-centric approach to which most sociologists/historians are prone) that by themselves fail to account for the diversity of immigration patterns. "The historical, economic, and political relationships between the United States and the country of origin, as well as the social and economic conditions in the source country, have to be examined to explain the major differences in immigration streams" (Cariño and Fawcett 305). Robert Blauner's point that the status of any Asian American group should roughly equal the status of its country of origin in relation to the United States bears remembering (Takaki, *Race and Ethnicity* 159). Conceptually useful for the Philippine case, both of these views also expand American immigration, ethnic, and cultural studies beyond their parochial purviews of American nation-building, acculturation, and settlement.[5]

Invisibility and (Non-)identity in History

Among the various Asian countries of origin, the Philippines holds the sole distinction of being drawn into a truly colonial and neo-colonial relation with the United States, and for this reason it has been absorbed almost totally into the vacuum of American innocence. It was the founding moment of colonialism, "a primal loss suffered through the Filipino-American War (1899-1902) and the resistance ordeal of the First Philippine Republic up to 1911, that opened the way for the large-scale transport of cheap Filipino labor to Hawaii and California [and inaugurated] the long, tortuous exodus from the periphery to the metropolis" (San Juan, "Boundaries" 117). Hence, while rooted in the earlier period of Spanish rule, the spectre of "invisibility" for Filipinos is specific to the immediate and long-term consequences of American colonialism.

The invisibility of the Philippines became a necessary historiographical phenomenon because the annexation of the Philippines proved to be constitutionally and culturally problematic for American political and civil society around the turn of the century and thereafter. (A consequent case in point was the anomalous status of migrant workers and students for much of the formal colonial period when they were considered American "nationals" but without the basic rights of "citizens.") To understand the absence of the Philippines in American history, one faces the immense task of charting the intense ideological contestation that developed in the United States around the Philippine question at the point of colonial conquest, and the active rewriting of American historical records from then on that articulated and rearticulated the verities of "American exceptionalism."[6] As Amy Kaplan suggestively notes, "the invisibility of the Philippines in American history has everything to do with the invisibility of American imperialism to itself."[7]

Discursively, the unbroken continuity of this historic amnesia concerning the Philippines has had real invidious effects. Note the repetitious and unreflective use of the modifier "forgotten" to describe, even renew, this curse of invisibility which may be said to have been bestowed on the Philippines as soon as the bloody war of conquest and resistance began to require stringent official/military censorship in the United States around 1900. No one has bothered to ask some of the more unsettling questions: Who is doing the forgetting? What is being forgotten? How much has been forgotten? Why the need to continue forgetting?

Contemporary examples abound. An historiographical essay by the American historian Peter Stanley bears the title, "The Forgotten Philippines, 1790-1946" and sticks out in a retrospective survey of American-East Asian studies, a field which has always revolved around China and Japan (May and Thomson 291-316). Quoted in Russell Roth's journalistic account of the long and costly Filipino-American War, one writer admits that "our movement into the Philippines is one of the least understood phases of our history, one of those obscure episodes swept under the rug, and forgotten" (1981). In a truthful exemplification of the workings of hegemony, a chapter of Takaki's *Strangers From a Different Shore* is devoted to "The Forgotten Filipinos" (314-54) and one Filipino American documentary work itself, *Filipinos: Forgotten Asian Americans*, finds the term as unproblematic and adequate (Cordova 1983).

Genealogies of Exile and the Imagined Community

So it is that "in the Philippine experience, History has provided its own despotism" (Gonzalez, *Kalutang* 32). It is in the various forms and manifestations of this despotism that one can locate the productive conditions of possibility for Filipino writing and the making of Filipino identities. For something as specific as Filipino writing in the United States, the banishment of the Philippines and Filipinos from history, the global dispersal of Filipinos, the migrant realities of Pinoy workers and urban expatriates, and "the alienation of the English-speaking intellectuals from workers and peasants speaking the vernacular" (San Juan, *Ruptures* 25) must constitute the set of tangled contexts. They amount to a common orientation of the experiences, writings, and identity politics toward a "national mythos," following the creation of a "Filipino diaspora . . . the scattering of a people, not yet a fully matured nation, to the ends of the earth, across the planet" by the colonial moment (Brennan, "Cosmopolitans" 4; San Juan, "Homeland" 40).

Through a coordination of the expressive tendencies and impulses of Filipino and Filipino-American writers in the U.S., a "literature of exile and emergence" can be constructed from the normally separated realms of the old and new countries. I see the obsessive search for identity that marks Philippine literature in the colonial language (and the vernacular, which is not possible to cover here), and the identity politics articulated by first- and second-generation Filipino American writers (after the social and ethnic movements of the 1960s and 70s) as specific streams with certain points of confluence.

In recognizing the intimate connection between Filipino nation-building and the problematics of Filipino-American community-formation, and hence, the radical contingency of both processes, the seeming scarcity of "published literature" (sometimes attributed to the smallness of the Filipino-American second-generation) ceases to be a problem. That "we still don't have anyone resembling Maxine Hong Kingston for the Filipino immigrant community here"[8] begins to make sense and points us to the many writers who write about the situation in the Philippines and the Filipino American writers who may be U.S.-grounded, yet articulate this same ancestral focus. The orientation toward the Philippines prevents prevailing notions of Asian American literature from reducing Filipino writing in the United States to just another variant of the immigrant epic, even if this in itself must be seen as an ever-present and partial possibility as time passes and Philippine-American relations change.

In what follows, I examine some expressions of exile and gestures towards return—either explicit or latent—that typify the available writings. How do they characteristically respond to, or even embody, the experience of exile and indeterminacy and the question of redemptive return? Put another way, what are the intersections between historical experience and literary history, between subjection and subject-positions? I organize my review around several interrelated issues: exilic experience and perspective, exilic identity and language, and exilic sensibility and attitude toward history and place, all of which account for the forms of indeterminacy and visionary resolutions in the writings.

The writers may be clustered into three "cohorts" that need not necessarily coincide with the migration and immigration patterns or cycles documented by historians and sociologists (see, for example, Cariño and Fawcett 305-25; Pido 1986). There is the pioneering generation consisting of Bienvenido Santos, N.V.M. Gonzalez, Jose Garcia Villa, and Carlos Bulosan for the period 1930s to 1950s; a settled generation that matures and emerges by the 1960s who, after Penaranda, Tagatac, and Syquia, may be called the "Flips"[9]; and the politically expatriated generation of Epifanio San Juan, Linda Ty-Casper, Ninotchka Rosca, and Michelle Skinner from the 1970s to the present. These writers whom I have specifically mentioned must be taken as demarcating, rather than definitive, figures for each group.

This periodization has obvious limits. Bulosan died in 1956 and Villa ceased to write nearly three decades ago, while Santos and Gonzalez continue to be prolific and have exhibited significant shifts in their perspectives and writings after extended residence in the United States as professors. Bulosan, with the intervention of U.S. cultural workers, has earned some critical attention and student readership in ethnic studies courses, yet to be matched in the cases of Santos and Gonzalez whose exilic writing did not fit with the immigrant ethos. Villa has languished in self-selected obscurity even as Sollors recently and curiously recuperated him as an "ethnic modernist" (253-54).[10] My concern here is much more in comparison than in contemporaneity since their works are uneven in quality, their developments divergent in pattern, and their influence diffuse in reception. By "comparison" I mean their styles of coping with the experiential reality of exile—given their initial and subsequent ties with, or alienation from, each other— and their relevant self-definition and development of certain forms of writing on this basis.

I also make the "Flips" assume a kind of corporate existence although this is suggested itself by their self-designation as "Bay Area Pilipino American Writers" and their networks that are rooted in the ethnic movements of the late 1960s and 1970s. Of these writers (mostly poets), I find a few who exhibit tendencies to outgrow the agonized temporizings associated with that historic juncture, namely Jeff Tagami, Virginia Cerrenio, and Jaime Jacinto. What concerns me here is their search for kinship with their predecessors in the pioneering generation and their symbolic appropriations of Philippine history and identities from the perspective of a second, or consciously American, generation (hence, "Pilipino American").

Not all those who may belong to the "politically expatriated" were literally so, by the yardstick of martial law politics and the sensibility of nationalism that grew out of the social and political turmoil of the late 1960s and the subsequent period of authoritarian rule in the homeland. It is the peculiar elaboration of the theme of exile from a more troubling historical moment and its consequent suspension of Filipinos within a more ideologically and politically bounded sphere that distinguish the actions and predicament of this group. San Juan shifted to Philippine and Third World literary and historical studies from traditional literary scholarship and creative writing in the conjuncture between his initial residence in the United States as an academic, and the politicizing movements in the United States and the Philippines in the early 1970s. Skinner came to the United States with the sensibility of her martial law generation back home but did not exactly flee from political persecution as Rosca did. And yet again, their relationships of affinity and alienation as a group, and with the other two, may be divined in what they have written and how they have defined themselves.

My groupings are not chronological but synchronic, concerned with what Benedict Anderson has called "the deep horizontal comradeship" that enables widely dispersed populations to imagine peoplehood and community, to overcome historically disabling differences, and to occupy new spaces of historical, literary, and cultural possibility (15-16). Writers can find a home in the relevant pattern or cohort of affinity specific to their emergence in any of these three historical moments of colonial generation, ethnic identity politics, and political expatriation. The groupings need not be rigid since certain movements between them are possible, within defensible bounds, and depending to some extent on the stronger sentiment of the writer or reader.

Exile and Return: Literary and Experiential Parallels

In looking at the plurality of Filipino experiences, positions, and writings in the United States as a generalized condition of exile, I refer to the ensemble of its many relations, degrees, and forms, and not its easy reduction to a single thematic. One cannot succumb to the homogenizing assertion that "Immigration is the opposite of expatriation" (Mukherjee 28) or the tendency to construe the west as only a base for "cosmopolitan exiles" and not a place "where unknown men and women have spent years of miserable loneliness" (Said 359). The need is to "map territories of experience beyond those mapped by the literature of exile itself" (Said 358) and, if I might add, the areas of exile and writing overlap.

Sam Solberg notes that "if there is one indisputable fact about Filipino-American writing nurtured on American shores that sets it apart from other Asian American writings, it is that it is inextricably mixed with indigenous Filipino writing in English" (50). He adds that Carlos Bulosan, Jose Garcia Villa, Bienvenido Santos, and N.V.M. Gonzalez did not find the distinction between writing in the Philippines and the United States meaningful. Yet, also, their common experiences of migration to the United States and the vicissitudes of their careers in this setting consigned them to the same state of indeterminacy and limbo of invisibility as their less noted kinfolk.

Bharati Mukherjee posits that "exiles come wrapped in a cloak of mystery and world-weariness [and in] refusing to play the game of immigration, they certify to the world, and especially to their hosts, the purity of their pain and their moral superiority to the world around them" (28). Aside from making exile sound like a choice, this view fails to consider that there is nothing to romanticize about this condition even if it might sometimes generate romantic visions of one's "origins." "Exile is a grim fate and its recourses equally grim" (Seidel x). Although exile gives birth to varieties of nationalist sentiment, even imagined communities and unlikely kinships among peoples with enduring differences, "these are no more than efforts to overcome the crippling sorrow of estrangement . . . the loss of something left behind forever" (Said 357).

Just as it has been for similarly-situated peoples, the exilic experience for Filipinos and Filipino Americans has engendered such "enormously constructive pressures" (Gurr 9) as self-recovery and the critical distance from a putative homeland whose outlines are sharpened from the perspective of their new or "other" home in the metropolis. More, for Filipinos as "colonial exiles," the "search for identity and the construction of a vision of home amount to the same thing" (Gurr 11). In turn, this "identity" (now in the sense of specular experiences and visions), condenses itself in the institution of creative genealogies, mythic reinterpretations of colonial history, and reevaluations of the linguistic and cultural losses caused by colonialism. These may be seen as notations of redemptive return to a "home" in the imagination, with specific inflections for Filipinos and Filipino Americans.

When Bienvenido Santos declares that "in a special sense I, too, am an oldtimer" ("Pilipino Old Timers" 89) and a Flip poet like Jeff Tagami (1987) memorializes these Pinoys in his work, there is already this particular reciprocity of self-representations among unlikely "allies." Distances are being bridged here among generational locations, social classes, and particular experiences, from the pioneering experiences and enduring ties to native territory of those migrant workers in the Pacific Coast states as the privileged point of reference. Documentary works have described the exilic conditions of these Pinoys in paradigmatic terms because of the complexity of their displacements: "between themselves and their homeland, between themselves and their children who have known only America, and between themselves and recent arrivals whose Philippines is, in some ways, drastically different from their own" (Santos, *Apples* xiv).

Santos's claim of affinity with the "survivors of those who immigrated in the 1920s or even earlier, through the 1940s" ("Pilipino Old Timers" 89) may seem ill-considered because of the large wedge in class, migratory pattern, and education between this former "pensionado" and resident writer of a Kansas university and the faceless, nameless "Manongs." Carlos Bulosan—valorized as the supreme chronicler of the Pinoy story and claimed as an immigrant writer even while moved to state once that "I think I am forever an exile" (*Falling Light* 198)—particularly lamented this great divide. Regarding the pensionados of his time (and the ruling/middling classes they helped form in the Philippines) with suspicion and contempt, Bulosan foregrounded his shared peasant background with the oldtimers in his identity as a writer. Among many expressions of affiliation with them are his controversial letter to a friend concerning his critique of Filipino writers in English and their "contrary feelings" for him (*Falling Light* 228) and his narrator Allos's discovery of the estranging and demarcating stance of the middle class in regard to the Philippine peasantry in *America is in the Heart* (1946/1973), in the humiliating encounter between the narrator's mother and a middle-class girl (37-38).

This great wedge partly derived from the institution of education as a form of social hierarchy in the Philippines during the colonial period (the pensionados or colonial government scholars were trained in the United States for colonial/cultural administration) and threatened Bulosan's own close kinship with the migrant workers as his writing career took off in the 1930s and 1940s. He obviated this successfully with a symbolic return to their ranks and their lives in his writing and by articulating a Pinoy critique of upper/middle class conceit: "There is no need for Filipino writers to feel that . . . they are educated because they went to colleges, nor should they think that I am ignorant because I lack formal education" (*Falling Light* 228). If Bulosan's "return" to the oldtimers is warranted by an original class affinity, this makes Santos's gesture from the other side toward this group striking.

The sense of indeterminacy conveyed by Santos in his many stories, essays, and in interviews, resonates with the Pinoy's suspension in eternal time and alien place, "deracinated and tortured by the long wait to go home" (Gurr 18). Like Bulosan, he has codified this linkage in his work, as in the symbolic kinship between the Michigan farmworker Celestino Fabia and "the first class Filipino" in the moving story, "A Scent of Apples" (*Apples* 21-29). Especially revealing is Santos's juxtaposition in an essay of his fictional transfiguration of the oldtimers' characters and lives and their documentation in oral and social history to illustrate his point—when asked "to explain the difference between the old timer as character in fiction and in real life"—"that there is nothing to explain because there is no difference" ("Pilipino Old Timers" 91).

These heroes with all their little triumphs and tragic losses as exiles but "survivors" populate Santos's tightly crafted stories, endowing his identity as a writer and his writing with a pointed specificity. One detects the origin of Santos's notion of the struggling exilic writer as a "straggler"—doomed into irrelevance and hermitage for writing in English—in the condition of the migrant worker as a "survivor [who] lives through years of hiding [and waits] until a miracle of change happens in the homeland and in this, our other home" (Personal Saga" 399, 404, 405). That the construction of kinship and identity among Filipinos is fraught with difficulty and paradox is also in the foreground of much of the writing, but as especially emblematized in Santos's "The Day the Dancers Came." While Santos finds common cause with his Pinoy subjects, he also confronts the tensions of this affiliation on the level of symbolism.

Like "Scent of Apples," this story concerns the re-encounter of the Pinoy with the other-self, a representative of one's time-bound vision of home, in visitors from the islands. "Identity," as in similitude, in mutual recognition as Filipinos, is sought by the oldtimer Fil in the young members of a dance troupe from the Philippines who stop by Chicago for a visiting performance. But just as the middle-class girl reduces Allos's mother to humiliation in Bulosan's *America is in the Heart*, the visiting dancers reduce Fil to an "ugly Filipino" (Santos, *Apples* 116), subtly spurning his attempts to communicate with them and his offer to entertain them in his humble abode (an eventuality foreseen by his fellow oldtimer and roommate Tony, who is dying of cancer). There is none of the natural affinity that develops between Fabia and the visiting lecturer in "Scent of Apples," only the edge of class hierarchy and generational or experiential difference. While making his overtures to the dancers in the Chicago hotel lobby where they milled after the performance, "All the things he had been trying to hide now showed: the age in his face, his horny hands . . . Fil wanted to leave, but he seemed caught up in the tangle of moving bodies that merged and broke in a fluid strangle hold. Everybody was talking, mostly in English" (120).

The frequent impossibility of "identity" (as similitude) between Filipinos expatriated by colonialism, placed in different social/historical rungs, and separated by trans-oceanic timelines, is figured by this story in specular instances. Focused in the predicament of Fil, these compounded mirrorings of the other-self reflect the many dimensions of Filipino exilic identity and perspective. A memory that Fil associates with one of his many jobs—as "a menial in a hospital [who] he took charge . . . of bottles on a shelf, each shelf, each bottle containing a stage of the human embryo in preservatives, from the lizard-like fetus of a few days, through the newly-born infant, with its position unchanged, cold, and cowering and afraid"—is of "nightmares through the years of himself inside a bottle" (114). This reflection of himself in these aborted, disowned, and arrested lives, mediated by the figure of the "bottle" that both exhibits and encloses them, is a powerful statement on the utter disconnection of the old timer from the flow of time and from a Philippines whose birthing as a nation itself has been aborted by American colonialism. (Perhaps it is significant that his name is "Fil," almost "Filipino," but attenuated into an American nickname.)

The relationship between Fil and Tony also takes this form of allegorical doubling. When Fil castigates Tony in one of their playful spats: "You don't care for nothing but your pain, your imaginary pain," Tony retorts: "You're the imagining fellow. I got the real thing." Tony's skin not only "whitens" from the terminal ailment that is inexplicably but slowly consuming him but he also feels "a pain in his insides, like dull scissors scraping his intestines" (115). Yet, if Tony's pain is indeed excruciatingly physical, it only seems to be the correlative for Fil's pain which, in a sense, is more real. For after being denied his last few memories of home by the dancers' disavowal, the pain that guts him is similar but more keen: "Was it his looks that kept them away? The thought was a sharpness inside him" (121); and then, again, in recounting their rebuff to Tony, "The memory, distinctly recalled, was a rock on his breast. He grasped for breath" (124).

The identity between Fil and Tony (they are both oldtimers wrapped in pain and warped in time) stands for the singular problem of constructing Filipino/American identity in light of colonialism. The doubling of colonizer and colonized, its conflictedness, is signified in Fil's specular but contrastive relationship with Tony, even as this is also kinship forged by their history of shared banishment. Tony stands for one's translation into a colonial: "All over Tony's body, a gradual peeling was taking place . . . . His face looked as if it was healing from severe burns . . . . 'I'm becoming a white man,' Tony had said once . . . ." (114). Note also that Tony is figured as looking young. "Gosh, I wish I had your looks, even with those white spots," Fil says to him (116)—Fil, who feels and looks old and ugly in the company of the *young* dancers. Where Tony "was the better speaker of the two in English," Fil displayed "greater mastery" in the dialect (117), although Fil's prepared speeches for inviting the dancers "stumbled and broke on his lips into a jumble of incoherence" in their presence (120). If Tony is his other-self, a desired ideal of being, then even turning to him for identity is unsuccessful as the reader knows that Tony will die for Fil's own rebirth.

As the dancers board their bus for the next destination and Fil imagines or sees them waving their hands and smiling towards him, Fil raises his hand to wave back. But wary of misrecognition one more time, he turns to check behind him but finds "no one there except his own reflection in the glass door, a double exposure of himself and a giant plant with its thorny branches around him like arms in a loving embrace" (122). Here, the reader is being alerted to the strength of an identity that is reflected in and by the constituted self, the spectral but appropriate figure being a "a giant plant with its thorny branches."

In vowing to commit the performance and memory of the dancers to a tape recording in what he calls "my magic sound mirror" (he loses the "record" by accidentally pushing the eraser near the end, symbolizing the fragility of his "memories" of home), Fil wonders if the magic sound mirror could also keep "a record of silence because it was to him the richest sound . . ." (117). This implicit recognition of himself as the supreme record, the actual referent of his identity, is brought to the fore at the conclusion of the story when he exclaims: "Tony! Tony! . . . I've lost them all." The last glimpse the reader has is of Fil "biting his lips . . . turn[ing] towards the window, startled by the first light of dawn. He hadn't realized till then that the long night was over" (128). Looking through the bottle at "frozen time" early in the story, Fil looks through a window at "time unfolding" by the end. Fil is somehow restored to history, to the sufficiency of his silence and resilience.

The interposition of "English" in the story (Tony speaks better English, he is turning into a "white" man; the dancers talk mostly in English, they are all beautiful) as the radical mode of difference for and among "Fils" (Filipinos) implies the organizing relation between exilic identity and language. Recall the symptomatic link or parallelism in Solberg's argument between the exile experienced by Filipino writers of English in the Philippines and that expressed by the "writing nurtured on American shores"—or between literary and experiential exile, generally. But this historically interesting nexus, this "inextricable link," is usually disarticulated in universalizing formulations like "the human condition" or the "alienation of the soul" (Gonzalez, *Kalutang* 64-65). Language has a historical specificity in relation to the development of "indigenous writing, writing nurtured on American shores," and the migratory movements of writers and laborers to/in the United States that these careless oversimplifications flatten out. The result has been to compound these literatures and experiences imperceptibly or to explain them away in terms of the inescapable alienations that afflict the dislocated, as if there were nothing more to say about their historic concurrence or recurrence.

As Santos's work suggests, writing in English, the colonizer's language, and migrating to the United States, the colonizing country, are analogous and fundamentally imbricated processes, or are parallel while related forms of cultural translation and historical exile. Carlos Bulosan's consummate piece, "The Story of a Letter" starkly embodies such relationships in aesthetic form and supplies another paradigm for beholding these various writings and experiences together. In this allegory of the epic of migration and expatriation, the narrator is a peasant son who finds himself heading for the United States as part of the migratory waves of workers in the late colonial period, but also as a consequence of a letter to his father written in English—a language alien in history and social class to his father and his people—by the narrator's brother Berto who had migrated earlier. Simply, the letter remains unread until the narrator himself has gone through the linguistic, cultural, and historical translation necessary for him to decode the letter for his father and himself. The letter reads: "Dear father . . . America is a great country. Tall buildings. Wide good land. The people walking. But I feel sad. I am writing to you this hour of my sentimental. Your son.—Berto" (*Bulosan Reader* 44). It is an attempt by an exiled son to bridge the distance between him and his origins in truncated language that aptly mirrors Berto's and his family's truncated lives.

The narrator's voyage is propelled by various developments (climaxed by the loss of the family's small landholding), and prefigured by the father's plea to the narrator "to learn English so that [he] would be able to read [the letter] to him" (41). After landing in the United States, and after he is whirled into the vortex of displacement, labor exploitation, and fragmentation of Pinoy life, he accrues the experience needed to make sense of the letter and develops some mastery of the language that it speaks. In this process of personal translation (experientially and symbolically), he sustains a series of losses, for one always risks losing the original matter substantially in the historic passage from one experiential/cultural realm to another. The father dies before the narrator reaches the point of linguistic and historical competence and therefore before he can read his son's translation; the narrator himself experiences the deep-seated removal from origin and the past that acquiring such a competence entails; and he is only able to glimpse (not to reunite with) Berto in the United States.

With the letter returned to him after a series of disconnected deliveries, the narrator muses: "It was now ten years since my brother had written the letter to Father. It was eighteen years since he had run away from home . . . . I bent down and read the letter—the letter that had driven me away from the village and had sent me half way around the world . . . . I held the letter in my hand and, suddenly, I started to laugh—choking with tears at the mystery and wonder of it all" (44). Being able to decode the simple message of the letter (couched in his brother's fractured English) endows him with an expansive consciousness, agency, renewed memory, and the sign of redemptive return to his moorings.

The story of the letter then can be read allegorically, whereby one's search for self or identity is enabled and simultaneously codified in the trans-Pacific voyage to the United States, condensed here primarily in the demarcating and analogic role ascribed to "English." But particular stress must be placed on the symbolic weight of language in the story and in cultural history itself. By viewing English as a material and symbolic mode of alienation and transformation, one can account for the "inextricable link" as well as the great wedge among various classes, generations, and experiences of Filipino peoples. In surveying the thematic landscape of contemporary writing, David Quemada concludes that the recurrent themes of rootlessness indicate "a spiritual dislocation which is nurtured by the act of writing in a foreign language" (428). "Spiritual" here suggests that one's translation and transformation *through* the colonial language is fundamental and all-encompassing.

Albert Memmi refers to this phenomenon as "colonial bilingualism," describing it also as a "linguistic drama" because it is the struggle between the colonizer's and colonized's cultures in and through the linguistic sphere (108). The "possession of two languages" means immersion in "two psychical and cultural realms" which, because "symbolized and conveyed in the two tongues [of the colonizer and colonized]" generates an irremediably conflicted and complicated condition for the colonial subject. Memmi qualifies that most of the colonized are spared this condition since their native tongue is not given the same level of circulation and status in the colony itself (108). This can be extended to mean that not every Filipino can be allowed through the gates of immigration or his/her impossible dream of statehood for the Philippines. Yet, English becomes a mechanism of social hierarchy and thinking that ensnares the colonial/neocolonial natives or immigrants/citizens into the same circuit of exilic suspension while also segmenting them from each other in class or experiential terms.

In his many creative and scholarly works, N.V.M. Gonzalez has dwelt extensively on the linguistic alienation of Filipino English writers from their people and what he calls its "national and historical dimension" ("Drumming" 423). He specifies the period "when English was adopted as a national language" in the Philippines as the inaugural moment for the complicated American reconstruction of the Filipino, recalling Frantz Fanon's metaphor of consequent "changes in the flesh, even in the composition of the body fluids" of the colonized (*Kalutang* 32, 34). Quoting the writer Wilfrido Nolledo, Gonzalez avers that with the "receiving" (the term he uses to reckon with the American imposition) of English, the Filipino writer was converted into a "domestic exile," an expatriate who has not left his homeland

("Drumming" 418-19).[11] Yet this also locates the writer at a particular remove from his subject since, as Raymond Williams argues, "To be a writer in English is already to be socially specified" (193).

For Gonzalez, writing in English about the *kaingineros,* the peasant folk of Mindoro and the other islands of his imagination "separated each actuality from me at every moment of composition . . . . Rendered in an alien tongue, that life attained the distinction of a translation even before it had been made into a representation of reality through form . . . . The English language thus had the effect of continually presenting that life as non-actual, even as it had affirmed the insecurity of its making" (*Kalutang* 40-41). Like Santos, however, Gonzalez shortcircuits these multiple determinations of linguistic/cultural exile and seeks identity with and in the "poor folk going from clearing to clearing, island to island, working in the saltwater sweat of their brows for whatever the earth will yield" (Guzman 111). Consequently, his writing has been critiqued for creating a literary brand of nativism and ethnography about a "bygone rural Philippines . . . no longer mapped by American anthropologists . . . but by insurgents" (San Juan, *Ruptures* 31). But like Santos, Gonzalez has also reflected upon the contradictions of his identity claims and codified several important categories of the exilic sensibility.

From *Seven Hills Away* (1947) to his most recent writings, Gonzalez has lyrically valorized the people of the "backwoods, barrio, and town," graphing their lifeways and folk culture in styles, rhythms, and forms of storytelling that express a pointed fidelity to this point of origin. Like Santos in his oldtimers, Gonzalez mirrors his exilic condition in the patterns of migration, dispersal, and selfhood of these people who populate the past that he remembers: "Although they might become city folk, I seem to see them at their best against the background to which they eventually return" (*Kalutang* 66). In a parallel vein, Gonzalez returns to this life and place by the power of a language that renders his gesture always already imaginative. A most early piece, "Far Horizons," harbors the beginnings of Gonzalez's model and vision of exile. As in his other stories that feature the sea, voyaging/sailing, and island-hopping lifestyle of his past as metaphors for exilic distances, departures, and arrivals, this piece involves characters who find themselves ineluctably separated from their habitat by seafaring as a way of life.

Juancho, the surviving crewmember of a sailboat sunk off Marinduque island recalls that among the casualties is Gorio, a sailor from a remote barrio in Mindoro. He surmises that the news of his death will have not reached his village at all and this worries him until he meets a fellow-sailor, Bastian, who turns out to be Gorio's brother. Bastian finds himself making an unintended homecoming after so long, but as a bearer of sorrowful news for his mother and kinfolk. When the sailboat (suggestively called "Pag-asa" or hope) bound for Southern Mindoro comes to lie at anchor off the coast leading to his village, Bastian convinces Ka Martin, the *piloto*, to let him ashore for one night to make this important visit.

What sets off this story is a classic scene in exilic writing: the actual and transient return and the first glimpse of home after one's absence for many years. In seeing the first familiar landmarks of home, "A strange feeling swept over him. There came some kind of itching in the soles of his feet and his heart began to throb wildly as though trying to get out of his mouth . . . Then it occurred to him that it was some seven or eight years since he had left home" (*Mindoro* 24).[12] Yet mindful of the tragic news that he brings with him and the grief it may cause his mother, Bastian reflects: "Perhaps it would be better to tell her nothing at all. Should she learn of his brother's death, it might prove difficult for him to go to sea again. And how he loved the sea although it might claim him too" (24). Bastian loses his nerve and, at the call of Ka Martin's horn, stealthily heads out to sea. He entrusts the news to the boatman who ferries the villagers across the river and trusts him to spread it after he, Bastian, is gone. The mother, Aling Betud, receives the news of the death of one son and the sudden disappearance of another with a curious response. It occurs to her that "it must have been Bastian himself who had died and what had come was his ghost" (26).

In this act of substitution, Aling Betud nurses her "hope" for her other son's apparition and return, and she irritatedly responds to the villagers' disbelief: "We shall know all, we shall know all. For my other son Gorio will come—and we shall ask him, and he will tell us" (26). In this instance of "identity" (as similitude), the dream of return as formed from the site of departure reflects back the idea of exile's loss and gain—signified here in the dialectic between sorrow and hope, when the mother represents to herself the incalculable transience yet worth of her sons' "imagined" and imaginable returns.

Indeed, "the sea might claim him too" and it is the idea of homecoming as ever-deferred for the pleasure and curse of voyaging (miming the ever-deferred nature of representation of loss and gain in language) that Gonzalez suggests here. Still, for Gonzalez, it is placed as the locus of rootedness, the islands from which sailboats and sailors flee and to which they return, and the clearings between which peasant folk shuttle, that supply the coordinates and the orientations for these movements.

In many stories including "Children of the Ash-Covered Loam," "Seven Hills Away," and "Hunger in Barok" (*Mindoro* 49-61, 32-42, 27-31), Gonzalez also foregrounds the tensions of Philippine social relationships, the difficulties of mutuality and kinship. He maps this historical geography by paraphrasing John Kenneth Galbraith's description of India as not a country but a continent: "understanding the Philippines begins in the realization that it is one nation made up of three countries . . . . Manila is the capital of the first country of the City. The second country—the Barrio—has a capital known by many names: Aplaya, Bondok, Wawa, whatever . . . . The third country—the Mountain—by its very nature needs no capital or center, although it shares with the Barrio a calculated distance from the city." (*Kalutang* 29). Whether concerned with the calibrated frictions between the citified and the folk or the benign feudal paternalism of landlords over their tenants and its illusion of reciprocity, Gonzalez recognizes the problems of constructing a unitary notion of national identity.

The movements are defined by the location of gain and loss in the oppositional relationship between places of power and disenfranchisement: "We of the Barrio—for it is to that country that I belong . . . trudged in the direction of the country of the City" (*Kalutang* 32). By figuring his expatriation as always already determined by the uneven development of the colonized homeland, Gonzalez restores a dimension of internal conflict that gets lost in the accustomed antimony between colony and metropole. His memorialization of "the country of the Barrio" (a particular revision of the Philippines) constitutes what Said calls a "cartographic impulse" since "for the native, the history of his or her colonial servitude is inaugurated by the loss to an outsider of the local place, whose concrete geographical identity must thereafter be searched for and somehow restored" (Eagleton et al. 77). Yet the dispossession creates a rhetoric of placelessness, nostalgia, and wandering, and in Gonzalez's case, one drawn from the "local place," the *kaingin*: "It is enough that solid ground, whether illusory or real, lies under our feet, and that not too far away is the next clearing, and the next, and the next . . . " (*Kalutang* 74).

These pioneering writers have constructed literary analogues of the national mythos that are not without their dangers. The mythic tropes of natives and native territory in Gonzalez's work, like the sense of suspension endemic to the oldtimers of Santos, or Bulosan's uneven idealization of peasant folk, stop short of becoming "demagogic assertions about a native past, history, or actuality that seems to stand free of the colonizer and wordly time itself" (Eagleton et al. 82). What these gestures map is a "new territoriality" that recovers or repossesses the colonized land imaginatively, and from which, in turn, the countercolonial "search for authenticity, for a more congenial national origin than provided by colonial history, for a new pantheon of heroes, myths, and religions" should emerge (Eagleton et al. 79).

It is to the younger and more recent writers that one must turn for an extension of these suggestive tendencies in the exilic identities and writings of the pioneering writers. Recent writers (nearly all women) are turning their own exilic condition into a powerful stance, an engagement with the reality of invisibility that is doubled by their absence or their appropriation as a metaphorical presence in the historical antecedents and models of the pioneers. (Here I have in mind Bulosan's dualized representations of women, or even specifically, the gendering of the homeland as female in Santos's "Scent of Apples," among countless instances.) The Flip poets are writing from an alienation that is double-sided as they address their own historical absence in the United States and remain implicated in the historic invisibility of the nation that permanently identifies them.

With a set of concerns and questions determined by their own historical conjunctures and different from the pioneers, recent writers view "History [as] the rubbish heap in which lie hidden the materials from which self-knowledge can come" (Gurr 10). This is a disposition that the Flips share with politically expatriated writers because their politics of emergence builds from a dialectic between past and present, not "a past sealed off from the vigorously altering effects of contemporary events" (Brennan, "Cosmopolitans" 17). For example, although the oldtimers continue to serve as figures of affinity for many Flip poets, there is a research into their social history for a stronger genealogical link. It is an attempt to "turn over the rubbish heap of history by studying the past and in that way fixing a sense of identity" (Gurr 10). This is an impulse codified in Virginia Cerenio's "you lovely people": "ay manong / your old brown hands / hold life, many lives / within each crack / a story" (Bruchac 11). History is inscribed in, is an imprint on, the appropriated Pinoy body: "and it is in his hands / cracked and raw / that never heal. / Shotgunned stomach. One-kidney Frankly. / One hot day he revealed / that stomach to me, slowly raising / his T-shirt, and proclaimed it the map of California" (Tagami 13).

The probing of history for Flip poets also takes the form of social analysis, but of the conditions in a country as alien to them as they are to it. Perhaps this critical distance is what allows Jaime Jacinto to dramatize, in measured tones of grief and tension, the enduring inequities of Philippine life as sanctioned by the Church and the semi-feudal order, and as symbolized by the burial of a peasant woman's little daughter: "As the blonde Spanish priest / anoints you, touching your / lips and feet with oil, / your mother wonders if ever there was enough to eat or / if only she had given in / to the landlords's whispers, / that extra fistful of rice / might have fattened the hollow / in your cheeks." (Ancheta et al. 48-49).

Nearly all the emergent writers are women although this amplitude of women's writing is a development observable for other emergent literatures in the United States and the postcolonial world. Compared to the two other groups, it is the Filipina writers who recognize that "the relationship to the inherited past and its cultural legacy has been rendered problematic by the violent interference of colonial and imperial history" (Harlow 19). As Filipino historical crises are intensified by the authoritarian rule of Ferdinand Marcos and its aftermath, history and its countermythic writing become their own forms and visions of return, identity-building, and self-recovery.

Linda Ty-Casper returned to early colonial Philippine history and showed the way for this group with *The Peninsulars* (1964). The novel has been critiqued for its "ill-advised" revisions of some historical documents but also commended for setting "certain precedents that are bound to affect subsequent efforts" (Lumbera 202). In fact, Ty-Casper went on to handle Philippine historical subjects more boldly, seeking to make material out of the moral atrophy and political intrigues that mark the period of authoritarian rule by Marcos (see, for example, *Wings of Stone* 1986; *Fortress in the Plaza* 1985). One can profit from examining the intertextuality between Ty-Casper's and Ninotchka Rosca's ventures, specifically as borne out by Rosca's historical novel *State of War* (1988). This novel alerts the reader to Rosca's indebtedness to Ty-Casper's pioneering efforts, establishing certain genealogical links between both writers on the narrative level.

In *The Three-Cornered Sun* (1979), Ty-Casper turns to the Philippine Revolution of 1896 against Spain, creating a somewhat indecisive picture of national identity through the members of the Viardo family whose individual traits are unevenly endowed with allegorical weight. As N.V.M. Gonzalez notes, the call is for "a depiction of private lives that would encompass Philippine experience within living memory," and as Rosca herself qualifies, "the problem is how to tell a story that was not anybody's story yet was everybody's story" (Gonzalez, "Filipino and the Novel" 962; Mestrovic 90). In *State of War*, Rosca re-visions the whole stretch of colonial history in the context of the period of Marcos's dictatorship through a melange of dreamy sequences, historical vignettes, and hyperrealized characters and events. She balances allegory with personal history in the triadic relationship of her main characters, Anna Villaverde, Adrian Banyaga, and Eliza Hansen, whose genealogies and symbolic stories intertwine in a series of historical wars and developments that are symbolized by a 24-hour period of festivity and political conspiracies. The interrelated carnivalesque of merrymaking and political conflict is emphasized by narrative pattern and design, as supremely exemplified by the three-part structure of the novel ("Acts," "Numbers," "Revelations").

An obvious footnote to the triangulated characteristic of Ty-Casper's *Awaiting Trespass* as "a small book of hours about those waiting for their lives to begin, . . . a book of numbers about those who stand up to be counted, . . . a book of revelations about what tyranny forces people to become; and what, by resisting, they can insist on being" (author's preface, n.p.), Rosca's organizing stratagem also directs the reader to incremental and interreferential layers internal to the work of either author. In Rosca's case, for example, Eliza and Anna (along with Colonel Amor, incarnated as the Loved One in *State of War*, symbol of the authoritarian and military reign of terror), first make their appearance as character sketches in the piece "Earthquake Weather" (see *Monsoon Collection* 129).

This movement continues outward as Michelle Skinner packs her extremely short stories in *Balikbayan: A Filipino Homecoming* (1988) with powerful allusions and subtexts concerning the life under dictatorial rule as it was subtended by American neo-colonial support for Marcos; or as Cecilia Manguerra-Brainard compresses into a story ("The Black Man in the Forest," *Woman with Horns* 21-25), the many historical ramifications of the Filipino-American war which had concerned Ty-Casper in *Ten Thousands Seeds* (1987).

Experientially, these writers create from the same sense of expatriation from the past and their history that stems quite immediately from the founding moment of American colonization and the cultural translocation through the master's language. But the distance is not crippling, as they invert its anthropological commonplaces from their perspective as colonized natives or immigrants/citizens who regard from the outside that is also the country of the colonizer the whole spectacle of their transhistorical movements and displacements. Return for them is redefining and rewriting "history" from the perspective of banishment: "Physical departure from the scene of one's personal history provides a break in time and separates the present from the past. History then becomes what preceded departure" (Gurr 10-11).

For these writers, the pioneers serve as stark examples and models. Either one is disabled and "waits for miracles to happen" as Santos seems to express when recalling how his writing teacher Philip Roth excised his desired ending image for a short story: that, significantly enough, of "floating in a shoreless sea" (Alegre and Fernandez 245); or one is enabled, moving on, as the narrator in Bulosan's story does, to tell the "story" (history) of the "letter" (one's transcription or codification of the self-in-history) through the language and experience of one's subjection.

*Many thanks to Epifanio San Juan Jr., Robert Lee, Roland Guyotte, Barbara Posadas, and Neil Lazarus for their comments and suggestions, and to Yuko Matsukawa for suggesting some important references.

NOTES

1. Asian American literature is remarkably under-theorized when compared to African American, Chicano, and Native American literatures. Yet one can intuit from existing anthologies/bibliographies and prevailing notions of Asian American literature a pronounced but unacknowledged focus on Chinese- and Japanese-American writings and their telos of immigration and settlement, to the unintended exclusion of other Asian American writings and their concomitant logics. The *Aiiieeee!* group (1974/1983), David Hsin-fu Wand (1974), Elaine Kim (1982), and many others reflexively include Filipinos or Filipino Americans as part of the Asian American triad of major communities, but because of their preoccupation with Chinese and Japanese American writers, they are hard-pressed to list "Filipino American" writers other than Carlos Bulosan, the "Flip" writers who figured prominently in the identity politics of the 1960s, or the younger California poets. A singular exception to this is Kai-yu Hsu & Palubinskas (1972). Cheung and Yogi (1988) recognize the problems with this implicit theoretical center of Asian American literature when they note that "the influence of overseas Asians—be they sojourners or immigrants with American-born offspring—cannot be ignored [and that there are] authors who may regard themselves as expatriates or as regional writers rather than as Asian Americans (v)."

2. There has been a similar but related "neglect" or "invisibility" of Filipinos and Filipino Americans in the sociology of American immigration, ethnicity, and communities (Posadas, "Filipino American History" 87-88).

3. The anthology featured a short excerpt from Carlos Bulosan's *America is in the Heart* (1946/1973) and two short pieces by Peñaranda and Tagatac. The writers themselves went on to construct a "literary background" from the history of Philippine literature in English, choosing Carlos Bulosan and Bienvenido Santos from "five authors [who] left the Philippines and wrote about Filipinos in America" even as this extremely limited pool consisted of "already mature men whose psychology and sensibilities were Filipino." Cf. 44-47 with Bienvenido Santos, "The Filipino novel in English" (Manuud 634-38).

4. Here, I certainly do not wish to subsume, even to reduce, the identity and community politics of immigrant and native-born Filipino Americans into a totalizing structure. The historians Barbara Posadas and Roland Guyotte warn against the dangers of this facile move (26). Rather, I am interested in how Filipino Americans and exiled Filipinos are caught in a web of mutual implication with each other

and with their groups of affinity in the country of origin when faced with the question of American colonialism within a U.S. context.

5. Recent efforts in various fields recognize the need to coalesce around such possibly comparative issues as American Imperialism and Orientalism. Mazumdar (1991) calls for a dialogue between Asian Americans studies and Asian studies on this score and many others, while Cheng and Bonacich (1984) has initiated a parallel dialogue of these fields with studies in political economy. Hunt has called the attention of diplomatic historians to the centrality of the immigration question and "the intellectual currents among the elite and popular views in the regions intimately involved in trans-Pacific contacts" to any fresh work in American-East Asian international relations (18, 29-30).

6. In historiographical terms, this doctrine was codified in many ways, but most relevant for us here, through the "aberration thesis" of Samuel Flagg Bemis in diplomatic history—the notion that American imperialism was merely a blot in an otherwise spotless and incomparable political tradition. This dominated the literature for many years and (although debunked by subsequent paradigms) continues to assume many lives in different works and cultural expressions. Some prior but exemplary incarnations include the notion of "Manifest Destiny" which naturalized the expansive thrust of American nation- and empire-building, and "Benevolent Assimilation" which distinguished American imperialism as "humanitarian" and "tutelary." For a critique of the historiography, see San Juan, *Crisis* (1986) esp. 3-5, and Miller (1982) 1-12, 253-67. For recent renewals of this sacrosanct view of American imperialism, see Welch (1979) Ch. 10; May, *Social Engineering* (1980) 170-83, and the Pulitzer Prize-winning book by Karnow, *In Our Image* (1989) 12-15, 227ff, 323ff.

7. Letter, October 10, 1989. Kaplan's work on American imperialist discourse announces a much-awaited cultural turn in the study of American imperialism; see, for example, "Romancing the Empire" (1990). Rydell (1984) preceded Kaplan with his pioneering work on American world fairs and their focus on the Philippines. Institutional developments that indicate the wholesale submergence of the Philippines in various American historiographies include its erratic and tokenistic positioning in East Asian and Southeast Asian studies and the absence of a strong Philippine studies tradition in the United States. See May's half-hearted critique of this benign (or active?) academic neglect of the Philippines in *Past Recovered* (1987) 175-89, but also Alice Mak, "Philippine Studies in Hawaii" (6 & 9), which notes that in instituting a formal Philippine studies program at the University of Hawaii in 1975, the university faculty observed that no other U.S. institution "had a program focusing on the Philippines." Mak adds: "After many decades of [so-called] close political, historical and social ties, it seemed odd that no American university had made an effort to encourage research on the Philippines."

8. Letter from Epifanio San Juan, Jr., April 24, 1990.

9. Peñaranda et al. uses this term to refer to Filipino Americans born and/or raised in the U.S. (49).

10. San Juan critiques Sollors's uninformed and ahistorical appropriations of Villa in "The Cult of Ethnicity." For an account of Villa's autocanonization and self-obsolescence see his "Reflections on U.S.-Philippine Literary Relations" 47-50.

11. Or as Memmi describes the situation unambiguously, "the entire bureaucracy, the entire court system, all industry hears and uses the colonizer's language; . . . highway markings, railroad station signs, street signs and receipts make the colonized feel like a stranger in his own country" (106-7).

12. Compare with Bulosan, "Homecoming," where the protagonist Mariano's first glimpse of his hometown and the family hut after twelve years in the United States evokes a quickness of step and powerful emotions (*Bulosan Reader* 64).

WORKS CITED

Ancheta, Shirley, et al., eds. *Without Names*. San Francisco: Kearny Street Workshop, 1985.

Anderson, Benedict. *Imagined Communities: Reflections on the Origins and Spread of Nationalism*. London: Verso, 1983.

Brennan, Timothy. "Cosmopolitans and Celebrities." *Race and Class* 31.1 (1989): 1-19.

Bruchac, Joseph, ed. *Breaking Silence: An Anthology of Contemporary Asian American Poets*. Greenfield Center, N.Y.: Greenfield Review Press, 1983.

Bulosan, Carlos. *If You Want to Know What We Are: A Carlos Bulosan Reader*. Minneapolis: West End, 1983.

_____. *America is in the Heart*. 1946. Seattle: University of Washington Press, 1973.

_____. *Sound of Falling Light: Letters in Exile*. ed. Dolores Feria. Quezon City, Phils.: University of Philippines Press, 1960.

Cariño, Benjamin and James Fawcett, eds. *Pacific Bridges: The New Immigration from Asia and the Pacific Islands.* New York: Center for Migration Studies, 1987.

Cheng, Lucie, and Edna Bonacich, eds. *Labor Immigration Under Capitalism: Asian Workers in the United States before World War II.* Berkeley: University of California Press, 1984.

Cheung, King-kok and Stan Yogi. *Asian American Literature: An Annotated Bibliography.* New York: MLA, 1988.

Cordova, Fred. *Filipinos: Forgotten Asian Americans.* Dubuque, Iowa: Kendall Hunt, 1983.

Eagleton, Terry, et al. *Nationalism, Colonialism and Literature.* Minneapolis: University of Minnesota Press, 1990.

Fernandez, Doreen and Edilberto Alegre. *The Writer and His Milieu.* Manila: De La Salle University Press, 1982.

Fuentebella, Cielo. "What is Filipino American Culture?" *Philippine News Magazine,* August 9-15, 1989.

Galdon, Joseph, ed. *Philippine Fiction.* Quezon City, Phils.: Ateneo de Manila University Press, 1972.

Gates, Henry Louis. *The Signifying Monkey: A Theory of African-American Literary Criticism.* New York: Oxford University Press, 1988.

Gonzalez, N.V.M. *Kalutang: A Filipino in the World.* Manila: Kalikasan Press, 1990.

_____. *Mindoro and Beyond: Twenty-One Stories.* Quezon City, Phils.: University of Philippines Press, 1979.

_____. "Drumming for the Captain." *World Literature Written in English* 15.2 (November 1976): 415-21.

_____. "The Filipino and the Novel." *Daedelus* 95.4 (Fall 1966): 961-71.

_____. *Seven Hills Away.* Denver: Alan Swallow, 1947.

Gurr, Andrew. *Writers in Exile: The Identity of Home in Modern Literature.* New Jersey: Humanities Press, 1981.

Guyotte, Roland and Barbara Posadas. "Unintentional Immigrants: Chicago's Filipino Foreign Students Become Settlers, 1900-1941." *Journal of American Ethnic History* (Spring 1990): 26-48.

Guzman, Richard. "'As in Myth, the Signs Were All Over': The Fiction of N.V.M. Gonzalez." *Virginia Quarterly Review* 60.1 (Winter 1984): 102-18.

Harlow, Barbara. *Resistance Literature.* New York: Methuen, 1987.

Hsu, Kai-yu and Helen Palubinskas, eds. *Asian American Authors.* Boston: Houghton Mifflin, 1972.

Hunt. Michael. "New Insights But No New Vistas: Recent Work in 19th Century American-East Asian Relations." In *New Frontiers in American-East Asian Relations,* ed. Warren Cohen. New York: Columbia University Press, 1983.

Kaplan, Amy. "Romancing the Empire." *American Literary History* 3 (December 1990): 659-90.

Karnow, Stanley. *In Our Image: America's Empire in the Philippines.* New York: Random, 1989.

Kim, Elaine. *Asian American Literature: An Introduction to the Writings and their Social Context.* Philadelphia: Temple University Press, 1982.

Mak, Alice. "Development of Philippine Studies in Hawaii." *Philippine Studies Newsletter,* October 1989.

Manguerra-Brainard, Cecilia. *Woman with Horns and Other Stories.* Quezon City, Phils.: New Day, 1988.

May, Ernest and James Thomson Jr., eds. *American-East Asian Relations: A Survey.* Cambridge, Mass.: Harvard University Press, 1972.

May, Glenn. *A Past Recovered.* Quezon City, Phils.: New Day, 1987.

_____. *Social Engineering in the Philippines.* Westport, Conn.: Greenwood, 1980.

Mazumdar, Sucheta. "Asian American Studies and Asian Studies: Rethinking Roots." *Asian Americans: Comparative and Global Perspectives.* eds. Shirley Hune, et al. Pullman, Wash.: Washington State University Press, 1991.

Memmi, Albert. *The Colonizer and the Colonized.* Boston: Beason, 1965.

Mestrovic, Marta. "Ninotchka Rosca." *Publishers Weekly,* May 6, 1988.

Miller, Stuart Creighton. *"Benevolent Assimilation": The American Conquest of the Philippines, 1899-1903.* New Haven: Yale University Press, 1982.

Mukherjee, Bharati. "Immigrant Writing: Give Us Your Maximalists!" *New York Times Book Review,* August 28, 1988.

Peñaranda, Oscar, et al. "An Introduction to Filipino American Literature." *Aiiieeeee! An Anthology of Asian American Writers* eds. Frank Chin, et al. Washington, D.C.: Howard University Press, 1974.

Pido, Antonio. *The Pilipinos in America: Macro/Micro Dimensions of Immigration and Integration.* New York: Center for Migration Studies, 1986.

Posadas, Barbara. "At a Crossroad: Filipino American History and the Old Timers' Generation. *Amerasia* 13.1 (1986-87): 85-97.

Quemada, David. "The Contemporary Filipino Poet in English." *World Literature Written in English* 15.2 (November 1976): 429-37.

Rosca, Ninotchka. *State of War.* New York: Norton, 1988.

_____. *Monsoon Collection.* New York and Sta. Lucia: University of Queensland Press, 1983.

Rydell, Robert. *All the World's A Fair: Visions of Empire at American International Expositions, 1876-1916.* Chicago: University of Chicago Press, 1984.

Said, Edward. "Reflections on Exile." *Out There: Marginalization and Contemporary Cultures.* eds. Russel Ferguson et al. Cambridge, Mass.: MIT Press, 1990.

San Juan, Epifanio, Jr. "Mapping the Boundaries, Inscribing the Differences: The Filipino in the U.S.A." *Journal of Ethnic Studies* 19.1 (Spring 1991): 117-31.

_____. "The Cult of Ethnicity and the Fetish of Pluralism." *Cultural Critique* 18 (Spring 1991): 215-29.

_____. "Farewell, You Whose Homeland is Forever Arriving As I Embark: Journal of a Filipino Exile." *Kultura* 3.1 (1990): 34-41.

_____. *Ruptures, Schisms, Interventions: Cultural Revolution in the Third World.* Manila: De La Salle University Press, 1988.

_____. "Reflections on U.S.-Philippine Literary Relations." *Ang Makatao* (1988): 43-54.

_____. "To the Filipino Artist in Exile." *Midweek,* August 19, 1987.

_____. *Crisis in the Philippines.* South Hadley, Mass.: Bergin and Garvey, 1986.

Santos, Bienvenido, "Pilipino Old Timers: Fact and Fiction." *Amerasia* 9.2 (1982): 89-98.

_____. *Scent of Apples.* Seattle: University of Washington Press, 1979.

_____. "The Personal Saga of a "Straggler" in Philippine Literature." *World Literature Written in English* 15.2 (November 1976): 398-405.

_____. "The Filipino Novel in English." *Brown Heritage: Essays on Philippine Cultural Tradition and Literature* ed. Antonio Manuud. Quezon City, Phils.: Ateneo de Manila University Press, 1967.

Seidel, Michael. *Exile and the Narrative Imagination.* New Haven: Yale University Press, 1987.

Skinner, Michelle Ma. Cruz. *Balikbayan: A Filipino Homecoming.* Honolulu: Bess Press, 1988.

Solberg, Sam. "Introduction to Filipino American Literature." *Aiiieeeee! An Anthology of Asian American Writers.* Chin, Frank et al., eds. Washington, D.C.: Howard University Press, 1983.

Sollors, Werner. *Beyond Ethnicity: Consent and Descent in American Culture.* New York: Oxford University Press, 1986.

Tagami, Jeff. *October Light.* San Francisco: Kearny Street Workshop, 1987.

Takaki, Ronald. *Strangers From a Different Shore: A History of Asian Americans.* Boston: Little, Brown, 1989.

_____, ed. *From Different Shores: Perspectives on Race and Ethnicity in America*. New York: Oxford University Press, 1987.

Ty-Casper, Linda. *Ten Thousand Seeds*. Manila: Ateneo de Manila University Press, 1987.

_____. *Wings of Stone*. London: Readers International, 1986.

_____. *Awaiting Trespass*. London: Readers International, 1985.

_____. *Fortress in the Plaza*. Quezon City, Phils.: New Day, 1985.

_____. *The Three-Cornered Sun*. Quezon City, Phils.: New Day, 1979.

Wand, David Hsin-fu, ed. *Asian American Heritage*. Boston: Houghton Mifflin, 1974.

Welch, Richard. *Response to Imperialism: The United States and the Philippine-American War, 1899-1902*. Chapel Hill: University of North Carolina Press, 1979.

Williams, Raymond. *Marxism and Literature*. New York: Oxford University Press, 1977.

SEVEN

Speaking of AIDS: Language and the Filipino 'Gay' Experience in America

MARTIN F. MANALANSAN IV

THE GLOBAL ETHNOSCAPE: AIDS, GAY MEN, AND LANGUAGE

In an increasingly seamless world, modern communication and transportation technologies continuously carry objects, people, and ideas across land, air, and water. Appadurai (1991) calls this terrain a *global ethnoscape*. He describes it as a "landscape of persons who make up a shifting world in which we live, tourists, immigrants, refugees, exiles, guestworkers, and other moving groups" (*ibid:* 192). This reality has brought people from diverse and disparate contexts together, even those that are deemed as marginals such as gays and lesbians. In a New York City gay bar for instance, it is not unusual to find a man of Colombian descent dancing with a Japanese businessman in town for the weekend or an African-American cruising a French tourist. These cosmopolitan encounters have given rise to gay magazines devoted to interracial gay issues (e.g., *Passport*), inter-cultural organizations (e.g., Asians and Friends), and other artifacts of gay "international" life. However, amidst all these iconic examples, lay a specter that also goes beyond borders and lifestyles, the AIDS epidemic.

AIDS as a transnational biological and cultural force poses problems for scholars attempting to understand its dynamics among diasporic or migrant gay men. While studies of Western gay men and mass media (Watney 1987; Crimp 1988) have presented a monolithic view of the strategies by which these men have represented AIDS, there is no study that problematizes the mercurial character of gay men from minority and immigrant groups. This is especially crucial in a world where boundaries of culture, identity, and community continually shift. A clearer understanding of the AIDS epidemic as well as of gay men must acknowledge the fact that crossing physical or geographic borders do not necessarily mark the point of cultural disjunctures.

The *cultures* of gay men, particularly their linguistic habits, reflect the global impact of the pandemic. "T-cell counts," "PWA or person with AIDS," "serostatus" and "antibody" have become part of the gay lexicon. This study presents a case analysis among Filipino[1] gay men and how many of them have constructed a unique symbolic system around AIDS through the use of "swardspeak" or the Filipino equivalent of gayspeak or gayslang. This paper is a result of my work as an AIDS service provider and fieldwork in the gay community in New York City as well as some interviews with several Filipino/Filipino-Americans in San Francisco.

Several issues arise out of a fieldwork situation involving Filipino gay immigrants, exiles, and guest workers in America such as: How is Filipino swardspeak, displaced through migration, practiced in a different context? What are the continuities and discontinuities in the linguistic and cultural practices of these men? This paper will not provide comprehensive answers but will sketch very broadly the numerous aspects of the issues.

To begin, I first describe and analyze the Filipino construction of male homosexuality in order to establish the context in which swardspeak operates. Then I present the basic features of the gay argot. The next section is a discussion of issues of immigration, displacement, and AIDS in relation to gay Filipinos in New York City. I focus on the way gay Filipinos have established linguistic practices around AIDS when they talk to each other. Gay Filipinos have effeminized and personified AIDS by calling it Tita Aida or "Auntie Aida." I will describe how swardspeak made this idiom possible and how it is constantly being reworked or reconstituted according to various contexts. To illustrate the various points, I present two cases. The first case is a life narrative of a gay Filipino who has contracted HIV. The second case is a discussion of how AIDS prevention efforts in the Filipino community in San Francisco has reconfigured the notion of Tita Aida. In the final section, I attempt to analyze the implications of the idiom of Tita Aida in terms of the issues of gay identity and community in the cosmopolitan arena.

The Social Construction of the *Bakla*

Filipinos are a people of paradoxes and contradictions. The Philippines was a colony of Spain for more than three hundred years and of the United States for the first half of the century. The cultural landscape therefore bears the scars of colonialism and the fresh wounds of postcolonial conditions. Dreams of America merge with the prayers and rituals to the Infant Jesus and the Virgin Mary. The Catholic Church as well as strong values on family relations dominate the topography of Filipino lifeways. American popular culture (movies, television, magazines) co-exists with the recent rise of Bible cults (born again Christians, Catholic orthodox, etc.). In such a situation, scholars are perplexed as to how male homosexuality is accommodated into a seemingly forbidding Filipino sexual discourse.

In light of this issue, I use the term "gay" as a provisional term to describe the Filipino men I am studying. Gay identity involves a cultural and politico-economic milieu that allowed this concept to become a hegemonic category for describing individuals as well as groups of individuals (see Herdt and Boxer 1992). These conditions are conspicuously absent in the Philippines. I will use the Tagalog term *bakla* in the succeeding parts of the paper to express more adequately the social realities and the sexual ideology that give rise to swardspeak. By using the term I do not assume that Tagalog adequately addresses the internal social and linguistic differences within Philippine society. However, Tagalog (or Pilipino as it is officially designated) is spoken in most if not all of the islands (apart from English and the regional languages) and *bakla* is an enduring social category. These two realities justify formulating the discussion on the concept of the *bakla*. As the section on swardspeak will show, my usage of the term does not preclude any cross-fertilization between regional languages and cultures with the Tagalog language and Manila-centric culture.

In most instances, *bakla* is an emotionally-ladened as well as a potentially derogatory term. It does not have the political implications of "gay" as an identity. Scholars and writers have translated the term *bakla* to homosexual (Whitam 1990), queer (Itiel 1989), and gay (Mathews 1987). This practice distorts the term's social dynamics. By understanding the social construction of the term, one is able to better understand the travails and struggles of the social being called *bakla*.

Bakla is a problematic Tagalog term. Its etymology is popularly seen to be a result of the contraction of the first syllable of the word for woman (*babae*) and the first syllable of the word for man (*lalaki*). A Tagalog dictionary defined *bakla* as hermaphrodite. In addition, it is also seen in terms of the in-between or *alanganin* (which was also another term for Filipino male homosexuals in the sixties and fifties).[2] The interstitial and epicene quality attributed to the *bakla* illuminates the social script. Indeed, while *bakla* conflates the categories of effeminacy, transvestism, and homosexuality and can mean one or all of these in different contexts, the main focus of the term is that of effeminate mannerism, feminine physical characteristics (i.e., small, frail bodies, delicate facial features, etc.) and cross-dressing.

Most of the translations of the term view it as non-condemnatory and descriptive (Hart 1968; Mathews 1987), except for a lone Filipino woman who started her article by describing *bakla* as an emotionally-charged word (Raquiza 1983). Phonetically, *bakla* ends with a glottal stop. In the Tagalog sound system, it is abrupt and not euphonious compared to other terms that mean the same thing (i.e., *sward, badaf,* etc.). Nobody, except in moments of extreme camp and self-effacement, will call another a *bakla* as a way of describing or naming him without malice.

A good example is the translation of the Broadway play "Bent" into Tagalog at the University of the Philippines in the early eighties. The play was about homosexuals in Nazi concentration camps and the word *bakla* was hurled several times even in the most intimate moments between characters. Many commented that this usage of the term "hurts the ears" (*masakit sa tenga*). The inappropriateness of this usage shows how the term is emotionally-ladened and is potentially condemnatory.

Sexual relations of the *bakla* are not integral to this popular conception. Despite the views of the previous writers, Nimmo and Mathews, who focused on the sexual aspects, the linguistic and social construction of the *bakla* primarily centers on two closely related images—the cross-dressing queen and the pseudo-woman. The cross-dressing *bakla* is a "man" who exhibits the proclivities for women's garb and mannerisms. The pseudo-woman is one who exhibits the "weaker" emotions and needs of "real women" and therefore, looks for a "straight" man. This image is not based on sexual desire alone, but a desire shaped by the gender hierarchy, and of the view that women like the Virgin Mary were meant to suffer for men. It is the imitation of the stereotypical female role that proves crucial in the social script of the *bakla*.

Judith Butler (1990) defined drag or cross-dressing as transparent lies in public. This is useful in trying to understand the role of cross-dressing in the social construction of the *bakla*. Cross-dressing is an integral part of the visible *bakla* social network. Apart from the *karnabal* (carnival) and *perya* (fair), any public occasion from a church festival to a village dance creates an opportunity for the cross-dressing *bakla* to show off his "wares." In Bacolod, a major Philippine city in the south, the most important religious occasion and social event of the year is the Christmas eve pageant. The queen of this pageant is usually a cross-dressed *bakla* (Whitam and Mathy 1986). In Pasay (a city in the Metropolitan Manila area), one of the attractions of its May festival or Santacruzan is the procession of *bakla* who dress up as female religious and historical figures from Mary Magdalene to Empress Helena. National television has its share of these "men." In the early eighties, a popular noontime TV variety show had a popular segment called "Miss Gay Philippines" (which had all the accoutrements of the traditional beauty pageants such as bathing suit and talent portions).

The spectacle of the cross-dressed *bakla* has been woven into the social fabric. A stereotypical neighborhood or village in the popular imagination would include its usual families, gangs, wayward girls, old spinsters, idiot, and *bakla*.

Village idiot? Village *bakla*? What is the difference? Very little if we closely examine what even the most meticulous scholars failed to observe. Writers have described the light teasing and public scoldings of these men (Hart 1968); however, what were never mentioned were the beatings and bashings. These were not in any way hidden from public view.

In television shows and movies, especially the comedies, there would usually be one or two incidents where the *bakla* is beaten up in a Marx Brothers-like melee. Dolphy, an actor who is seen as the premier Filipino comedian, has made a career of appearing as a *bakla* in movies. There is a formula in the celluloid representation of the *bakla* which is to include the bashing of the *bakla* by some thug or an irate father or brother. These beatings almost always are met with laughter and approval by the audience. This is followed by a sexual awakening to heterosexuality. On one level, the beatings of the *bakla* is seen as therapeutic—to subvert the lie. On another level, it is seen as natural. A *bakla* is bashed because of who he is (*bakla kasi*).

The cross-dressed *bakla* is both tragic and comedic. His fate is to suffer the life's pains much like a stereotypical woman. At the same time, he is a source of amusement and humor for people. This is the way Philippine social discourse accommodates this "transparent lie."

This is further elucidated by the problematic category of the "masculine" *bakla*. Indeed, there are *bakla*s who do not cross-dress nor exhibit effeminate mannerisms. The masculine *bakla* is the cassowary (anomalous category) in the Philippine taxonomy of sexual behavior. The popular notion about the *bakla* is that there is a "real" screaming queen beneath the masculine facade. It is not true that the Filipino public is disinterested with the masculine *bakla*. There is no social discourse by which to discuss these kinds of "men." These *bakla*s are met either with puzzlement or suspicion. Two good examples to prove this are the movie "Macho Dancer" and a short lived all-male singing group in Manila called "Charing."

"Macho Dancer," a film about male prostitutes in Manila, was previewed in Los Angeles and New York City in the spring of 1990. The film radically departs from the formula of Philippine movies about *baklas* that I have just discussed. Here, two masculine looking and acting male prostitutes (the paragons of machismo) become intimate with each other after a night of drunken abandon. However, this breakthrough dissolves as the film utilizes another tragic ending for such a topic. One of the men is gunned down and the other is left to pursue (though unsuccessfully) a woman and leave the city.

The singing group "Charing" included five well-groomed middle to upper class youths who at first glance were straight-appearing and masculine acting. Their hit song was called "Badaf Forever" (*badaf* is another term for *bakla*) which dealt with coming-out to parents. Audiences were puzzled at the fact that no one was in drag yet all of them acknowledged being *bakla*. However, when these men started wiggling their behinds and started dancing with limp wrists, then the applause came. The initial novelty wore off and the group's popularity died. Their mixture of non-cross dressing and overt proclamation of being *bakla* did not integrate well into the popular consciousness.

The female dress is only an external shell of the popular image of the *bakla*. It functions both as iconic and as indexical symbols of the man's pysche. The *bakla*'s body is not his own. An informant from Quezon province, in the southwestern part of Luzon, told me that another euphemism for *bakla* in his hometown was *manyika ng Panginoon* (doll of God). While the drag paraphernalia form the outer shell of the *bakla*, his physical self is the plaything of God. Again, the image of the *bakla* as a spectacle and as a passive object for somebody's amusement is elevated into divine fate.

The *bakla* as pseudo-woman supposedly expresses stereotypically female emotions (like maternal feelings of nurturing, tenderness, etc.). He possesses what is called the "female heart" (*pusong babae*). This idiom encapsulates what is perhaps the core of the social construction of the *bakla*—that of the male body with a female heart. The yearnings and needs of the *bakla* are seen to be similar to women's. This construction explains why most *bakla* would say they are looking for a "real" man. By "real men," they mean straight (being married and having a girlfriend boost the masculinity of a man). There are very few reported cases of sexual relationships between *baklas*. It is seen as incestuous, unnatural, and weird. Some *bakla* view the act in cannibalistic terms (*kumakain ng sariling laman*—eating one's flesh) or as lesbians doing it (*lesbiyanahan*—verb form of lesbian). When a *bakla* discovers that his boyfriend is also *bakla*, he is said have been fooled or *natanso* (which literally means "bronzed" and is used to describe the treachery involved as opposed to "real" golden masculinity). The humorous saying goes that if a *bakla* does it with one of his own, he will be hit by lightning (*Tatamaan ng kidlat*) as if such an act goes against the divine order of things.

Thus unlike his American "counterparts," the *bakla's* predilections are seen to be focused on the straight male population. This is manifested in a thriving tradition of male prostitution. Whitam (1990) suggests that about 80% of men from working and lower class origins have participated in some kind of prostitution with some *bakla*. Most if not all gay bars in Manila and other tourist spots are hustler bars. It must be noted that outside Manila and the tourist areas, there are no organized male prostitution rings. There will be mostly informal "transactions" between *bakla* and a seemingly "straight" males. The flow of money and gifts goes from *bakla* to the callboy or "boyfriend."

While there is no stigma for the callboy/prostitute in this kind of relationship, the *bakla*, on the other hand, is seen as a reckless "crazy woman" or a "woman" embarking on a futile mission to establish a relationship with a straight "man."

This is further clarified by the ideal type of male prostitute the *bakla* would interact with as opposed to the gay foreign tourist. Mathews' (1987) study of male prostitutes focused on those who catered to foreign tourists and most of his informants presented effeminate mannerisms. Filipino clientele of male prostitutes insist on masculine acting and looking men. Indeed, for the *bakla*, the male prostitute or the callboy should represent the paragon of masculinity.

Callboy-*bakla* relationships are not the same as the Latin-American *activo* and *pasivo* which are based on the roles each may play in anal intercourse (Murray 1987). Actual sexual practices by both parties (*bakla* and callboy) can vary according to whim, negotiation, and bargaining abilities of those involved.

Despite being in a country where more than 80% of the people are living under the poverty line, it is expected that the *bakla* must fare better economically than the rest of the population. This is the social script of the *bakla*. In order to fulfill his inscribed role, a *bakla* has to slave away at work in order to survive and get what he is told he should "desire"—the "straight" macho man. He is told to suffer and not expect to have his needs filled. The ideological rationale for this situation is that like a woman, he must suffer, but unlike a woman— being a pseudo-woman, he must pay.

This is the sum of the social construction of the *bakla*. However, this construction must not be seen as an all-encompassing body of ideas and practices. Class cleavages is manifested in how such practices and ideas about the *bakla* are perceived. Most *bakla* from middle and upper classes see cross-dressing as a symptom of a lack of breeding and education. This is not to say that *bakla* from the upper classes never cross-dress. The differences in perception shows how a sense of belonging or community is not based on sexual preference alone but rather, common class origins and social experiences. This is seen in the ways *bakla* call themselves. For example, Whitam and Mathy (1986) noted that among male homosexuals in central Philippines, those from the upper classes call themselves *sward* while those from the lower classes call themselves *bayot*. But class differences are not quite clear-cut. This is further illustrated in the features and use of the gay argot or swardspeak.

The Contours of Swardspeak

Swardspeak reflects the epicene representations of the *bakla*. In Tagalog, pronouns or indexicals are not gender marked, however, adjectives are usually categorized according to male (*panlalaki*), female (*pambabae*) or non-gendered (*walang kasarian*). Most of the time, gender is indicated (as in Spanish) by word endings. Those ending in "a" are usually feminine while those adjectives ending in "o" are masculine. For example, in many conversations I have observed, *bakla* informants would describe themselves as *maganda* and not *guwapo* (handsome) or more popularly—beauty/*biyuti* or B.Y. to designate physical attractiveness for both sexes. Masculine adjectives were usually reserved for their boyfriends or crushes.

When asked why swardspeak exists, many *bakla* informants said that it was one way of communicating with each other in a way in which the outside (straight or *diretso*) world is unable to make sense of it. An informant observed that an air of conspiracy is involved in the use of the argot. He said, "When we (*bakla*) talk about *min* ("straight" men), no one will be able to know even if we talk in public."

The issue of who uses swardspeak is more problematic because of class and generational differences. Ironically, swardspeak, (from the Bisayan upper class term *sward*) is perceived by idiom of lower class *bakla*. Joel, (a fictitious name) an informant who went to the Ateneo de Manila (an exclusive Catholic institution for boys), mentioned that while growing up, one of the things he and his *bakla* friends attempted to consciously avoid was using the argot because they viewed it as the way *bakla* beauticians and manicurists talked. They perceive it to be the mode of speaking used by the *baklang talipapa* (*bakla* of the wetmarket) or the *baklang palengke* (*bakla* of the market). In this situation, the notions of wetmarket and market are construed to be an index of lower class status. Joel said that they were more prone to speaking in Taglish (combination of English and Tagalog) and even used what they perceived to be current American camp terms like "girlfriend" or "divine."

There is a sense in which the argot cuts across some class lines. Those who came from the lower classes reported that the use of swardspeak was not an issue of *bakla* identity but also a matter of pleasure or fun. Robert, a hairstylist from a southern province said that using the argot was a pleasurable way of keeping sane in an otherwise maddening existence. He said, "*Dati, pagkatapos akong awayin o bugbugin o imbiyernahin ng mga maton, nakikipagdaldalan ako sa aking mga amiga na nagsaswardspeak. Nakakagaan ng loob.*" (Before, after thugs have fought with, beaten, or irritated me, I talk to my friends [female form of the Spanish noun] using swardspeak—it brightens my mood).

As a counterpoint, another informant, Rico, from the same background as Joel's said that those who thought like Joel were *patago* (in hiding or in the closet) about their identity and were *paclass* (snobbish). Rico said, "*Wala akong paki, que magsalita silang napaka-cheap ko, kung type kong maglandi—nagsa-swardspeak ako.*" (I don't care if people think I am cheap (tacky), if I want to camp it out (acting queenie), I talk swardspeak.") Therefore, while class is an important factor in the use of the argot, exposure to *bakla* lifeways is equally important.

Generational differences is another issue. It is important to note that swardspeak and other gay argot undergo faster transformations than mainstream linguistic forms. Since it is basically expressed verbally, swardspeak is in perpetual flux. Studies have shown how the use of the argot or at least parts of it have crossed over to the general population with its use in the Filipino film as well as its inscription in movie tabloids. Despite this situation, the fashionable terms and phrases come and go.

A form that was popular in the sixties and seventies was what is called *ipis* talk. *Ipis* is the Tagalog word for cockroach, but it is the phonetic not the semantic elements of the word that are crucial in this form of swardspeak. In Tagalog or any regional language like Cebuano, the main strategy of this style of speaking was to change the sounds of f or b to v, and a, u and e to i (Hart and Hart 1990:29). For example the phrase, "*Ano ba ito?*" (What is this?) is expressed as "*Inis viz itis?*" An informant said the fascination with *ipis* talk was with the way the i and v sounds shape the lips when they are used were "so *bakla*" or queenie.

Many *bakla* in their thirties and forties are aware of the existence of this form of swardspeak, and depending on their exposure to the lifestyle are proficient in it. In fact, many of them saw proficiency or skill in using *ipis* talk as an accomplishment. These men use to have impromptu competitions in which the goal was to speak fast using the rules of *ipis* talk. However, many of those in their twenties or younger report that while some of them are aware of its existence, many of them do not use *ipis* talk.

The words in swardspeak change more rapidly than speech styles like *ipis*. If one were to examine the contents of the vocabulary, one would find a multiplicity of linguistic sources. Among the dominant influences are Tagalog, Cebuano (a southern Philippine language),

English, and Spanish. Inter-regional differences become less apparent due to the cross-fertilization of terminologies from the different languages. More than three fourths of Hart and Hart's (1990) vocabulary of Visayan (the central group of islands in the Philippines and south of Manila) gay argot are also used in Manila even if some of the words are non-Tagalog in origin. The contents of the vocabulary are basically compounds, alliterations or double entendres (*ibid*:30).

Hart and Hart (1990) indexed lexical items in swardspeak in several categories namely; sex act and organs; terms of address and endearment; words for male homosexuals, lesbians, and straight people; and physical attributes. *Bakla* are called sward, bakling, badaf, jokling, jokla, and bading. Lesbians are called tomboy, t-bird, T'boli or tibo, and portugesa. Tomboy comes from the English term while t-bird, t'boli or tibo are puns on the same word. Portugesa is a play in geography and sounds. Portugesa is a female native of Portugal and the capital of Portugal is Lisbon. Lisbon can be seen phonetically suggesting lesbian. *Dakota* is a word for a man with a huge penis (Hart 1990:37) which is a play on what is believed to be a big American state or based on the belief that anything American is big. Heterosexuals are called *diretso* which is a direct translation of "straight" *Sing and dance* is used for the sexual acts of oral and anal intercourse.

Another popular feature of swardspeak in the eighties was the use of prefixes ma (for present tense) and na (for past tense) plus English words and adding an s or tsing/tsang to the end. For example, one way of saying that Roberto got a man last night, a swardspeaker may use the word *na-gets* or *na-getsing*. Another example would be to use the word "do" in reference to having sex as *na-do*, *ma-do* or *na-dutsang*.

Swardspeak continually changes. Some changes in swardspeak can be idiosyncratic such as a play on previous words, but most of the time the changes are in response to specific social, economic, political, and cultural shifts in the environment. Nowhere is this more evident than in the predicament of swardspeakers in America.

Crossing Over: Cultural Transfer or Amalgamation?

Studies on diasporas and language (Landau 1986) emphasize the importance of examining the links between homeland and host country to better understand the continuity and disjuncture of diasporic language. Immigration to America has been a consistent part of Filipino life since the American annexation of the islands at the turn of the century. This can be only understood in terms of the long historical relationship between the Philippines and the United States. Even with the dismantling of the American military bases in the Philippines (two of the biggest outside the U.S.), this relationship has influenced and is still influencing much of the cultural, political, and economic milieu in the Philippines. For example, in Manila, American movies and television shows abound. Taglish, a combination of English and Tagalog predominates most conversations and some written texts in the urban areas (in the south it is a combination of English and another language). PX or post-exchange, a term derived from the U.S. military presence, is still used by many Filipinos to talk about imported items. America is still seen to be the important land of opportunity despite the economic allures of the Middle East. These scenarios among many others are among the reasons why the lines at the American Embassy in Manila for immigrant and non-immigrant visas are continually replenished by Filipinos dreaming of a better life.

The traffic of people between the U.S. and the Philippines is manifested in words that have become part of the everyday speech. For example, *balikbayan* is a term that literally means "back to the country" and is a designation for people who are returning back to the Philippines from abroad, usually from the U.S. The word can also be used as a verb to designate the act of coming back home to visit. "T & T" is a term for "*tago ng tago*" which literally means "always hiding" and is used for Filipino illegal immigrants in the U.S.

Swardspeak is no different from the mainstream language. Filipino *bakla* also have responded to the reality of American presence in Filipino society as well as to the immigration process in linguistic terms. For example, *afam* is used to designate Americans and usually other Caucasians. *Bay* (pronounced bai or bi) is used to call the *bakla* who has immigrated to or visited the U.S. This is in reference to the

San Francisco Bay area which has one of the highest concentrations of Filipinos in America.

The Filipino diaspora is necessarily multi-directional. The institutionalization of Filipino immigrants visiting the Philippines in what is called the *Balikbayan* program, sending some dollars back home, and the use of long distance telephone services have made "comings and goings" virtual realities. A.T. & T. has created a special series of advertisements directed at the huge Filipino market in the U.S. who clog the overseas phone lines during special holidays. Several airline and shipping agencies have also provided services and discounts to attract the same market. Filipino stores abound in cities like Jersey, Daly, San Diego, Chicago, and Seattle which are laden·with foodstuffs, handicrafts, magazines, and videos from the Philippines.

These developments have created a cultural bridge or a borderland where the intense exchange of ideas, practices, and people from the homeland and the U.S. is made possible. *Bakla* cultural practices such as beauty pageants and religious processions are still strong. In the New York City gay scene alone, beauty pageants from the prestigious Miss Fire Island to those sponsored by different gay organizations have a plethora of Filipino gay participants and winners. A Filipino gay group, *Kambal sa Lusog,* produced a Santacruzan at the Gay and Lesbian Community Center in August of 1992. Visiting the Philippines or having visitors from the homeland provides opportunities to renew or replenish one's sward vocabulary. "*O ano ba ang bago?*" or "so what is new" in swardspeak is necessarily an important part of the conversation in such encounters. This is not only true among Filipinos born, raised, and socialized in the *bakla* scene in the Philippines. It is a common practice for Filipino immigrant families to send their college age kids to universities in Manila because of the English medium of instruction, the American system of education, and the low tuition especially in medical schools. There were two American-born informants who were sent to Manila, one for college and another for an extended visit of six months. Both reported that it was during this period that they were initiated to swardspeak. The Philippine-educated informant spoke swardspeak well, while the other one understood most of it and frequently practiced it with a wide number of Philippine-born gay friends.

Most informants, residents of New York City, reported that the type of swardspeak spoken here in America is usually out of date, *luma*, or passe. Indeed visitors from Manila have complained and/or were amused by the styles of swardspeak being spoken here. Most of these visitors say, "We don't use that anymore." This kind of perspective constructs the argot as an object that is passively being transferred from the "original" source in the Philippines and passively accepted by those who practice it in America. Swardspeak's lexical items and speech styles are seen to be nothing more than native terms used in any situation. However, any kind of linguistic system, including this argot, responds to particular changes in the social arena. Filipino gay immigrants are not passive users of swardspeak but are crucial agents in the construction of what can be seen as a supralocal or cosmopolitan gay argot.

This can be seen in several lexical items which are seen as linguistic responses by gay Filipinos to the American (white) gay culture. Most lexical items in what can be considered to be American-based linguistic construction in swardspeak are usually translations or literal translations of particular words. For example, the word for transvestite or someone who goes in drag can be *transvestita* or *dragon*. Sadomasochism or leather culture does not exist as a tradition in Philippine homosexual life. However, in New York, some *bakla* have terms for "leather queens" such as *mananakit* or *mahilig sa balat* (literally "those who hurt" or "those who like leather").

Ethnic or racial categories which are virtually non-existent in the Philippine based gay argot become crucial in mixed gay scenes like New York's. The word that is sometimes used for Puerto Rican is *purico* which is both a contraction of the two words and also a popular brand for lard in the Philippines. This term hints at the racist outlook of some Filipino gay men in how they view Latinos as being "greasy." Terms such as "rice queens" and "rice bars" which are terms for men (usually Caucasians) who desire Asians and places which cater to Asians become part of the argot. A rice queen can be called *mahilig sa kanin* or "one who likes rice" in a conversation between *bakla.*

Influences from other gay men from different ethnic groups such as Latino and Blacks are also manifested linguistically. Some Filipino gay informants use the endearment "girl" or "girlfriend" instead of the terms *manay, tita, manash* or *inday* for other gay friends.

The most crucial arena where swardspeak in America becomes a virtual amalgamation of supranational processes is in the symbolic and linguistic aspects of AIDS among Filipino gay men. This has to do with the history and epidemiology of the pandemic among Filipinos. Filipino gay informants in New York reported being aware of the epidemic as early as 1981 not only because they were here when the first cases were being reported, but most importantly they were among the first to witness or know other Filipinos who came down with the illness. As late as 1984, most Philippine newspapers were either silent about the epidemic or were publishing articles about the genetic immunity of Filipinos to the disease. In fact, the first documented case in the Philippines was from a Filipino guest worker from abroad. Most of the AIDS cases among Filipino gay men in the U.S. were usually regarded as statistically insignificant until 1987 when a dramatic increase in cases was seen among Asian and Pacific Islanders. Filipinos have one of the highest number of AIDS cases among Asian-Americans (Woo et al 1988). AIDS until that time was a reality only among other Filipino gay friends and family members of Filipinos with AIDS in the U.S. These realities have created a unique gay Filipino discourse about AIDS in America.

AIDS and Swardspeak: Tita Aida Goes to New York

Informants who were born and raised in the Philippines and who migrated as adults to America before the eighties have various theories on how Filipinos started talking about AIDS. Among my informants in New York City, most agree that it was after the change from GRID (Gay Related Immune Deficiency) to AIDS that there was a noticeable change in talking about the disease among Filipino gay men. It was during this time that many Filipino gay men in both countries were using *tita* as an endearment for other gay friends. *Tita* is the Tagalog word for aunt and this kinship term is extended not only to gay friends and hangers on but to inanimate objects or social institutions. For example, the INS or the Immigration and Naturalization Service of the American federal government (an office that is a source of fear and is central to the lives of Filipino immigrants both legal and otherwise), is called *Tita Imee*. This term is both a play on the first two syllables of the word immigration and a political joke because daughter of then Philippine president Ferdinand Marcos was named Imee.

Many informants said that the logical step in talking about something especially as frightening and mysterious as AIDS was to give it a female name and the kinship term *tita*. For example, names of Filipino beauty queens are used instead of English words such as *Nelia Sancho* for somebody who is effeminate or acts nelly. However, around the name Aida, which is a play on the acronym for the disease, a more intricate and confusing lore has been constructed. One informant who immigrated in 1979 said that the name Aida is from Aida Atutalum, a woman raped in the sixties. Another informant whose life narrative follows said it was from a movie star. The exact place of origin of the name Tita Aida may never be actually known. However, it is among the Filipino gay men in the U.S. where awareness of the disease is paramount and where a unique structure of meanings surrounding the illness is continually being deployed and re-worked.

The unique situation of AIDS among Filipinos who are immigrants, residents and/or American citizens has produced a unique discourse. Lexical items are continually being reconfigured to represent various experiences during this epidemic. For instance, there is a practice of cremating the bodies of Filipinos who have died of AIDS outside the Philippines and who will be buried there because of specific Philippine laws. Cremation has become an ordinary practice that is part of the gay Filipino discourse on AIDS. Consider the text of this conversation between two *bakla* informants.

> A: *Nadinig mo na ba? Si _____ ay nasa _____. Na-Aida. Sinampal ni Tita!*
> Have you heard? (Name of a person) is in (name of a hospital). He has AIDS (here the speaker is using the prefix na to convert Aida into a verb). Auntie [Aida] slapped him!
> B: *O kailan siya lalabas ng ospital?*
> When is he coming out of the hospital?

> *C: Wiz na siya lalabas. Malapit na raw siyang matigbak.*
> *Pagkatapos ay polvoron na ang biyuti niya.*
>
> *He is not coming out [alive]. (Wiz is swardspeak for noth-*
> *ing or not). He is near death. Then he/his body will become*
> *polvoron. (Polvoron is a Filipino confection made out of flour,*
> *butter, and powdered milk and is used to symbolize cremation*
> *in this context. Biyuti is swardspeak for physical attractiveness,*
> *self or demeanor.)*

Conversations and interactions such as these show that AIDS has become not only an intrinsic part of the gay argot among gay Filipinos in America but also as a catalyst for the creation of more elaborate linguistic and social practices. Conversations at Filipino gay parties and other social activities usually are punctuated by gossip and conversation around the disease. Between Filipino gay men, Tita Aida has become an ordinary figure in their encounters with each other.

To illustrate this point I will present two case studies. The first is a life narrative of a Filipino who has been diagnosed with AIDS. The second, is a description and analysis of AIDS prevention texts in California directed to Filipino and Filipino American gay men.

Rene/Amalia: A Life

I met Rene in mid-August in 1992 at a lower East side hospital in Manhattan. He had just undergone a surgical procedure on his lungs two days previous and was suffering high fevers the night before. On that day, he seemed very ebullient and talkative. I was not prepared for the outpouring that happened when I introduced myself both as a Filipino *bakla* and as an anthropologist. I explained my mission. He readily accepted and before I could ask him what day would be good to conduct the interview, he started talking about his life.

We code-switched using English and Tagalog and sometimes used words from Tagalog "gayspeak/swardspeak." He first described himself in this way:

> *My [bakla] friends call me Amalia . . . you know . . .*
> *Amalia Fuentes [a Filipino movie actress]. Do you know why?*
> *First of all, she is pretty and so am I [laughter]. Secondly, she*
> *and I are both streetsmart (butangera) and brave (matapang).*
> *My friends back home [in Manila] will tell you how I used to*
> *pick fights and how I will run after tenants in our apartment who*
> *were delinquent with their rent. So when the bakla are hanging*
> *out and they see me approaching, they say, "Here comes,*
> *Amalia." Even my friends in California will call me that when*
> *we go cruising in those parks. I will be with someone, [having*
> *sex] and I will hear them call, "Amalia, Amalia, you loose bitch,*
> *(malanding puta) where are you?"*

He was 34 years old and was born in Manila. He grew up in a lower-class neighborhood with his mother, sister, and a maternal aunt. His father abandoned his family when Rene was about two years old. In fact, he and his sister took their mother's maiden name.

During the early seventies, his mother married an American citizen and left for the U.S. He and his sister stayed with their aunt. Through their mother's sponsorship, he and his sister immigrated to America in 1980. They settled with their mother in California where a number of their relatives lived. He did a lot of part-time work. During the first year in America, he met a Caucasian who was thirty years older than he was and almost two years younger than his mother. They eventually became lovers. Rene's lover was a teacher and he encouraged Rene to finish college. With his lover's encouragement he went back to school and finished an accounting degree. They broke up in 1988 after his lover found a younger man.

Rene intermittently visited the Philippines, sometimes staying for as long as three or four months. He steered the discussion about conditions in the Philippines by asking if I had gone "home." After I said no, he proceeded to discuss political corruption and how bad things were the last time he was in Manila. He compared conditions between the Philippines and the U.S., and he realized that he was in a relatively comfortable condition compared to most Filipinos.

I remember being in downtown Manila and I saw this boy
vending cigarettes on the busy streets. A young kid. He was
skillfully avoiding cars when a policeman accosted him. The
boy gave him twenty pesos and the policeman let him go. Can
you believe that? That kid will never recoup the money. I used
to complain about being poor, but I realized that being here [in
America], I don't have it so bad. I am not poor.

AIDS for Rene and his Filipino *bakla* friends was always couched
in feminine terms. He said that they called it, "Tita Aida," "Aida" or
"Aida Roxas." According to Rene, Aida Roxas was a Filipino B-movie
actress who became a nun. He used the term in this way:

I used to tell my friends every time they went out to party
to be careful because Tita Aida might be lurking in the corner
(nandiyan sa kanto). You know, sometimes if you are not care-
ful, Tita Aida might pick a fight with you. She [Tagalog does not
have gender-specific indexicals] is a formidable foe. Well, some
of my friends used cocaine . . . some of them are so careless, I
still keep telling them if they persist on taking drugs, Tita Aida
might come to fetch them. And you know where she may lead
you.

Religion played an important role in Rene's life both in the Philippines and in America. Rene said that his religiosity can be traced to
both his mother and aunt and has been an essential part of his experience with AIDS.

My life did not really change when Tita Aida touched me
(kinalabit ako ni Tita Aida). I have always been religious . . .
although I say more prayers now and I do novenas to Our Lady
of Perpetual Help . . . you know at Our Lady of Pompeii Church
in the [Greenwich] Village. I do that. I was brought up in a very
religious household, my mom and my aunt . . . oh those women
should have been nuns. My aunt would take us to mass every-
day . . . yes everyday. My mother became a born-again Chris-
tian when she came here.

Rene tested positive for the HIV antibody in 1989. He had bouts of sudden weakness and unexplained fatigue. He came down with PCP a month later. He described his initial reaction to these developments in this way:

> My first reaction was that my infection and illness was a punishment from God. He was punishing me for being bakla. However, I thought it over and I realized that he is not punishing me for who I am but for what I have done. I was so promiscuous (taratitat) especially when my spouse was away, I would just go wild and pick up men. So I now believe that God is punishing me for my unfaithfulness and rather loose ways.

Rene was able to tell his sister and other members of his family right away except for his mother. He found it extremely difficult to tell his mother about being *bakla* and having AIDS since she was old and was a born-again Christian. He was afraid of how his mother would react. He finally told his mother when they went to view the AIDS quilt when it came to California in 1990. He came out to her about his sexuality and diagnosis at the same time. He said:

> We were walking around looking at the different panels. We came upon one panel where the man had the same birthdate as I did . . . same day, month and year. I pointed it out to my mother and she agreed. Then I said that I wanted her to make my panel and I wanted to see it before I died. She broke down crying. Volunteers in the area helped us. We finally came to terms with it. She is very supportive right now.

In August, 1990, Jimmy, a *bakla* childhood friend of Rene who was living in New York invited him to move east. Jimmy was called Pilar, after Pilar Pilapil, another Filipino actress. They had a happy reunion in the city. After a few weeks, they both confided about each other's AIDS diagnosis. Jimmy/Pilar became sick a few months after Rene's arrival. Rene remembered the ordeal.

I took care of him. Pilar just got sicker and sicker . . . . We were like siblings. He and I were such a beautiful pair. Our bakla friends would say, "There goes Amalia and Pilar." Do you remember, both Amalia Fuentes and Pilar Pilapil were in a magazine article years ago . . . in the seventies I think. Well, they were so beautiful, like Jimmy and I . . . We were really close . . . It was a very difficult time for me. I saw his slow deterioration. Somehow I knew I must fight this. Pilar . . . Jimmy died in March [1991].

A few months later, in July, Rene became sick again. He entered the hospital with respiratory problems in August. He felt that this time, the opportunistic infection was more virulent than his initial bout in 1989. He noted that he was having more physical difficulties and he said, "when I came to the hospital a few days ago, I felt that this was it. I prayed, 'Lord if it is my time, I am ready.'"

Inscribing AIDS: Tita Aida and AIDS Prevention

AIDS prevention experts in California have used the idiom of Tita Aida in several pamphlets and brochures targetting Filipino gay and bisexual men. They have appropriated the symbolics of Tita Aida and taken the personification process further. In two major pamphlets, *Hoy Loka—Importante Ito* and *Dear Tita Aida*, the AIDS as the image of the wise aunt takes over the image of the dangerous woman. Both of these brochures use some form of swardspeak.

In *Dear Tita Aida*, AIDS acquires a Dear Abby persona. The disease becomes the benevolent wise and caring aunt who provides advice to people about safer sex and sexual identity. The initial page has Tita Aida saying:

How my informants tell me na hanggang ngayon (until now), many still engage in risky behaviors, primarily by not using condominiums. Again take it from someone who deeply cares about the beauty of my nieces and nephews: don't take any unnecessary risk.

In the succeeding pages, problems about safer sex, sexual identity, and AIDS are answered by Tita Aida. Paradoxically, she becomes an authority on relevant problems during the pandemic as well as becoming the focus of a discourse that aims to eliminate her.

In "Hoy Loka," *ipis* talk is used to convey basic AIDS information. Tita Aida is inscribed as a wise old woman mouthing Philippine proverbs and sayings (*salawikain*). In the brochure, Tita Aida is written to have said, "will you rush into the rain without a raincoat?" (*lulusong ka ba sa ulan ng walang kapote?*) in allusion to the need to be well protected in sexual encounters and to avoid bodily fluids such as blood, come, and vaginal fluids. Another section has Tita Aida saying, "AIDS is not like steaming rice that you can easily spit out once you have placed it into your mouth" (*Ang AIDS ay di parang kaning mainit na kapag isinubo ay madaling iluwa*). In the last paragraph however, there is a warning which says, "remember that anyone can be fetched by Tita Aida." The notion of "fetch" is an allusion to death which when personified is usually described as a figure coming for her victims. In these two brochures, Tita Aida is constructed in a dysphoric manner. The first facet of this construction is that of a wise and friendly kin who is ready to dispense advice while the other is a menacing if not ominous sign of death itself.

The dual nature of this construction led to some problems when a Filipino AIDS prevention group in California attempted to have a fund-raising activity utilizing a standby in *bakla* tradition, the beauty contest. This contest was called the "Miss Tita Aida Contest." Trouble ensued because nobody wanted to enter the contest. Many gay Filipinos were afraid that if they participated and won the title, people might think that they have the disease.

Tita Aida: An Unpacking

The two cases presented the different ways the idiom, "Tita Aida," have constructed constellations of meanings in numerous gay Filipino cultural and linguistic practices. These ways enable gay Filipinos to talk about the disease within their own terms. Tita Aida, like all other

AIDS discourses, is not neutral (Leap 1990). To better understand this term it is important to unpack the layers of meaning behind the idiom.

Philippine sexual ideology focuses on the cross-dressing practices and effeminate qualities of the *bakla*. The words gay or homosexual do not adequately translate the Tagalog word *bakla* because this concept foregrounds gender inversion and decenters sexual behavior and desire (see Mathews 1987; Raquiza 1983; Hart 1968). *Bakla* is what Murray (1992) categorized as "gendered homosexuality." The term, *pusong babae* or "one who possesses the female heart/soul" is central to the social construction of the *bakla*. The *bakla* is one who exhibits female emotions, looks for "real" (straight) men[3] (not other *bakla*) and is fated (as in the female stereotype) to suffer. Suffering is a subtext that is part and parcel of the epicene quality attributed to the *bakla*.

The notions of gender hierarchy in the Philippines have inscribed suffering within the social script of the woman and by default, the *bakla*. The Roman Catholic Church with its coterie of female saints, martyrs, and most importantly the Virgin Mary has provided the models par excellence of suffering. The *sinakulo* and *pasyon*, two of the most important Catholic rituals in the Philippines, chronicle the suffering and death of Jesus Christ. It is interesting to note that in these texts, the Virgin Mary is an integral character and that Jesus Christ is described in many instances using feminine adjectives (Ileto 1979: 17). Philippine society's conflation of the feminine with suffering is given religious dimension.

In Philippine popular culture, movies, and television shows often portray women as sufferers particularly in dramas. The *bakla* on the other hand is seen in two extremes as marginal comedic figures or as tragic fall guys. In many interviews I have conducted with other *bakla*, there has been a tendency, even with those who contend they are happy, to acknowledge the existence of a "cross" they have to bear for being who they were. In some cases, these *bakla* referred to the Tagalog melodramas in television and movies and saw themselves as the tragic heroines.

The intersection of suffering with sexual orientation, religion, and gender can be better understood with Philippine cultural conceptions of illness and disease in general and venereal diseases in particular. The Tagalog word for illness and disease is *sakit* which can also mean pain. The same word but with a stress on the first syllable means suffering. Venereal diseases are euphemistically called *sakit ng babae* or illnesses of women. In swardspeak, the names of Filipino beauty queens such as *Vida Doria* sometimes are used for these diseases. This notion of venereal diseases is not unique to the Philippines (see Gilman 1988: 248-57), but it ties in with other Philippine notions of suffering.

This is the cultural tableau which informed in part, Rene's experience of AIDS. First, his sense of self-definition has been effeminate/feminine and the persona he presented was that of a "woman." His role model, Amalia Fuentes, was a Philippine actress. Second, the major figures in his life, his mother, sister, and aunt have been female. Third, his religious training and devotion particularly to Our Lady of Perpetual Help shaped his perception of AIDS as suffering inflicted by God.

Rene was able to accommodate his effeminate/feminine persona by utilizing the idiom of Tita Aida. By engendering AIDS, Rene and other Filipino homosexuals are able to talk about AIDS without creating a discursive upheaval or reconfiguring the notion of *bakla*. By utilizing "tita" which is both a kinship term and camp term of endearment, Rene symbolically included AIDS into his own circle of friends and kin. Since other *bakla* are not potential sexual partners, the term "tita" as camp endearment in Tita Aida enabled Rene to skirt the tricky issue of sexuality and sexual desire within the AIDS problematic.

The idiom also accommodates Rene's fascination with the movies and Filipino actresses in particular by exchanging Tita Aida with Aida Roxas, a Filipino actress turned nun. Here, both religious and cinematic images and symbols merge to form a kind of spectacle of the feminine, suffering and AIDS.

The use of Tita Aida in AIDS prevention literature utilizes the ambivalence inherent in the idiom. The brochures directed at Filipino gay men in California allowed public health officials to tap into a discourse that constructs the disease with the use of inclusive and friendly tropes. Tita Aida as an idiom permits the use of humorous and effective channeling of information without becoming preachy or too ominous.

Despite the use of the kinship term *tita,* the idiom has another side which is the image of death. Rene's warning about Tita Aida lurking in some corner or coming to fetch the careless *bakla* equated AIDS with death and personified AIDS as the grim reaper. The failed beauty contest "Miss Tita Aida" is another example where the stark biological realities trespass the otherwise friendly borders of the Tita Aida discourse.

Tita Aida could be seen as an anomalous category that comes in between what Gilman (1988:6) saw as the two reactions individuals have to images of illness, denial or affirmation. Tita Aida oscillates between these extremes, between being the kind wise kin to the dark ominous figure of death.

The ambivalence of the idiom parallels the position of the disease in the lives of gay Filipino immigrants like Rene. To many who have come in search of a better life in America, some gay Filipinos might see AIDS as a punishment. However, set within the contours of a gay transnational life like Rene's, the disease may sometimes be located within a bifocal vision, that of America and of the homeland. Rene's anecdote of the small boy selling cigarettes matches other narratives from Filipinos who have AIDS. To them, the disease becomes another part of the balancing scales of life. For gay immigrants, this vision is a necessary component of seeing most life events. "If I stayed in the Philippines . . ." or "I don't have it so bad . . . " may be to some just frantic attempts at justifying their predicaments, but in the context of the reality of a globalizing world, these are necessary panoramas in which to situate diasporic lives.

Studies of immigration and exilic populations have often focused on the assimilation or violent resistance of groups. More often, the creative responses of the groups utilizing resources from both countries are not dealt with. Tita Aida is one such creative response. AIDS and a gay diasporic argot such as swardspeak have created this cultural amalgamation that has been effectively deployed in numerous communication arenas. Tita Aida is a paradoxical "package of meanings" that continues to be reconfigured and reshaped by the continuous flow of ideas and people between the U.S. and the Philippines.

NOTES

Versions of this paper were presented in the 1990 and 1991 American Anthropological Association annual meetings. I would like to thank the following for their comments, suggestions and insights that enabled me to complete this paper: Vince Rafael, Tom Gibson, Eufracio Abaya, Jane Po, Rick Bonus, Mike Tan, Steve Murray, Joey Almoradie, and Walter Williams. This paper was written in memory of several Filipino and non-Filipino friends who have died of AIDS.

1. I use the term Filipino to designate the population of Philippine born immigrants as well as U.S. born individuals to Filipino heritage. I am aware of the new designation Pilipino/Pilipina, but I find that in most situations in the Philippines, the use of Pilipino is for designating the national language and not citizenship.

2. I am indebted to Mary Jane Po for this analysis.

3. In most of my interviews, most Filipino *bakla* found it abhorrent to have sex with other *bakla* or effeminate men because doing so would be akin to "lesbianism," cannibalism, or incest. Many of them said that such an act would be (jokingly) "frowned upon by God." "We will be struck by lightning" was a sentence most often heard as if to say that sexual relations between *bakla* were unnatural.

WORKS CITED

Appadurai, Arjun (1991). "Global Ethnoscapes: Notes and Queries for a Transnational Anthropology," in R. Fox (ed.) *Recapturing Anthropology*. Santa Fe, NM: School of American Research.

Butler, Judith. 1990. *Gender Trouble: Feminism and the Subversion of Identity*. New York: Routledge.

Crimp, Douglas. 1988. *AIDS: Cultural Analysis/Cultural Activism*. Cambridge: MIT Press.

Gilman, Sander L. 1988. *Disease and Representation: Images of Illness from Madness to AIDS*. Ithaca: Cornell University Press.

Hart, Donn V. 1968. "Homosexuality and Transvestism in the Philippines: The Cebuan Bayot and Lakin-on," *Behavior Science Notes*: 3(4) 211-48.

Herdt, Gilbert and Andrew Boxer. 1992. "Introduction: Culture, History and the Life Course of Gay Men," in G. Herdt (ed.) *Gay Culture in America: Essays from the Field.* Boston: Beacon Press. 1-28.

Ileto, Reynaldo C. 1979. *Pasyon and Revolution: Popular Movements in the Philippines, 1840-1910.* Quezon City: Ateneo de Manila University Press.

Kleinman, Arthur. 1988. *The Illness Narratives: Suffering, Healing and the Human Condition.* New York: Basic Books.

Landau, Jacob M. 1986. "Diaspora and Language," in Scheffer (ed.) *Modern Diasporas in International Politics.* New York: St. Martin's Press.

Leap, William. 1990. "Language and AIDS," in D. Feldman (ed.) *Culture and AIDS.* New York: Praeger.

Marzan, Lourdes. 1991. *The Filipino Community in New York City.* Asian/ American Center RE-910105. New York: Asian/American Center, Queens College. (information sheet)

Mathews, Paul W. 1987. "Some Preliminary Observations of Male Prostitution in Manila." *Philippine Sociological Review* 35 (3-4): 55-74.

Murray, Stephen O. 1992. *Oceanic Homosexualities.* New York: Garland Press.

Nimmo, Arlo. 1978. "The Relativity of Sexual Deviance: A Sulu Example." *Papers in Anthropology.* Norman, Okla.: Department of Anthropology, University of Oklahoma.

Po, Mary Jane. 1991. *Hoy, Loka Importante 'to!* (Hey Crazy Woman—This is important!) San Francisco: San Francisco AIDS Foundation (pamphlet)

Raquiza, Marie Antonette. 1983. "Bakla: do they have a chance?" *Diliman Review* 31 (5): 35-37.

Watney, Simon. 1986. *Policing Desire: Pornography, AIDS and the Media.* Minneapolis: University of Minnesota Press.

Whitam, Frederick. 1990. "Philippines." *Encyclopedia of Homosexuality* Volume 2. Wayne Dynes (ed.) New York: Garland Publishing Co.

_____ and Robin M. Mathy. 1986. *Male Homosexuality in Four Societies: Brazil, Guatemala, the Philippines and the United States.* New York: Praeger.

Part 4

Aesthetics and Politics of the Everyday

EIGHT

The Power of Appearances:
Beauty, Mimicry, and Transformation
in Bicol

FENELLA CANNELL

THIS PAPER BEGINS WITH SOMETHING SO ELUSIVE THAT IT IS RARELY CONSIDered as a social fact; the expression on somebody's face. To be more precise, it begins with the expression on the faces of some friends of mine in a ricefield and at a wedding, and continues with the facial expressions of the aspirants for the title "Mrs. Calabanga 1989," through the somewhat similar expressions, more or less professionally fixed, of various beauty and talent show contestants in small Bicol towns and villages, to the most spectacular of these contests which is the *Bakla* (male transvestite) beauty contest in Naga City. Since the significance of these particular, dazzlingly made-up and glamorously-disguised faces is especially ambiguous, it contains something about the meaning of being a *bakla* in Bicol. There are other faces too, barely glimpsed here or for which this essay cannot even make room, faces whose owners figure more substantially elsewhere.[1] The faces of the players of religious games seated round a table on Good Friday night deep in debate: the healer from Libmanan who had himself photographed nailed to a cross; finally some almost ghostly faces, those of the Tagalog film stars, which exist only in two dimensions hanging on the screen or on posters, and have no substantial person behind them at all. All these faces are engaged in performance, and the creative, defiant, sad, and funny meanings behind their various expressions are linked by the workings of imitation and transfiguration in Bicol.

These people, wearing the facial expressions which caught my attention and seemed to demand response and understanding, are all standing in different places. They do not all know each other, and in fact they aspire to rather different lives in many ways. But I think their expressions are connected. I shall argue that in the different performances on which they are engaged, all these people are attempting to come to terms with an idea of beauty and glamor which refers to images of a mostly unattainable West. The performances in which they are engaged are all to some extent imitative of "Western" culture as Filipinos see it or have it thrust upon them. But imitation in the Philippines, I shall argue, has a particular meaning and the fact that it incorporates "Western" models should not lead us to confuse it with mere derivativeness; in Bicol, imitation of content can constitute a self-transformative process which is itself part of Bicol culture and its historical continuity.

The material I shall be discussing in this paper is based on 20 months' fieldwork in Bicol, Southern Luzon, part of the lowland Philippines and still predominantly Roman Catholic. The regional language is Bicol, and standard Bicol is the language spoken in all normal circumstances, although here as elsewhere people understand some Tagalog and receive some English teaching in the local primary school.[2] The places in which I worked, and to which this paper refers, are respectively "San Ignacio," the village or barangay where I lived, Calabanga, the little market town at whose margins San Ignacio is situated, and Naga City, which is the regional capital for Bicol, and which is less than an hour's journey by jeepney from Calabanga.

The main occupation is rice farming, which has traditionally been combined with smallscale inland and coastal fishing. In the face of increasing scarcity of access to land,[3] and reduction of fishing yields, many people also try to make a living from small buy-and-sell operations or service sector work of various kinds. Nevertheless, they remain marginal to the capitalist economy. The average day-wage in 1988-89 for labor in the ricefields was 50 pesos, while the cost of a kilo of rice at that time was P8.-8.50. Since a family may need four kilos of rice per day just as a staple, it can be seen how little leeway rural people have to negotiate in a cash economy or to purchase the range of manufactured goods available in the markets.

In Bicol, as in much of the rural Philippines, the most visible reminders of the Spanish colonial period are the churches, but physical signs of the continued American influence on politics and the economy are ubiquitous. The houses, clothes, tastes, and educational aspirations of Filipino people bear a strong evidence of both the colonial and post-colonial link. In Bicol as in much of the lowlands, the architecture of public buildings, and the luxury goods, clothes, food, and films which are available in the cities, are things that are thought of as being in the American style, even if some of the goods actually come from Taiwan.

Bicolano people of all classes are in fact extremely interested in thinking about the Philippines with reference to somewhere else. Usually, that somewhere is America, and usually the comparisons stress that the "outside" or distant place—the imagined America—is a place of power, wealth, cleanliness, beauty, glamor, and enjoyment. Opinions differ on whether it is a more moral place than the Philippines, according to the context of the discussion. Some people express a wish to emigrate and live in the paradise of abroad. Others point out the advantages of coming home to one's family. But the central point, I think, is that people see the imagined "outside" as one source of power,[4] and as a key source of wealth. Making the voyage to America as a migrant worker is thought of as one of the only ways in which one can transform one's life at home, becoming wealthy, prosperous and freed from the burden of subjection which poverty brings. More recently, the relevant work destinations have changed, so that one is now more likely to go to the Middle East or Japan, but although a keen interest is taken in these locations, the United States still occupies the paradigmatic position in the imagination of "abroad," and I take it as such for the purposes of this paper.

Given the history of the economic and political relations between the United States and the Philippines, this interest is quite solidly founded in financial facts. But if the Philippines has been in some ways forced into dependence on America (a dependence summed up by the size of its national debt), it is hardly a surprising observation that this has not affected all Filipinos in the same way. Setting aside the Filipino international elite, it is clear that in contemporary Bicol as elsewhere middle-class people and poor rural people have different relations to the lure of "America." In the area in which I lived, it was most often middle-class people who were able to mobilize connections and pay agency fees to seek migrant work. In the barangay itself, only one man had work abroad in 1988-89, and his circumstances were unusual. Another family had lost all their property on an agency-fee swindle. Thus both the income and the experience of migrant work remain unaffordable for most people.

Similarly, although middle-class people are more able to seek jobs and educational opportunities outside the Philippines, they are not exclusively reliant on doing so, for they can better afford the goods and services which offer the advantages of "America/abroad" *within* the Philippines. Schools and colleges run by American Jesuits are an obvious example.

For the people living in San. Ignacio, on the other hand, these things were perpetually known and visible, but almost always quite inaccessible to them. This was brought forcefully home to me whenever I accompanied women from the barangay on their trips to the city market to sell fish.

If the men returned from night fishing with a catch of a kilo or more, the women would take it in buckets and walk at four in the morning to catch the jeepney to Naga, arriving while it was still dark. Their only equipment was a piece of plastic sheeting on which to spread the catch in priced piles (*atado*). Naga has a concrete multi-storey market, with different goods available on each floor, but the women from San Ignacio cannot afford a license, and even the ₱1. temporary ticket eats into their small profits. They all climb to the roof of the building, known as the "squatters' market"; after dawn, the heat becomes unbearable and the police are likely to arrive, so most people leave by 7 a.m. Occasionally, there is a police raid, and several women had lost their catch, or a precious bucket, when they had to make a run for it.

To get to the squatters' market, the fish sellers pass through Naga's main squares. In Naga one is never far from riceland, and any unoccupied lot is likely to be squatted by someone growing vegetables. Nevertheless, the center has its big churches, public monuments to national heroes, and several buildings on a glossier scale. Banks and Chinese-owned department stores loom behind smoked-glass doors, their air-conditioned interiors guarded by the inevitable security man with dark glasses and gun. The women from San Ignacio walk past these buildings, but they never go into them. Local office workers eat at the several fast-food restaurants (Filipinized versions of McDonald's) or Chinese restaurants, but if the fish-sellers eat anything at all, it will be bought from a small stall selling ordinary local dishes. During my fieldwork, it was an exceptional event if anyone from the barangay went to the cinema or was taken to eat in Naga, and many people had never done so. People from the rural areas inhabit a different space; they see the gloss of the city, but they do not consume its products.

To be poor in any society is always to be excluded. In the Philippines, as Pinches has shown in his work on Manila slum dwellers, poverty is experienced most definitely as personal subordination as well as material lack. It is "the experience of not being valued, of . . . constantly having one's dignity challenged" and of "being shamed" (Pinches, 1991:177). While life in the rural barangay may support one's dignity rather better in some ways than life in the slum, the exclusion from urban facilities and foreign foods is, I would argue, doubly painful; once because you are not rich, and once because you cannot afford to buy a piece of America-in-the-Philippines.

"Symbolic capital" in Bourdieu's sense (1972:6) is clearly tied up in the Philippines with command over the goods, gestures, and language of America. The hierarchy of access to these things is neatly illustrated by the different kinds of films shown in rural and urban cinemas. While local picture houses show exclusively Tagalog films (melodramas, comedies, and violent action movies), the grandest cinemas in Naga also show some English language films. English language goes with air-conditioning in the auditorium. Even the local cinemas, however, already have their own glamor and their own linguistic shifts, since the films they show are made in the language of the capital. There are no Bicol films, although there are Bicol radio stations and newspapers. Anyone familiar with Tagalog movies will know that they too seem to offer a variant of the America-in-the-Philippines idea, with their mingling of folklore elements and exaggeratedly luxurious Manila-American settings. It is no accident that the directors so often choose stories which pit poor and virtuous characters against wealthy ones. Emerging from scenes of brocade armchairs and villains listlessly toying with plates of hotdogs and tropical fruit, my companions and I would return to the bamboo houses of the barangay, where imported canned goods are saved for fiesta, and where sometimes there is nothing to go with the daily rice.

As a result of these kinds of observations, and the apparent paucity of "traditional culture" in any easily visible form, it has often been suggested that Filipino lowland culture has been eviscerated by the American colonial experience. Even a sympathetic commentator like Neils Mulder, for example, has written that:

> The Filipinos were mentally colonized in a discourse that not only extolled American culture . . . but that also degraded the Spanish colonial past . . . aborting what could have grown into a distinct Filipino civilization. (1990:6)

Many nationalist-minded writers would agree with Mulder on the balefulness of American influence, and its result, it is argued, has been to reduce lowland culture to a "colonial mentality."[5]

I would never question the damaging effect which the political and economic subordination of the Philippines has had, nor the insidiousness of some of the cultural processes of colonization. What this paper is concerned with, however, is an argument that the people with whom I did my fieldwork engaged in a series of performances ranging from the most casual (a joke) to the most elaborate (the gay beauty contest). In these performances, the apparent "imitation" of American forms actually constituted a subtle and ironic exploration of the possibility of accessing the power of the imagined American world, through self-transformation.

These performances are largely concerned with the process of becoming beautiful (Bicol, *magayon*). The Bicol term for beauty is heard constantly both as adjective and as exclamation (*ang gayon!*) in daily conversation. It is the usual term of approval for any performance well-done, and can be stretched from a direct reference to personal attractiveness to a term almost as vague as the English "really good." I will argue that the most pertinent aspect of its meaning in Bicol is that it refers to a successful self-transformation in which one appropriates a small part of "America," and/or its many derivatives and stand-ins. Beyond that, however, I will also argue that in their focus on a learned, transformative personal aesthetics, Bicolanos are just as much like the Javanese as they are ever like the Americans.

I. "Beauty" in the rice-paddy

I will begin with the women working in the rice paddy. It was the rice planting season for the second yearly crop. A group of women had gone down to plant out two large fields for the farmer, Maria, in return for a share of the harvest. Rice planters always joke among themselves, but sharecropping produces an endless stream of jokes about the size of the harvest, the number of strips of the field the planters can cover, and whether they are going to "lose" or "win" on the deal with the farmer. When I joined them towards sunset, it was clear that the women would not finish in one day, but my friend Ilar in particular began working even faster. My appearance in Ilar's team was a fresh source of inspiration for jokes, this time on the theme of how wealthy Maria must be to hire "imported" workers from England, mixed with a lot of advice to me; "You'll have to say: I planted this, and so I'll be the one to harvest it . . . will you remember?"

As the mood of hilarity increased, so did the volume of pop music, which had been playing from a distance all afternoon, and could now be heard coming incongruously over the green expanse of the rice fields. It was a dance for young people, which was being held in the neighboring barangay. The young people's organization had hired a cassette-player and loudspeakers, and they had been playing in advance so as to advertise the evening's event, the latest Tagalog and American pop. The women in the fields began to joke about the dance (which of course as married people they would not attend), asking each other what they were going to wear, and making fun of their own ragged and muddy planting clothes by holding them out as if they were dancing-skirts. Gradually, Ilar and several others began to do a pop dance in the rice fields, wiggling their hips but with their feet stuck in the paddy.

This way of dancing as a joke and parody is something often done in Calabanga, but almost always just between women, never between men and women. Women dancing with their friends and relatives will mime romantic cheek-to-cheek clinches and passionate embraces. Dancing with real male partners is usually a much more stiff and formal business, even husbands being held at an elbow's length, or else it can sometimes be a serious display of virtuosity; tangos, sambas, and two-steps. At the same time, women dancing together will mimic Spanish and English musical idioms. A wedding I attended in the summer of 1989 between the two founding families of the barangay will serve as an example.

This was an endogamous wedding between the two main families of the barangay. As is usual in these weddings, there was a second day of celebration held by the bride's family rather than the groom's.[6] During the afternoon, men and women remained in separate groups and passed beer around. After they had been drinking for an hour or so, the women had begun to sing in turns, and to dance with each other. Women say they cannot sing unless they are "drunk," and a drinking group always reaches a point where everyone or some members of it are declared drunk. In this case, Ilar was the self-appointed first woman to become drunk, together with another friend of hers, and she went to the microphone and began to sing solos. There is a special emphasis in Bicol weddings on the solidarity of kin and on courtesy between affines; barangay-endogamous weddings mean that many people attending are both kin and affines, and consequently the stress on cooperation is especially intense. To sing a solo in Bicol is to put oneself forward, abandoning the group, and there is a slight frisson associated with being the first person to do so, though others will usually follow.

In Lent, Ilar is a skilled singer of Bicol songs, and of the Bicol Passion (the story of the death of Christ), but in this sort of mood she has a variety of party turns which are American songs in English. Her favorite ends,

> ". . . But I miss you most of all, my darling,
> When autumn leaves start to fall . . ."

Like all people in her generation, Ilar was taught some English at school, but she is not confident in the language. She has learned the song painstakingly by rote, as Bicolanos usually do. Nor is the idea of falling autumn leaves very clear to anyone there.

Ilar sings her English songs in a very different way than her Bicol ones. To begin with, she only sings them when "drunk," whereas at the opposite extreme she rarely drinks even a sip when "reading" the Bicol *Pasion*. In fact "Manay Iling is singing in English . . ." is understood by all her friends as a synonym for "Manay Iling has got drunk." This is understandable when one remembers that one drinks in order to overcome *supog* (shame, embarrassment), and hence to sing. Ilar's singing-English gestures are both more self-conscious and somehow more daring than her singing-Bicol gestures. She stands in dramatic poses which must imitate singers she has seen at singing contests, or dances, in the cinema or on her neighbor Salvaccion's T.V. She makes hand-gestures. When singing Bicol songs she usually sits relaxed and joking with other women, and when singing *Pasion* she is still and seated at the house's altar table, able to keep calmly wakeful all night, marking her turns in the long text. The riskiness and daring are conveyed as by Ilar's giggling and conspiratorial looks at the other women as she stands up to sing, and by her willingness to accept her "drunk" status. Of course, it is risky to sing solo in a language which she doesn't speak, and like many Bicolanos speaking English, Ilar must feel she is potentially exposing herself and her lack of mastery of the language so often associated with status and education.

So when Ilar sings in English, she is making herself conspicuous on an occasion which emphasizes kinship and togetherness. Secondly, the riskiness stems from the fact that she is choosing a song, one aspect of which is that it represents "high" culture, education and glamor, and which is therefore "beautiful." To overcome the risk, she has to be especially "drunk." Ilar always ends up weeping when she sings these songs. Although Bicolano songs are generally poignant and sentimental, it is not usual to weep while singing them.

I do not want to imply that the fact that the song is in English is all that it means to Ilar and her audience; of course, she chooses it because it pleases her; she likes its melancholy tune and she knows she sings it well. But its being in English does, I think, alter the song for Ilar and the other women. There is a particular élan about carrying off well a song in this foreign language, especially solo. It is, it appears, a small act of triumph; a small act of possession of this culture which largely excludes the poor. At the same time, there is a kind of nostalgia which attaches to it when sung in this context; not the nostalgia for an autumn leaf in a place on the other side of the world which evades the imagination, but a nostalgia for the fragility of this act of possession, perhaps of any acts of possession; the difficulty of appropriating fragments of this culture as your own.

Combined with this nostalgia, though, is the sense of daring which comes from performing the song—the taking part in a shared joke. Ilar and all her friends know she is not American, not a glamorous singer or film star or even a local chanteuse for a dance band, but a poor farmer with T.B. and old clothes even at a wedding. The performance is therefore partly a conspiratorial joke, a sending-up by both audience and performer of the incongruity between the standards of American stardom and the circumstance of life in the barangay. It is this kind of joke which figures constantly in daily conversation. It marks the giving of nicknames (*bansag*) for instance. One woman was introduced to me as *Maria Mayaman* (Wealthy Mary). "It's because her house is filled with radios, fridges, and electric fans," I was told. "Yes," said Maria, "If one of my fridges gets a little old, I throw it out, just like in the States." Needless to say, Maria's house does not contain even an electric point; it is one of the poorest in the barangay, with an earth floor and a leaking roof. Maria has a handicapped teenage son whom she supports by making and selling snacks among her neighbors and working in the fields.

Other jokes too play on the gap between imagined wealth, Western-style, and Bicolano realities. Typhoon damage which tears holes

in houses is ironically referred to as "air-conditioning"; feet muddy from the paddy-fields as "my manicure" and so on. Anyone who has an imminent birthday is likely to be teased by her friends dancing around her in imitation of the *pantomina*, the "love-dance" performed by bride and groom at a wedding, during which the guests are urged to pin money on their clothes. These references to splendid celebration and high living were often performed in contexts which pointed them up by contrast—when a group of women, dressed in the work-clothes, had gone to look on at a local dance they had decided they couldn't afford to attend, for instance.

Conversely, joking and teasing also takes place whenever someone does dress up or offer hospitality. One party with noodles and beer was remembered with relish for months afterwards, as people exclaimed how delicious it was, and compared it to the products of the most expensive American-style restaurants in Naga. The usual reaction when someone appears dressed for a barangay dance, wearing shoes and carefully-pressed clothes, is to suck one's teeth, make appreciative clicking noises and exclaim with emphatic admiration on the splendor of the wearer's outfit and their transformation into a beauty: *"Aba-aa na ini, an gayon-gayon mo! Ay, naka-highheels na si Manay, ay! Naka-beauty na!"* (That's too much, you're so beautiful! Ay, Elder Sister's put her high heels on! She's put her beauty on now!")

This was addressed to Celia by her neighbors and friends. She is in her late fifties and her face and body show the years of hard work, planting, harvesting, and gleaning in the fields. But although it may be partly a levelling tease, those who comment are not mocking her sarcastically, but enjoying her transformation and their own (they were all sharing the same powder puff and on the way to the same dance). Dressing up is of the greatest importance in Bicol, and costumes and uniforms, whether for religious plays, folkdances, or the schoolchildren's majorettes band, are matters for serious concern and sources of intense enjoyment.

II. The *amateuran*

If references to performance are part of the everyday currency of communication in San Ignacio, this is not surprising considering the number of opportunities to watch or take part in amateur singing contests, beauty contests, pageants, dances, and school shows. Some such event takes place in the immediate neighborhood at least once a month, and more often near fiesta.

The *amateuran* or singing competitions, attract contestants from a wide area. They arrive carefully dressed with their "minus one" tapes—tapes on which the vocalist can be turned down so that you can sing against the backing track. This is important for two reasons: firstly, it means they will have learned the song (I have watched several people do this) by literally mimicking the performance of the singer on the tape over and over again; secondly, it is the explanation for the frequent minor disaster of Bicolano *amateuran*, in which the ropy sound equipment is not equal to the task of eliminating the vocal track, and the contestant sings a duet with the artist on tape. This is not popular with audiences, and even less so the attempt sometimes made by weak competitors to "lip-sync" by miming to the sound of the original artist rather than singing themselves.

During the contest, the judges' table is gradually and ineluctably surrounded by dozens and dozens of little boys who creep forward in a squatting position until periodically shooed back by some irate barangay member or local teacher. Each judge is provided with paper and pencil, and a list of criteria on which to mark the contestants, including Voice, Diction, Artistic Interpretation, and Presentation.

The key figure at the *amateuran* is the master of ceremonies or *emcee*; there may be two male *emcees* or a man and a woman, but never a woman alone. An *emcee* is a curious mixture of folk character and figure from media entertainment. The person chosen for the job is always someone Bicolanos describe as *masuba* (jokey). Being *masuba* often implies an ability to get away with sexual joking without causing offense; for an *emcee* it means an ability to play with the potential shame and embarrassment of the situation of performing. As Apolinar Mendosa, a barangay captain and one of the two male *emcees* there, put it in part of his patter to the audience:

"Dapat sa emcee daing supog, ano?" ("An M.C. should never feel shame, should he . . . ?")

A reminder perhaps that the other situation in which Bicolanos habitually use *emcees* is at traditional weddings, when they have to set the pace of games in which guests are asked to give as much money as possible to the newlyweds. Since in most contexts in Bicol society, shame (*supog*) is positively valued, and to be classed as "shameless" is heavy criticism, the *emcee* clearly falls into a category of licensed transgressors. Demanding, giving, or refusing money is perhaps the quintessential situation in which feelings of *supog* come into play within the barangay, and the *emcee* has to dispense with shame in order to increase the pressure to give, but also mediate tensions and rivalries, as well as possible feelings of obligation and inadequacy, between the guests, so that neither donors nor recipients finally feels shamed by the amount given at the wedding. A wedding *emcee* is also *masuba*, and it would be quite possible for the same person to perform both kinds of *emcee* role.

Some contest *emcees* adopt a stylized comic manner, laughing hysterically or asking repeated stock questions. This was true of the *emcee* at the San Domingo *amateuran*, a local young married man known to be good at the role. As each contestant appeared, he would give a gasp and cry out to the audience (who were highly amused);

> *"Garo artista! Iba na an pagkaguapo kaini . . . garo mas guapo sakuya, pero kun nakaparigos ako, dai ako napadaog. . . ."*
> ("He looks like a star! The handsomeness of this one is really something else . . . could be he's more handsome than me, but if I had a chance to wash, he wouldn't have got the better of me. . . .")

This continued with each contestant, as he pointed to their shoes or suits, demanded to know whether they had fiancées and announced their availability to the young people of the barangay, and so on. Female contestants sometimes, but not always, got off more lightly than male. The teasing of the *emcee* does not stop with the introduction of each contestant, since after each entrant had sung his piece, and often in terms of fulsome praise whatever the standard of singing, which came close to sounding like mockery.

People I asked about the *emcee* would often casually remark that he was supposed to *hale an supog*—to remove their contestants' shame, by joking with them and putting them at ease. In the light of this comment, it was always striking how much *supog* the *emcee* seemed to be inflicting on the singers. In fact, I never saw a contestant attempting to match the *emcee*'s banter with their own; instead they would stand meek and still, politely answering the *emcee*'s questions with near-inaudible but formal sentences:

> *Emcee*: ". . . my goodness, this one looks like *si Richard Gomez* (a Tagalog filmstar) . . : Tell me, where did you get your *Americano* (suit)?"
> Contestant: "Sir, my brother lent it to me."

The rural teenagers thus embarrassingly compared to major Tagalog filmstars suffered it all with the same self-deprecating downcast eyes and partial smile.

The contrast is all the stronger, then, when the contestant begins to sing. They do not seem to sing as themselves. Rather, they become, as well as their (sometimes considerable) individual talents allow them, a singer, a star, the *artista* to which the *emcee* has just incongruously compared them. Gestures from Western pop performers and the Tagalog singers they influence are choreographed into the performance: careful expressions of emotional excruciation very different from the normal Filipino facial repertoire, and set-piece, conscious singer's gestures, spreading the hand with a crescendo or raising and lowering the microphone.

What is remarkable about this is the contrast between the "message" of this range of gestures which we see all the time in the West, where they lay claim to expressiveness, the outward signs of an inward (romantic and sexual) emotion demanding to be released in song and gesture—and the stiff, slightly creaky, obviously learned way in which many local singers in the Philippines perform them. This is not simply a matter of amateur versus professional, still less of degree of talent, for many of the performances are in fact of a high standard.

The best local performers go on to become the stars of the national media, achieving seamless performances of the idiom. But at the barangay *amateuran*, it is apparent that this is a learned idiom for Bicolano people, and though they may learn it well it is not the only idiom to which they are exposed, and it conflicts to some extent with the gestural language both of daily life and of other modes of performance, such as Bicol folksongs and religious performances. It is a personal transformation, and a shift in language—literally so, because Bicol songs are not used at *amateuran*, where the repertoire is always in English and Tagalog. Favorite songs performed during the summer of 1989 in Calabanga contests included (for women) a current hit called "Eternal Flame," and for men, besides several sentimental Tagalog hits, the ubiquitous "My Way," the anthem of middle-class male Filipino drinking sessions. One child performer with a precociously loud voice had been coached in a song in English called "While We're Still Young." The song had fairly explicit references to an adulterous affair which sounded odd to me coming from an eight-year old, but the audiences found the title made it appropriate enough. Two choices of song caused more of a stir: a pretty fourteen-year-old who won the contest by singing the Beatles' hit "Yesterday" (fairly new to the Philippines) in an enormously powerful voice, and a diffident young man who sang a famous Tagalog song from the 1960's star Victor Wood, "Bakit Di Kita Malimot?" (Tagalog for "Why Can't I Forget You?") This last caused a division of opinion among local audiences. This song, with a mournful, vaguely Latin-American orchestral accompaniment, builds up to a chorus in which Victor Wood was famous for ending each line on choking sob:

"Why can't I forget you?
Why can't I leave you behind? . . .
Why did you make me love you
If you only wanted to cause me pain?"

reproduced by the performer in Calabanga, sprung like the others out of his acute bashfulness. While some of the audience enjoyed this revival of an old favorite, others objected that it was unfashionable. One rival contestant disapproved of the high marks the singer had got for his technical abilities and took me aside afterwards (for I was one of the judges at this contest) to advise me that the choice of song was *badoy*-vulgar and unfitting. "He should have something classier, like Shirley Bassey," he reproved me.

The *amateuran* are enjoyable, but they are also taken very seriously, and blunders in taste, voice, or dress are very unpopular with the audience. The clothes of the performers are another area where they can triumph or be shamed. All the male contestants wore shoes, trousers, and a shirt or jacket—everyday dress is flipflops, shorts, and tattered shirts. The women wore dresses and carefully arranged hairstyles, or else the "American" teenage fashion of clean jeans and top, clothes which are otherwise kept for fiestas and other outings where it is important to be smart. Several girls attempted the look favored by Filipina filmstars and singers, of tailored skirts or dresses, *mestiza*-pale complexions and long hair held up with slides. This look is known as *simple lang* ("just simple") though in fact it is highly contrived. By this it is meant that the clothes do not have the respectable ostentation of wealthy matrons dressing in the Spanish style, with frills and decorations, nor the hard-edged bad-girl look which is associated with villainesses in film melodrama. The *simple lang* look is the look of the virtuous film heroine.

The vast majority of those who watch prefer to admire success than to laugh at blunders; what they want, it seems, is a degree of decorum to the proceedings, gravitas from the judges and a feeling that potential stars of the stature of Tagalog film celebrities like Sharon Cuneta are singing for them on the barangay stage. Indeed, I was often told whenever I went to these events, how Nora Aunor, famous since the sixties, had come from a poor family in the Bicol region.

As well as the *amateuran*, Bicol villages, towns, and cities hold large numbers of beauty contests, for girls and for married women, which are immensely popular and attract large audiences who come to assess the "beauty" of the contestants. There are also large numbers of entrants, all seeking the elation of being publicly feted as a beauty. The history of the contests is a complex one; while their current popularity seems to date back to the end of the Spanish period and the beginning of the American one (Barcenas, 1989:14), they may have developed partly out of the Catholic religious processions (many still performed) which include parts for Mary as the Queen of Heaven, for Queen Isabella or Queen Elena in the Santacruzan (Santos, 1982:35-36).

Small village contests still tend to be run as a form of bidding; whoever raises the most money for the church or a charity wins. Although the first, second, and third prizewinners keep part of the money they have raised, this system deters most poor people from entering for several reasons. Firstly, they need to find wealthy sponsors to back them with contributions; secondly, they may lose all or most of the money they raise if they are outbid by others wealthier than themselves; and thirdly, éven the winners will find their prize money expended on costumes, float for the local procession, and the obligatory "*blow out*" meal they must offer to friends, neighbors, and sponsors to celebrate their success.

In 1989, one of the main contenders for the Mrs. Calabanga title was a woman I had come to know quite well in another context, since she was also a practicing traditional healer. Nelda is large woman in her early fifties, with a reputation for being rather too clever at getting money out of people, and she was the only healer I knew of whom it was hinted that she might be a fake. Because of her husband's land-holdings and some influential connections of her own, as well as her healing, she was however a person of some power.

In the event in 1989, Nelda came third having handed in 11,000 pesos (about 300 pounds). The first place was taken by a woman who raised 63,000 pesos (about 2,100 pounds)—an enormous sum by rural Bicol standards. On the day of the parade, Nelda and her husband were seen making a special trip into Naga to buy balloons with which to decorate her float, and these alone were said to cost 500 pesos (15 pounds).

The presentation of the titles was held in the main square of Calabanga, on the evening of the town fiesta. Nelda wore a dress of yellow, spangled material which fit tightly over her matronly figure; in Bicolano's terms, she was properly dressed, but certainly not beautiful. The woman who won with her enormous bid was younger and quite pretty in local terms. Like the other winning candidates, she made a triumphal entry as a queen with entourage—though hers was much larger than anyone else's. Dressed in a long frilly white dress in the Imelda Marcos style, she was accompanied by her husband and three pairs of little children, each attired in a different form of Western or Filipino formal dress. To be eligible, the woman had to be a citizen of Calabanga, but her husband was a Chinese businessman, and it was the wealth of the Chinese community that had secured her triumph.

The audience, watching the square as the light was fading, were like all Bicolano audiences that I remember acutely interested in the poise and turn-out of the contestants, though the event was not so eagerly attended as either the young women's or the transvestite contests. People let out customary admiring comments of *magayon!* (beautiful!), but although the winner was personable, and audiences are very interested in that, there is another kind of beauty to which these contestants were here staking a claim—the beauty achieved by having grand clothes and complete make-up, a float and attendants, and the assurance and poise which come with having skills and connections enough to place yourself on the stage, to take yourself out of the barangay and to demand and receive acknowledgment and admiration.

By contrast, the larger beauty contests are run on principles thought to represent all that is American and progressive, and are known as "brains and beauty only" contests. They include both the major women's contest, the Miss Bicolandia, and the main *bakla* or male transvestite beauty contest, the Miss Gay Naga City and Miss Gay Peñafrancia title. Both are held at the time of the regional fiesta for the Virgin of Peñafrancia in Naga City, the regional capital of Bicol. But before I describe the Miss Gay contest for 1988, at which I was a judge, I need to clarify the position of *bakla* in Bicol society.

III. The *bakla* as experts in the creation of "beauty"

Like everyone else in Bicol, most *bakla* have parents who are poor farmers or farm laborers like the women with whom I started this paper. *Bakla* are regarded with a peculiar mixture of acceptance and potential lack of respect or even contempt in Bicol society. For the purposes of this essay, it is inappropriate to give a very full account of the lives of some the *bakla* who I knew in Bicol.[7] However, it is significant that although *bakla* sometimes call themselves "gays," using the English word, they entirely reject the Western understanding of gay sexuality, that is, that gay men are those who desire other gay men. Most *bakla* I knew had never heard of this definition of being gay, and they vehemently deny either that they would ever be attracted to each other, or that their boyfriends are gay in any sense. *Bakla* say they are men "with women's hearts" who therefore love men, and love to dress in women's clothing and perform female roles. Or else, in a curious adoption of another English term, they say they are a "third sex," neither men nor women. This, at least, is part of the discourse of being *bakla*.

Bakla generally say that, although their powers of attraction and seduction may be intense, their ability to keep a boyfriend will always be threatened by the fact that they have no womb and cannot bear a child; the sharing of children being the essential fact which makes Bicol marriage permanent. Because of this, they often look for younger boyfriends, to whom they become a kind of financial sponsor, paying for their education or to set them up in business, while nevertheless casting themselves in the role of housewife and emotional dependent. *Bakla* in public discussion claim an identification with female sexual identity in their relationships, but men who have been involved with *bakla* tend to cast them as sexual aggressors, almost as sexual predators, though in other respects they will boast that they had their *bakla* lover in a state of subservience and willingness to do whatever they asked which exceeds that of even the most devoted wife.

Inside the barangay, however, *bakla* are in some ways entirely accepted. Many mothers calmly admit that one of their children is *bakla*, and most people agree on the identifications: "That's just how he is," they will say, or "that's just what's natural to him." Although some *bakla* may never join the *bakla* subculture, most will do so, associating with other *bakla* in small town centers and especially in the cities. They may well be unable to leave their parents' homes and the ricefield work in the barangays entirely, but *bakla* feel a pull towards a more urban life, and tend to shun agricultural work if they can. They often try to look for money outside the barangay, possibly as a domestic servant, but more usually by setting themselves up in one of the very numerous small beauty shops which can be found in every tiny Filipino town, servicing the huge demand for dressing up even among the poor. Women and *bakla* in fact divide the beauty and dressmaking businesses between them, and public opinion holds that while women may be more trustworthy, *bakla* are more artful in altering appearances. They therefore occupy a very particular position as mediators of beauty and glamor. As all Bicolanos say, "*Matibayon mag-arog an mga bakla*", "The *bakla* are very clever at imitating things," implying a sense not just of being good at mimicry, but at making things look like other things. As hairdressers, dressmakers, and beauticians in an area which, even in the rural barangays, is intensely interested in putting on a different appearance, the *bakla* are the experts in transformation; they transform others into beauties in their professional lives, and transform themselves into beauties in their private—or at least their performative—lives.

The *bakla* in fact often seem to assimilate their identity to a language of visibility and hyper-visibility, referring to themselves as an "*apir*" (a word seemingly derived from the English "appearance") and talking about their power to seduce as "exposing ourselves." A common *bakla* greeting is to say "How is your beauty?" instead of "How are you?" and to substitute in ordinary conversation the phrases "my beauty" for "myself" and "your beauty" for "yourself." Little children in the barangays are taught another *bakla* greeting as a joke to amuse their elders; one person claps the raised hand of another and exclaims, "*Apir*, now, because you are a *bakla*!"

The elite among the *bakla* are often those who started out from wealthier backgrounds than the average. They may run successful businesses based between Naga and Manila, making enough money to enable them to become patrons of the gay community and prominent citizens. The dressmaker Bingbing Suarez, the founder of the Miss Gay contest, is an attorney's son who speaks English and has spent a period working abroad in Saudi Arabia; he also sponsors his own basketball team.

Most *bakla* make their livings in much cheaper and less sophisticated surroundings. A small town *bakla* beauty parlor is a place with a definite ambience. In Calabanga, the parlor was a small, open-fronted shop near the main market next to a grain dealer's. It had a mirror and a shabby dresser, which the *bakla* later sold to pay off a debt, even though it belonged to the landlady, causing her to launch a stream of complaints about the financial untrustworthiness of *bakla*. There was a fairly steady stream of female customers of all ages, though few adult men. The original hairdresser in this shop was a melancholic *bakla* with waist-length hair called Mona. But after the incident over the dresser, Mona was replaced by Linda. Linda's mother, a farmer's wife in her seventies, would drop into the shop each afternoon after shopping for food, and was always treated with politeness and affection by the *bakla* who used the shop as a meeting-place and base for their boyfriend-hunting forays.

When Linda's mother was not there, however, the shop was notable for the continuous card-playing which went on hidden under the table, the surplus of manicurists which meant that customers had to be shared out, not always without squabbles, and especially for the continuous performance of "being *bakla*" which Linda and her friends gave for each other. The following description is taken from notes from a hot afternoon in July.

Linda is in fairly usual form, keeping up a hysterical conversation while cutting the hair of a young woman into a fashionable bob. Apparently, Linda is paying no attention whatsoever to the haircut, casting occasional sidelong glances at the progress of the work as if it were something somebody else was doing. She pauses, on the other hand for long periods to strike a pose in front of the mirror and exclaim to the room; *"magayon!"* (I'm beautiful!) or *"Gi'till!"* (Vanity!). Her client, though, can see that the haircut is going well, and is gradually assuming a smug expression. Whenever she stops her strenuous mode of conversation, which consists mostly of shrieks, screams, and giggles, Linda looks rather exhausted. A woman friend comes in, with a new boyfriend and Linda screams a greeting:

"'My Jesus, *amiga*, you made such a clever choice! . . . He's so good-looking! . . . I'm falling in love . . . do you mind? Do you want a haircut? Let Tess do it—I'm going to do your boyfriend's nails myself.' Linda places a hand over her heart; 'What a choice,' she repeats, 'not like Tess, she'll take any man as long as he's big,' and then correcting himself with another shriek, 'O *kieme*! Don't be angry now, will you?'"

Of course, Linda's conversation is an act, but it's an act which all the *bakla* deliberately and rhetorically deploy: the idea that they are vain, trivial, charming, infuriating, flirtatious, and hysterical, an idea represented in talking *kieme*—the gay slang (*swardspeak*) for nonsense, mischief, and naughtiness. This process of continuously performing an identity was something Linda personally perhaps took to extremes, but all the *bakla* I knew would switch in and out of it according to who they were dealing with.

It is not only women's contests which are ubiquitous in the barangays and small towns of Bicol. The large Miss Gay contest, held annually, is part of a growing network of smaller contests throughout the region, all of which are proving popular with rural audiences. It is due to Bingbing Suarez the dressmaker, and a group of other elite *bakla* and their friends in Naga, that these contests have moved over the past 25 years from being private subcultural events, to being large scale public ones whose respectability is guaranteed by their appeal to progressive and sophisticated Western standards of organization and high levels of taste and skill. But it is equally only because of the responsive chord which Bingbing's shows struck with the public—most of whom are poor people who do not pay for seats—that Bingbing's claims were able to carry conviction. By 1987, for instance, a huge audience sat through a tropical downpour rather than miss the contest. My argument, therefore, is that the Miss Gay contest is essentially a popular festival, though its performers are drawn from a subculture.

I have said that *bakla* are known for their artistry in creating beauty. The crucial and extraordinary thing about the Miss Gay contests is that they create themselves as beauties. As *bakla* see it, the social respect they have won comes from their skill in achieving a dazzling self-transformation. A *bakla* trader, Titong, explained this;

"People say that if you put the Miss Bicolandia show against the Miss Gay contest it is altogether more beautiful than those of real women, and they say that the gays look more truly womanly in their movements when they are . . . modeling on the stage . . . ." And I did indeed hear people remark over and over again on the beauty of the *bakla*. It was a subject which fascinated most people who had seen the show: "The real women are defeated by them; they really look beautiful," was a typical remark. People would speculate on how they achieved their effects, or relate stories about men who fell in love with beautiful *bakla* and courted them as if they were women. Though there was some disapproval in the attitude to *bakla* and their "artful," flighty ways, there was also a genuine wonder and delight in their achievement of beauty.

The audience's recognition that they are like women—or even better—is terribly important to the *bakla*. But when I asked them about the experience of performing in the contest, they always replied in slightly different terms. The experience was always one of happiness, they said, "When I am up on the stage, . . . my feelings are really truly happy." But the reason for this happiness was not just that you felt like a woman, but that you felt like a star. "If you win," said Pablo, "it's as if you are famous (*sikat*) just for the evening . . . you feel as if you . . . will be recognized . . . if you have been Miss Gay." "Do you feel that you're a woman?" I asked. "I'm a woman then! And then, I'm really very happy . . . because . . . enough to say . . . it's like I'm becoming a *superstar.*" Or as Titong says "If you win, it means that you are *deserving. That night you're the best.* You're the most beautiful, the cleverest. . . . *That is once in your life* that you will have something to say for yourself . . ." This triumph, however, is achieved only by the exercise of all the *bakla*'s artistry and by the constant practice of walking, smiling, posing, and practicing English in the weeks before the contest. As Titong says, "You have to research how to be in a beauty contest." The greatest shame that a *bakla* contestant can imagine is that "People would find fault with you and say you hadn't studied it." The beauty of the *bakla* is artistry.

The following account is taken largely from my fieldnotes for the Miss Gay contest of September, 1988:

The preparations have dominated Bingbing's house for weeks. All Bingbing's seamstresses are employed making the contestants' orders. Several at once are bent over a violet and white sparkly evening gown with white and silver flowers embroidered down the front; it has a boned bodice and a tube skirt which break into layers of frills at the knees. This means it gives *bakla* figures a lot of shape, and so it will be popular with them. The seamstresses are also fielding *bakla* contestants turning up to register their applications from all over the province. These beauties, as yet dressed only in their everyday streetwear of jeans and feminine tops preen themselves in front of Bingbing's long mirror and make sudden little squeaks and exclamations.

Pablo, Bingbing's *bakla* domestic servant, has a slight squint and is a little thin. He dreams of entering the grand contests, but confines himself to the smalltown ones where competition is less intense. He spends hours trying the dresses against himself in the mirror; "I look like the Madonna of the Rosaries" he sighs, holding up a blue one.

The contestants have been whittled down to 22. Swimsuit heats, were held at the municipal pool, in standard high-cut red costumes which duplicate exactly the ones made for the Miss Bicolandia contest; Bingbing has made them. The contestants, naturally hairless, cunningly padded, genitals plastered flat with tape, are breathtakingly convincing as girls with few exceptions . They have learned the teetering walk in high heels, the pose with the hand on the hip, and the flashing smile, winningly sustained at all moments except when actually answering a judge's question.These smiles are in fact held with a terrible determination. I have seen Pablo practicing all these techniques at home; the *bakla* teach them to each other.

On the evening of the finals, the make-up artist Ray Mandong is rushing about between faces. I am put into one of Bingbing's formal creations in cream frills and covered in Revlon in order to pass muster as a judge. I notice that Ray and I have exactly the same make-up, but he can make my fringe stick up higher in the favored style, as I have more hair. When I joined the other judges (three female dignitaries including the vice-mayor, one male counsellor, and two female beauty-queens), the stage is brilliantly lit with expensive sound equipment in place, and the plaza is absolutely packed. As the evening wears on, more and more people cram in, leaning out of restaurant windows or peeking round the wings—to Bingbing's fury, as a video is being made, and the raggedy boys spoil the opulent view. The *bakla* who are not competing are mostly in women's clothes, and busy with arrangements. Ray has become "Renata." Bingbing says he is too old and fat to wear a dress anymore; possibly he is also a little too dignified these days.

In fact, the acts are highly accomplished, the dancing fantastic, the audience's admiration genuine. The *bakla* have chosen stage names—Barbra Ledesma from Ligao, Ging-Ging Padilla from Pili, Alice Robles Narvades from Naga—which recall Tagalog filmstars, and old Spanish elites. Most of them are simply dazzling. Jennifer de Asis appears looking fragile in a white, empire-line evening dress trimmed with silver; feeling the admiration of the audience, she lifts up her arms, spreading the cloth like wings, and gives an angelic smile. Claudine Louise Ferrari, with severe waxed chignon and a gown hand-painted with pastel-colored flowers (she has a rich sponsor in Manila, a boyfriend perhaps), provokes admiring comment even from Bingbing, who declares her turnout "quality." The close-up photos taken by Naga's photographers and sold in local shops for weeks after the event, reveal a little more the large hands or too-broad shoulders. But for the moment on stage, the *bakla* are beautiful and elated, and the audience is elated with them and caught in their triumphant beauty.

As the contestants begin to enter to show their daytime outfits, I notice a group of fantastically-dressed *bakla* sitting at a table to my right. One has flowing auburn hair and a peacock-colored satin dress; another is (in a country of short people) almost six feet tall and wears a streaked blonde chignon and a black and pink satin dress with a thigh-high split. These amazing creatures are last year's title holders, and members of the Naga-Manila beautician elite in their daytime jobs. They sit glamorously sulking at the thought of handing over their crowns in an hour or so.

After the talent section, which featured a lip-sync to Judy Garland's "New York, New York," and a scene lifted from a Tagalog melo-drama in which a famous star portrays a mad beggar woman, came the questions and answers. The questions, in declamatory English, had been carefully set by Bingbing to be "beautiful, not vulgar." Nevertheless, those on politics and ethics received only vague replies. Other questions, a little less beautiful, seemed easier to answer:

Q: What part of a man's body most attracts you and why?
A: The part of a man's body that most attracts me is . . . whatever part that you think it is.

Q: If you found out that your boyfriend is also gay like you, what is your reaction?

A: I would feel deteriorated (sic), but then we could get togeth-er, after all there are plenty of men and we could look for new ones together.

Q: If you were the first gay saint, what is the first miracle that you would do?
A: Well, if it was up to me, I would arrange it so that all the *bakla* would be made into real women!

At three o'clock in the morning, Barbra Ledesma is made Miss Gay Peñafrancia and receives her crown from the last year's sulking beauties, who are in tears. The audience begins to drift away, but the atmosphere is still one of lightness and festivity. Miss Gay Naga City has her picture taken with her old mother. Someone remarks to Ray the beautician, "What a waste of your beauty, Ray, that there is no dance."

Bakla often account for the imaginative appeal of their show in terms of its elite characteristics. "People like to see something un-usual," says Titong, "it is not an ordinary thing to see and so it has a more beautiful appearance . . . my group (of friends) here are elite people, they have very high taste. . . . People are happy to see some-thing so rare. . . ." This view of the show as high taste and artistry is also that adopted by those leading citizens who support the *bakla*, and wish to take a progressive standpoint. The young mayor of Naga, opening the 1988 contests, remarked that its huge popularity "Is a sign that gays are being rendered due recognition and respect in their chosen field and personality . . . the third sex is already accepted . . ."

IV. The power of appearances

What the *bakla* purvey on the stages of beauty contests is of course the same thing that is aimed at in women's contests and *amateuran*, that is, "beauty." But this "beauty," although one variant of it may be praised in terms of its apparent "simplicity" is actually far more than a particular series of culturally-approved bodily and facial features.

One of the meanings of this beauty is clearly what we would call glamor: the glamor of wealth in a poor country, of dazzling clothes and make-up, of poised and practiced, artificially-cultivated walks and voices; of feet balanced on high heels and hair held up with pins and spray; of imperfections cunningly disguised and seemingly vanished away; of different costumes for day and evening chosen with a cultivated taste, and creative interpretations of national dress which derive from a manufactured national culture. Of the ability to speak in foreign tongues, and the effect of a style of moving "more in *islow-motion*," which for *bakla* demands an English word to summon up its allure.

Clearly, this way of constructing beauty as glamor relates to the unequal histories and positions of the Philippines and America. What I have been stressing in this paper, particularly, is that these performances deal with the *imagined* America which is experienced as a key source of power and allure.

I would also argue, though, that the meanings of the *bakla* performance do not relate only to the West, but also to wider and more familiarly Southeast Asian themes. I would suggest that the beauty contest is very similar to what in other Southeast Asian cultures would be identified as a festival or ritual of *alus* (refined) culture, though in the Philippines this comes a bit disguised by the fact that the source of what is *alus* is not the courtly rituals of Geertz's Balinese Negara (Geertz, 1980) but America and the world of Tagalog films. However, the two are similar in that they propose a model of "beauty" which comes from the "outside," that this beauty confers and raises status, and that it is an idea of beauty as in part an aesthetic performance—a series of gestures and ways of dressing which have to be learned and practiced, and not simply physically inherited.

One implication is particularly important. The idea of voyages in search of power and knowledge which comes from the "outside" is one found in many cultures throughout Southeast Asia. What this means in the context of the continually historically changing nature of that "outside" is a point incisively taken up by Jane Atkinson in a recent article on the Wana. For the Wana, she notes, the sources of knowledge and power are various, spanning the forest and the state, and this state in turn includes "both the traditional *negara* and more recent colonial and national institutions" (Atkinson, 1990: 80). I have argued that the *bakla* place enormous importance on "studying" the techniques and knowledge of the beauty which they must perform, and in the processes of close imitation. It is more than possible, then, to see the *bakla* contests (and other similar performances in Bicol) as a transformation which depends on this process of gathering and mastering knowledge from the "outside." From the Southeast Asian angle, the whole performance can be seen as one which, for both contestants and audience, celebrates the acquisition of "exogamous powers" (Atkinson, 1990: 80).

In this sense, the *bakla* contest, and the "happiness" it creates for both performers and spectators, is an extraordinary achievement. The *bakla* allow the audience to see and delight in an impossibly audacious act of self-transformation, in which they put on not just the clothes of another gender, but of another culture. In doing so, the *bakla* overcome in a spectacular fashion the shame which afflicts all performers in Bicol, and which has to be transcended in order to become, temporarily, a *superstar*, integrating Western glamor into your own person. In attempting this transcendence through beauty, moreover, the contest can never be merely imitative of American standards, but must integrate them into what is really a different aesthetic, and one very characteristic of other Southeast Asian cultures, which aspires towards a cultivated, harmonious style of beauty.

Though the *bakla* may be able to create the moment of stardom much more vividly than the poor women, often including their own mothers, who still have their feet stuck in the paddy fields, there is a sense too in which their attempt to become glamorous, accomplished figures is bound to be frustrated. The aspirations of Southeast Asian transvestites towards the *alus* are always in tension with counterimages of them as vulgar, trivial, and kasar. James Peacock's book *Rites of Modernisation* (1987) on Indonesian transvestites provides an illustration of this. Bicolano *bakla* always have to reckon with the perception that they are artful, affected, and vain. They are, after all, it's said, only pretending to be women, and in a sense, the more elaborate and effective the pretence, the more risible they seem. It is also thought that *bakla* can easily slip over the line and become *bastos* (vulgar, obscene).

The illusion is always a fragile one. At amateur singing contests, the entrants are shamed by the *emcee* and transcend that shame in order to become stars for a little while. But the lives of *bakla* are constantly poised on the edge of shame and humiliation, their position and the respect they are given always ambivalent; they do not need to be specially shamed on the stage. The way the *bakla* show hovers between dazzling success on the one hand, and obvious failure on the other—for the *bakla* can never transform themselves into real women whatever arts they exercise—makes it an appropriate metaphor for the position of poor Bicolanos in general faced with the problem of confronting American culture. They may try on its clothes for a few hours, but for most people the transformation into an American singer—or an American resident—is as impossible as changing sex.

Lest this should seem to place too much emphasis on the ultimate frustrations of Bicolano performances let me add that there are aspects of these contests and competitions which suggest a certain degree of distancing from the imperatives of American culture. Firstly, as I have said, some of the immediate referents of the performances are not American models themselves, but stars and productions from the national film industry in Manila, made in Tagalog, the language of the Manila area. Without the space to describe different kinds of Tagalog films here, I can only say that although the visual imagery is heavily American-influenced, it also displays a certain domestication of Western standards, and the stars of the films are Westernized Filipinos, not Americans. It could be said, therefore, that the Bicolano performers are aiming at transforming themselves into a kind of star who already represents some degree of successful integration of foreign, American glamor.

Secondly, I have argued that there is an element in all Bicolano performances, from the most casual to the most formal, which, despite the skill and enthusiasm with which they are enacted, keeps the standards of American glamor at a distance by constantly pointing at its incongruity in the lives of "those who have nothing." It is this distancing which makes the *bakla* such powerful and appropriate performers of the glossiest and most striking enactment of American beauty. In so far as the *bakla* contest implies the impossibility of appropriating things American, it also does so in a way which can be seen as making a joke of it. The very distance which people keep between themselves and the *bakla*, the view that *bakla* are potentially ludicrous and vulgar, allows the possibility of making light of their failure. The *bakla* performance is merely the most spectacular of a range of Bicolano performances which become both serious and joking, as they deal with the possibilities and limits of self-transformation.

This brings us back to the experience of shame in performance, and what it is based on. Although again there is no space to describe it here, I should mention that Bicolanos say that they experience shame in many other performance contexts, not only in those which borrow American idioms. In particular, shame afflicts spirit mediums when they have to become possessed in seance by the "people we cannot see" or spirits. Because of this and other aspects of Bicolano life I discuss elsewhere,[8] I would argue that shame is essentially experienced in the process of claiming an identity or relationship with a person thought of as being hierarchically superior to oneself—whether this is a spirit or a filmstar. The whole network of Bicolano performances can therefore be seen in a wider context in which Bicol culture turns centrally on claiming and transcending asymmetrical relationships, though not always in the same way. In the case of the beauty and singing contest performers who experience the "happiness" of becoming "superstars," this transcendence takes the form of a transformation of identity, in which, by temporarily sharing in the identity of the powerful, distant, and much-imagined other, one also makes the other a little more like oneself, and so for a moment integrates a little of the imagined "America" into the Philippines.

In writing about the way Bicolanos deal with an imagined West, I am aware that I am touching on areas recently discussed by writers on "postmodernism" such as James Clifford, George Marcus (Clifford, 1988; Clifford and Marcus, 1986), and others. These authors have raised the problem of internationalization in terms of cultural authenticity and cultural innovation. Their critique calls for an anthropology which recognizes the reinvention of cultural difference by non-Western societies exposed to the often destructive invasions of the West.

Despite the obvious relevance of this to the situation in Bicol, in practice there is little ethnography of changing cultures in their books, and little to indicate concretely how they imagine innovation and continuity to interact, either in social process or in individual lives. The potential problem in focusing on a postmodern condition of "offcenteredness" is that it threatens to become a new kind of universalism, concealing rather than revealing the many ways in which difference can be reinvented. It is an obvious point that no culture, however drastic its invasion by Westernization, can come adrift from its own history, and no culture can undergo the same process of transformation as any other. In fact, in the apparent mimicry of Western forms in Bicolano popular performances, I would argue that we can actually see a contemporary manifestation of a long-standing way of formulating relations with the "outside" in the Philippines.

The history of performances which use imported texts brought by colonial powers is a long one in Bicol and the Philippines. Each of these kinds of performance has its own styles and historical development, and each deserves to be examined separately in its own context. There are, however, some striking continuities at least in the ways in which they have been assessed by outside observers. Spanish travellers in the 19th century tended to dismiss Bicolano *comedias* and other Spanish-derived folk dramas as crude, derivative, and ridiculous. Guerra described a play given in Spanish in Legazpi in 1856:

> The performers had chosen a play taken from Persian history. The language was Spanish and the dresses were, to say the least, eccentric . . . . The actors walked on, chattering their parts, which not one of them understood, and moving their arms up and down . . . their countenances were entirely devoid of expression and they spoke like automatons . . . . (quoted in Realubit, 1983:217)

Even when the plays were adapted and translated into Bicol, as was common from at least the 1860s, travellers such as Jagor "Found it difficult to understand how the latter were persuaded to spend so much time and money upon a matter they seemed so thoroughly indifferent to" (quoted in Realubit, 1983:218).

It is impossible to know what the Albay performers made of the plot from Persian history, but whether or not they were indifferent to it as a story, even to the meaning of the words they had learned in Spanish, they clearly were not indifferent to the act of memorizing and speaking those words, wearing the costumes and taking part in the performance.

The text of the *comedia* in Bicol was not known and performed by as many people as the text of the sung Passion story, to which I referred at the beginning of this paper. However, it was one of a range of performances in which the point and the pleasure was clearly derived from the fact of the performance itself and not from the (Spanish standards of) acting style or plot development.

I have suggested in this paper that this is also part of the pleasure of modern performances in Bicol which use idioms thought of as "American." The apparent mimicry of these performances overlooks the different meaning of imitation in the Philippines and in the West. To take part in such a performance is both to move towards the pleasures of empowerment which come with "knowing the words" of a text and making it one's own, and also to move towards a transformation in which what is distant, powerful, and oppressive is brought closer and made more equal. In transforming yourself, in the process of becoming "beautiful," one also transforms the other.

Perhaps I can end with just one more set of faces in performance. I have said that Ilar, my friend who sang at the wedding, is also a skilled singer of the Bicol-language Passion story, which is performed as a Lenten devotion. She and others are so skilled in the metrical text that they can play a devotional game with it known as the *pagtapat*, in which two teams ask and answer religious riddles improvised on the spot in the traditional meter, rhyme and tune of the Passion text. Watching the *pagtapat*, which is now performed less and less often, it seemed to me that the singers' faces showed a pleasure, a confidence in their control of the text which was a more real mastery than the nervous elation of the beauty candidates and pop singers. Yet the *pagtapat* (and other practices which are coming to be defined by local intellectuals as "Bicol culture") were colonial productions too, though they were introduced by the Spanish and not by the Americans. Though it is sung with such familiar authority, it may not even have existed in its present form before 1866 according to some authorities (Javellana, 1988:235). The *pagtapat* players had made that text their own, so they could voice it with confidence, and yet it was being displaced by other colonial texts which are perhaps less confidently mastered, but more imperative. The constant in Bicol history has been, perhaps, not content, but process, and part of this process has been the making and remaking of relationships with the colonial other and the learning and relearning of texts, which at some point become more one's own than what follows. In Bicol, it is sometimes hard to draw the line between the "happiness" of successful self-transformation, and the "tristesse" of dislocation and loss.

NOTES

1. Popular religious performances are discussed in section two of Cannell (1991).

2. In the barangay, all my research was conducted in Bicol, which was preferred even by local schoolteachers. Most people found the prospect of talking to me in English enormously embarrassing, and never did so. In a few cases, usually in the city, highly-educated people or those used to a high degree of "code-switching," would talk to me in English or a mixture of languages. Where people have used occasional English phrases, this is indicated in the text by italics.

3. The average riceland cultivated in San Lucas was less than 0.5 hectares (Jo Asug, personal communication), whereas local farmers estimate that between 1.5 and 3 hectares (depending on the rate payable to the landowner) is needed to make a living in the current conditions in which purchase of fertilizer, pesticide, and high-yielding seed is an inescapable part of farming.

4. The range of ways in which people imagine and relate to different kinds of sources of power are described in Cannell (1991).

5. For a full discussion of this literature, see Cannell (1991: 18-37).

6. It is usual throughout the lowland Philippines for the groom's family to bear the cost of the wedding, as well as gifts to the bride and her family. Brideservice was common in Bicol until the 1940s, but is now rare.

7. It is not my intention here either to make claims to an inside knowledge of the sexual lives of *bakla* people I knew (which would be presumptuous) or to write a paper on gender in Bicol (although I hope to do so in a future publication). This paper describes—and is intended to celebrate—the *bakla* performance and some of the public rhetoric of *bakla* identity.

8. See Cannell, (1991) and (1992) for further discussion, and comparison with the historical analysis made by Rafael (1988). This is a complex issue, which I hope to take up in future publications.

WORKS CITED

Atkinson, Jane Monnig. 1990. "How gender makes a difference in Wana society, " in *Power and Difference; Gender in Island Southeast Asia*. Jane Atkinson and Shelley Errington, eds. Stanford, Stanford University Press.

Barcenas, Diosdado C. 1989. "The Beauties of Yesteryears" in *Women's Journal* magazine, April 22, 1989. Manila, Philippines.

Berger, John. 1988. *Pig Earth*. London, Hogart Press.

Bourdieu, Pierre. 1986. *Distinction: A Social Critique of the Judgement of Taste*. Trans. by Richard Nice. London, Routledge

Cannell, Fenella. 1991. *Catholicism, Spirit Mediums and the Ideal of Beauty in a Bicolano Community, Philippines*. University of London, unpublished PhD thesis.

Clifford, James. 1988. *The Predicament of Culture; Twentieth Century Ethnography, Literature and Art*. Cambridge, Massachusetts and London, Harvard University Press.

Clifford, James and George E. Marcus. 1986. *Writing culture; the Poetics and Politicals of Ethnography*. Berkeley, University of California Press.

Geertz, Clifford. 1976. *The Religion of Java*. Chicago, University of Chicago Press.

_____. 1980. *Negara: the Theatre State in Nineteenth Century Bali*. Princeton, Princeton University Press.

Javellana, Rene B. 1988. *Casaysayan nang pasiong mahal ni Jesucristong panginoon natin na sucat ipag-alab nang puso nang sinomang babasa*. With an introduction, annotations and translation of the 1882 edition. Quezon City, Ateneo de Manila University Press.

Levi-Strauss, Claude. 1975. *Tristes tropiques*. New York, Atheneum.

Mulder, Niels. 1990. *Appreciating Lowland Christian Filipino Culture*. Bielfield, Southeast Asia Program Working Paper No. 141.

Peacock, James. 1987. *Rites of Modernization: Symbols and Social Aspects of Indonesian Proletarian Drama*. Chicago, University of Chicago Press.

Pinches. 1991. "The working class experience of shame, inequality and people power in Tatalon, Manila," in Benedict J. Kerkvliet and Resil B. Mojares, eds. *From Marcos to Aquino: Local Perspectives on Political Transition in the Philippines.* Quezon City, Ateneo de Manila University Press.

Rafael, Vicente L. 1988. *Contracting Colonialism: Translation and Christian Conversion in Tagalog Society Under Early Spanish Rule.* Ithaca, Cornell University Press.

Realubit, Maria Lilia F. 1983. *Bikolanos of the Philippines.* Naga City, A.M.S. Press.

Santos, Luz Mendoza. 1982. *The Philippine Rites of Mary.* Manila.

Wikan, Unni. 1990. *Managing Turbulent Hearts: a Balinese Formula for Living.* Chicago, University of Chicago Press.

NINE

Ideas on Philippine Violence: Assertions, Negations and Narrations

JEAN-PAUL DUMONT

ONE OF THE PROBLEMS WITH VIOLENCE IS THAT WE ALL KNOW INTUITIVELY and experientially what it means. It is immediately obvious and commonsensical, and this is clearly why it is problematic. In his attempt to answer the question, "is an ethnography of violence possible?" Jean Jamin (1984: 17 [my trans.]) with perhaps even too much assurance and certitude—for doubt itself must be doubted—makes this remark: "The notion of violence concerns phenomena that are sufficiently heterogeneous to make them sociologically inoperational; its proteiform and polysemic character almost prevents anyone from defining it" (Jamin 1984: 17 [my trans.]).[1]

And thus I shall not attempt to define what escapes definition. In a minimalist vein, however, I understand the word to refer perhaps to the use of, and always to the abuse of force. Because violence remains hopelessly entangled with the issue of legitimacy, it is fair and necessary to state, once more, that I have no pretension to objectivity. There are villains in my biased story, and I shall let them wear the black hats. This said, my concern here is limited to documenting violence in a specific context, although I shall focus less on the real thing than on the concept of violence, its virtuality.

If actual violence is necessarily the manifestation of a conflict, understanding such conflict and violence cannot be achieved without placing them in their cultural context. Anthropologists can assume that much. Violence is expressive. Violence is also expressed. It is at once representation and represented, at once manipulative and manipulated. It is the strength of such a manipulation that I would like to emphasize here, by reflecting on my ethnographic experience of the Philippines. Limited though it may be, it will allow me to be at once minute and concrete—in short, to be attentive to details that might otherwise escape the attention of those who focus too narrowly on actual events alone or exclusively on sociopolitical institutions. The thicker, fuller, or denser the description, presumably the rounder the hermeneutic yield.

What historically passes for the first encounter between the West and the Philippines—Magellan's arrival in Cebu in 1521—was violent from the onset. Humabon who ruled on Cebu was hastily converted to Christianity and encouraged to recognize the suzerainty of the Spanish Crown, or else. And Magellan never finished the first circumnavigation for which he is nonetheless credited, as he was defeated by Lapu-Lapu who ruled on the neighboring island of Mactan and thus became the first nationalist hero of the Philippines.

I might as well jump to Marcos's dictatorship since the history of the Philippine is nothing but an incessant succession of political conflicts and uncontrolled violence: piracy, abductions, revolts, revolutions, occupation, and resistance succeed one another. Ferdinand Marcos, elected President in 1965, declared martial law in 1972 and thus seized power until "people power" and the "revolution" of February 1986 brought him and his administration down, with Corazon Aquino's democratic but frail triumph.

To evoke the notion of violence when speaking of the Philippines seemed to me, in my fieldworking experience at the end of the Marcos regime and before the assassination of Benigno Aquino on August 21, 1983,[2] a little farfetched. Of course, I knew of the historical forces that had shaped the present Philippines. From Magellan's arrival and his demise in 1521[3] to the imposition of martial law by Ferdinand Marcos in 1972 and thereafter, a quasi-uninterrupted succession of violent political turmoils had given to the Philippines its identity and originality. The Moro raids,[4] the Dagohoy revolt,[5] the revolution of 1896,[6] the Japanese occupation,[7] the Huk rebellion,[8] or, today, the confrontation between the NPA[9] and the MNLF[10] on one hand and the troops of the regime on the other hand, were all sufficient reminders of a situation that year after year had been tense, if not explosive.

And yet, between such an abstract knowledge and my concrete experience of the Philippines as I lived it, there was a great deal of distance, a fundamental discrepancy. Certainly there were private armed and uniformed guards almost everywhere in the cities of Manila and Cebu, and I could not pretend to ignore them, even though there were hardly any on the small and altogether out-of-the-way province-island of Siquijor. And in front of my very own eyes, school children were regularly involved in elaborate and compulsory paramilitary exercises. But, at once, the posting of uniformed guards as well as the martial training of the young appeared to be undertaken with a substantial amount of bonhomie—with good humor and a sense of humor—which seemed to guarantee that presumably things would not get out of hand. After all, even the Philippine Constabulary Officer who had come to check on my wife and myself about a week after our installation had paid to us what he called "only a courtesy call." I perceived then and there little tension. Troubles were or seemed to be elsewhere. In this general social and political atmosphere, "martial law, Philippine style" was a phrase, the popularity of which was in tune with the famous or infamous concept of "smooth interpersonal relationship."[11] And most of my informants displayed the expected and proper modesty and shyness amidst a profusion of endless smiles.

In the isolation that our insularity guaranteed, it was all too easy to forget that perhaps our hosts' smiles, their suavity, their pretense to be light and merry, real as all this might have been, deliberately obfuscated a contrary aspect of their culture. All happened as if the Siquijorians made a special effort to impress on us that erratic violence was, if it had ever been anything else, a thing of the past. And indeed people, in town as well as in the *barangay*,[12] seemed to emphasize the same theme: "On this island of ours"—some 75,000 persons, more than 80 percent of them Roman Catholics and more than 99 percent Cebuano native speakers, inhabited its 350 square kilometers—"harmony is in order." It was a matter of *angay*, which signified the evenness of treatment between people, their equality. As a verb, this word connoted "agreement" and also referred to the tuning of musical instruments. It was in addition a matter of *uyun*. As an adjective, the word meant "parallel." In the present derivative sense, it referred to "getting along with," to "adjusting to each other." Both *angay* and *uyun* were concepts that implied a sentiment of achieved equality between people.

But the metaphor that people preferred to use for our benefit was slightly different. In fact, it was almost exclusively, but repeatedly, expressed in English, in one single stock phrase that suffered little variation: "Here we form one big, happy family." This was said in English not only because those who uttered it wanted to make sure that we understood their message but also because being uttered in the prestige language—Tagalog, the language of Manila, or Pilipino, the official national language of the nation-state, conveyed less prestige—the phrase acquired a special resonance that amplified its meaning and augmented its rhetorical suasion.[13]

In and of itself, the statement would have had little to attract attention, had it not been asserted over and over again, in a manner that could only beg for deconstruction. When I realized that my informants were not merely expressing their personal feelings, but repeating a stock phrase learned at school, I became enticed to prod further into the meaning of the phrase. When I asked my informants to gloss the same phrase in Cebuano, they did not retranslate literally the word *family* (I would have expected *kabayanan* or the Spanish, borrowing *pamilya*). Instead, they said "Dinhi sa Siquijor, madaiton mi" or "malinawon mi," that is, "here on the island of Siquijor, we are peaceful" or "we are at peace." The verb *dait* means "to have good personal relations" and has thus strictly positive and social connotations. The adjective *linaw*, often used to describe the state of the sea, means "calm," and therefore connotes the continuity between natural environment and social milieu.

But that imputed harmony, as I came to realize, had in fact a triple aspect: (1) a descriptive or referential one (as it reflected the way in which Siquijorians tended to perceive their society), (2) a programmatic one (as it formulated the way in which they wished their society to be), and (3) even a performative one (as it also purported to bring about such an idyllic order). As a consequence, allusions to or mention of violence were more or less eschewed from conversations with me, since it did not fit the model of self-presentation that the Siquijorians wanted to impress on us. In the same way, different informants made an all-out effort to protect, not to say overprotect us from any mishaps to which we might have been exposed. The first time I was about to witness a brawl between two inebriated adult males, I was quickly ushered away from the scene and sheltered "for my own good." Thereafter, not only was it difficult for me to get directly any detail about this incident, but its very occurrence was even questioned, if not flatly denied.

Nonetheless, such an illusory eradication of violence could only achieve its opposite effect: the displayed and proclaimed absence of violence could only point at its absconded presence. If violence was so forcefully denied, did it not reveal its importance in that particular cultural setting? Hidden as violence was, where and at which level did it enter into the praxis of villagers and townspeople of Siquijor?

It was commonsensical to explore the ways in which Siquijorians perceived the occurrence of death. Inasmuch as it was rarely, if ever, considered as simply natural, it was always, in part or in whole, a violent occurrence, brought about by someone else's evil will. Except perhaps for the very old, no one died exclusively of what we would call natural causes; nor were such causes ignored. Because there were two systems of reference—a traditional one to which the world of spirits, of witchcraft, or syncretic Catholicism belongs and another one to which Western medicine belongs—it was clear to everyone that Tasio had indeed died of old age (kay tigulan na siya), while "high blood" was responsible for Carla's demise. But there was something else, too, something "supplementary" to use a Derridian vocabulary.[14] "Kidney failure followed by cardiac arrest" may have been good enough to obtain a bona fide death certificate for Tasio, but the hacking of a chicken, followed by the examination of its entrails, revealed to his immediate family that some spirits had visited his liver. As for Carla, whose demise was untimely, high blood pressure may have led to a fatal stroke, but "someone" (*usa ka tawo*) whose identity I learned only later from a reluctant informant, had borne a grudge against one of her close relatives. This person had been seen—I was told—roaming around Carla's home a few days before the fatal stroke and was thus strongly suspected of witchcraft. As a matter of fact, was not her death the last episode in a feud to which two close relatives of her husband had already and prematurely fallen victims? In other words, neither Carla nor Tasio—albeit to differing extents—had just died. Each one had been killed: he by unspecified (and so vague as to be almost generic) spirits and she by the magical power of a jealous or revengeful, powerful and nasty, neighborly affine.

Although in my understanding neither death resulted from any act of violence, the villagers obviously saw it differently. Similarly, they tended to perceive the presence of the spiritual world among them with such acumen that it tended to blur—without completely eradicating —the difference to which I, for one, preferred to hold, namely, the difference between natural occurrence and supernatural intervention. When Zikil blew off his arm while fishing with a stick of dynamite, that was—and everyone agreed—a *disgrasya* (i.e., just an accident). But when Senio disappeared at sea, he had not just drowned in a fishing accident but had been the victim of a *kataw*, of a siren who had seduced him, kidnapped him, and ultimately killed him.

But most cases of violent death are highly ambiguous and susceptible to a wide variety of contradictory, yet equally accepted explanations. For instance, when Ime died quite prematurely in what seemed to me a straightforward accident—the teenager drowned while skin diving when he became entangled in a fishing net—no one denied the immediate cause of his death. In addition, however, some had supplementary thoughts: the fishing net had been bewitched, another diver had done him in, and the irate spirit of a neglected relative had longed to see him in the beyond—all of the above and more.

What should become obvious by now is that the world surrounding the Siquijorians could not be and indeed was not as harmonious as they pretended it to be. Within their very cultural constructions, they had wrapped themselves into constant potential aggression. They had to contend not only with natural problems such as typhoons and the all too banal intrusion of death but also with the supernatural world that they had constructed. The latter was full of undesirable beings, each one more eager than the next to bring harm and doom to human beings.

Furthermore, the ordinary and mundane tensions that life in a village or in a neighborhood necessarily entail may lead to accusations and suspicions of witchcraft, the utmost manifestation of an unspoken, silent, if not secretive aggression. Beyond direct physical aggression and beyond the more subtle manipulations of witchcraft, acts of violence could still be perpetrated between living human beings even in absentia.

One day, as I inquired about the cause of a young man's death in the *barangay* where we lived, I was told that he had been killed, that his body had just been brought back to the village from Mindanao. He had been killed by his enemies; they killed him during his sleep. Were there any bad wounds on his body? None whatsoever. You are telling me that his enemies killed him in his bed and that his body bears no mark? But then, how do you know he was killed? Because he was fighting. But I thought he was asleep. Yes, asleep and fighting. I was puzzled, indeed. How do you know he was fighting? Because of the picture. Did I want to see it? The immediate family had in its possession a snapshot that had been taken, as I understood, by the police who investigated the case. The body, half-naked, lay on its deathbed, presumably in the exact position in which death had taken him. You see, he was fighting. I could see no such thing. Can't you see, the room is in great disorder, his arms are folded, his fists are tight, his legs spread. It began to dawn on me that, had he been in an upright position, he would be in a fighting posture. More explanation came about. While asleep, souls[15] can take a stroll (*suroy-suroy*); this is why one can see others in one's dreams. The soul leaves the body and in fact goes and visits others, and normally returns to join the body just before the person wakes up. While he was asleep, he picked a fight with his enemies in his dream. They overpowered him, and this is how he got killed. This was obvious to everyone but me, although finding the murderer was a more formidable task, entirely left to the domain of speculation and suspicion.

In interpreting this particular death as the result of a deliberate and mischievous act of violence, the Siquijorians continued to project the fear that violence inspired in them. But, in the instances that I have presented so far, violence does not appear in action, nor even as a process. It is more of a passion, something to which they may be subjected rather than something that they may inflict. Moreover, they consider themselves more readily as its victims than as its perpetrators. In other words, violence is of greater concern to them than they are inclined to admit.

This ideological perception of violence reflects in part the different experiences of colonial and neocolonial dominations to which the Siquijorians have been submitted. About the dark aspects of their historical past, the Siquijorian social memory seemed to have been selective. Time had not softened but perhaps even amplified the Spaniards' misdeeds of the nineteenth century as well as the particular rigors of the Japanese occupation in World War II. For instance, I was told several times by informants who had not been immediate witnesses to such atrocities that Japanese soldiers in town had abducted at least several babies from their mother's arms, tossed them in the air so as to catch them better with their bayonets. Not only is this a story that, as I discovered later, has currency practically everywhere in the Philippines; no informant could be any more specific as to the identity of any such victim, nor could I find any evidence of such event in the death register of the local parish. My point here is not to deny, even less to justify, the occurrence of Japanese atrocities, but to underline that ideology can never be a mere reflection of experience. The experience of violence had structured the ideology of experience in such a way that the ideology, in turn, structured the experience.

This structured and structuring aspect of ideology and experience comes to the fore as soon as an example of proclaimed and enacted violence is introduced. This became apparent in a story that I was told at first in bits and pieces, although publicly and without any inhibition.

Toward the end of World War II, as the context indicates, a Japanese fighter pilot bailed out of his Zero, well in sight of the coastline. He swam ashore. And there he was safe and sound and hiding on Crocodile Point. Partisans had seen his parachute descent, looked for him, and picked him up without much difficulty. This was most unfortunate for the airman. They brought him back to town. He was fastened to a post in front of the Municipal Building, and without any water to drink, he stayed there, exposed to the wrath of the local population for three days according to some, for seven days according to others. After this, somehow still alive, he was brought back to the shore where he had landed. There was among them a woman who was so angry at what the Japanese had done in the Philippines that she took a *bolo* (a heavy weeding cutlass), opened up his belly, and ate his liver *kinilaw* (i.e., raw or seasoned only with coconut vinegar). Oh, yes, I could ask her if I wanted to, but she may not want to talk about it.

In many respects, it was a collective but piecemeal recitation as it had been purportedly a collective and spontaneous deed. The accuracy of the deed itself, its truth value, I could never establish because the successive narrators were not the participants, whose identity were always left in a blurred distance, save for the main character of the story. She lived somewhere in a neighboring *barangay*. But, discouragingly, she was much too old, too deaf, too unwilling to talk to be interviewed. I had been warned. I attempted several times to reach her but never could, as I was always at once encouraged and discouraged to pursue her testimony.

Amidst the conviction, suspicion, presumption of a revealed and unverifiable truth, a narrative experience of violence remained. It pointed at the Siquijorian preoccupation with, inclination toward, and justification of violence. Beyond the lost truth value of the event that it relates, and which structured the narration, the narrative, in turn, is bound to structure any possible future violence, giving it its value as argument. As such, English-speakers would say that it goes directly to the heart of the matter. For Cebuano-speakers, the heart of the matter is, in fact, a different organ, since the seat of emotions is the *atay*, the liver.

To take here a brief pause and bring to a temporary closure one panel of my diptych on Philippine violence, it seems manifest that violence in effect permeated the entire society. Despite assertions to the contrary, or perhaps because of such a denial, violence was omnipresent, at the very least as a forged memory, in everyone's consciousness. Time after time, and without much restraint, all forms of political authority had been able to manipulate to their own advantage the structuring value of its coercive argument, thus keeping the Siquijorians in line in their isolated insularity, fearful of their own nightmares and daydreaming of smooth interpersonal interaction.

When I first became interested in the Philippines, at least in Siquijor, one of the 7,109 islands that constitute the archipelago, the nation was under martial law. In my limited experience of the world, the mere utterance of the phrase "martial law," in and of itself, is sufficient to conjure images of great unpleasantness, with heel-clicking sounds, public executions, and other Orwellian horrors. I thus braced myself for the worst.

On arrival, I was surprised—I must confess—that the martial law atmosphere, pervasive as it may have been, was more diffused than I had anticipated. A province-island[16] in the central Visayas, Siquijor was poor, indeed. It was also small and isolated. Its homogeneity from any viewpoint was spectacular. And the KBL,[17] Marcos's party, had such a firm grip on the island that everyone and everything was calm, the peasantry complying, the bourgeoisie profiteering, and the political opposition either silent or under control. There was perhaps no great reason for the regime to exert an excessive surveillance, even though within a week of our arrival the Philippine Constabulary Commander paid me and my wife the visit of courtesy to which I have alluded above and thus welcomed us to the island.

Soon after, however, while in the market of the nearby town, I was approached by a drunkard who addressed me with insistence. What did I think of the political situation in his country? Eager to resist committing myself on this matter with someone I did not know, and unable to disengage myself, I felt I could at least learn something by returning the question. What did he think of it? I could not repeat here his exact words without being offensive. Suffice it to say that they were not entirely laudatory for the chief of state, and perhaps even less for his uxorial Minister of Human Settlements and Governor of Metro Manila.[18]

When four men drifted from a nearby coffee-shop table to ours, I expected trouble rather than their echoing, albeit sotto voce, my imbibing and original interlocutor. "You are not afraid of being arrested in saying that of Marcos?" I asked. "Oh no," someone replied, "this is martial law, Philippine style." As an outside observer, I could not help being struck by the paradox of a statement that affirmed and refuted itself, its own validity, as well as its very legitimacy in a modern—perhaps even postmodern in that it seemed to have been more parodic than ironic—display of disingenuous sophistry reminiscent of the lying Cretans.

This was indeed a curious phase, which I was to hear again and again, from many different quarters, until January 1981, when Mr. Marcos saw fit to lift martial law, a strictly pro forma maneuver, meant almost exclusively for American consumption. The political life of the country remained as stonewalled as ever and "Now it is democracy, Philippine style" began its career as a cynical replacement. Prior to that, however, "martial law, Philippine style" was in fact a chiché that everyone employed incessantly, and sometimes for no apparent reason, as if it were—and it probably was—perfectly commonsensical and transparent to anyone. Even in the most rural *barangays*, where most people did not have any real command of English, they would utter that expression with the same eagerness as they would repeat, to the great merriment of their audience, this other English joke: "Family planning? No, family planting!" Clearly, if the two expressions were constantly repeated with an apparently inexhaustible appeal, they must have meant something to those who uttered them.

In effect, both phrases functioned as narratives. Perhaps they were rudimentary ones, but this did not diminish in any way their saliency. Nor did their obligatory brevity, owing to the locutors' general lack of competence in English, make them stylistically any less crisp. On the contrary, they could have functioned rigidly, that is, in a formulaic way. They could have been uttered as statements, but they were not susceptible of any variation, other than contextual ones, of course, and even that was very limited.

In addition, such formulae were used almost as quotes. They were in fact often preceded by the particle *kono* (i.e., "they say, one says, it is said that"). In using this particle, Cebuano-speakers disengage themselves and thrust on a third party the responsibility of what they portend only to report. Such a lack of assertiveness is perhaps in step with a value system that pretends to favor smooth interpersonal relations (Lynch 1973), but it was also a rejection. It allowed speakers to place a distance between themselves as speaking subjects and the reference of their discourse.

This distancing was also a political disengagement that justified and revealed, vis-à-vis the government and its programs, a marvelously militant passivity. Being militant, this disengagement was thus paradoxically a form of resistance to the government, and therefore it was, indeed, a form of engagement, one of *The Weapons of the Weak* that James C. Scott (1985) has discussed with such lucidity in the Malaysian context. To the use and abuse of force by the government, the Visayan peasants could at least resist with irony, which was precisely the (only) rhetorical device that they chose and/or that was left to them. The rhetorical device that was used was manifestly ironical, because no other avenue was open to them who were not convinced, but forced into obedience and acceptance. To family planning, the peasantry objected—and still does—as government interference in their private life, although they were unwilling or unable to state it. They never went as far as rejecting it openly. They never accepted it, either. And so, instead, they turned it into ridicule. As for martial law, need I say that they were never consulted?

In evoking (or is it invoking?) a "martial law, Philippine style," they did not have the power—nor, of course, the determination—to resist it. But, once more, I should be prudent in this assertion. Even though it was not a joke, but an expression that was presented as a mere description, it was not—one would have guessed—a neutral, objective one. To start with, martial law is an interesting oxymoron, since it refers to the law of exception par excellence, that is, to the law that abolishes the law, to a sort of legal scuttling. Adding to it a style, be it a Filipino one, was a way of taking exception with the exception, without reverting to the status quo ante. It could only be a funny way of mellowing down the martial law and its rigors. But in so doing, it necessarily added the arbitrariness of a cultural flavor to the arbitrariness of the exception. And thus, turning to irony, the phrase at once underlined and ridiculed the imposed submission from which the speakers could not escape. Using English, a tool with which they feel at once familiar and clumsy (see Dumont 1991), the *barangay* people did not miss the pun, something they had not invented but were just repeating. Turning martial law into derision, they defused it, and thus passively disengaged themselves from its grip.

Yet, at the same time it should be abundantly clear that it was also wishful thinking, a mere invocation whereby passive resistance remained short of active rebellion. In fact, this also reflected a deep depolitization of the rural masses, who, with a sense of powerless despair, tended to satisfy themselves with turning everything into mockery, that is with the *simulacra* of their liberation, since either they pretended not to submit to martial law or they denied its rigor and thus its very existence. And thus all happened as if violence as abuse of power had no, or little, grip on the peasants of Siquijor.

This was 1980.

Let me jump to the end of 1985 and to the very beginning of 1986, and allow me the license of a little detour through Great Britain, Cambodia, and Hollywood.

The Killing Fields was a historico-political film in which the British filmmaker Roland Joffé presented his interpretation of two separate but related series of events, the American intervention in Cambodia in the early 1970s and the subsequent takeover of that country by Pol Pot's Khmer Rouges in 1975.[19] The two events were unmistakably distinct and yet clearly linked in *The Killing Fields*. The film condemned both events for their horrible and senseless violence. The depiction of such violence was so graphic that the film was rated "R." Part of its emotional appeal derived from the fact that the star of the film was a man who had no previous acting experience and who, in effect, played himself in it. Although a feature film, it aimed at truthfulness and at truth; and thus, without pretending to be a documentary, it had documentary qualities.

Any resemblance between the Cambodian tragedy and the turmoil that the Philippines had undergone in the mid-1980s does not seem a priori very compelling. Surely, the Philippines have suffered their share of violence. Popular uprisings and their repressions have run across the entire history of the archipelago. Still in the mid-1980s, the carryover of the Huk rebellion in central Luzon, of an Islamic nationalistic insurrection in Mindanao, and of a rural proletarian agitation in the Visayas—without mentioning the seeming itchiness of some segments of the military—tended to indicate that everything was not totally smooth in the islands. In addition, according to the Association against Detention and for Amnesty, or Selda, quoted in the *New York Times* on November 10, 1986 (p. 8, col. 3), "there [we]re 70,000 former political prisoners, 35,000 of whom suffered some form of torture" and "400 remaining political prisoners." At the risk of appearing cynical, I would have to say that, on the horror scale to which we have become accustomed, these numbers are almost low.

And yet, for anyone concerned with violence and its anthropological interpretation, there is a parallel that must be drawn, or at least sketched. Interpretive prudence commands it, since too many a Southeast Asian scholar was (should I say embarrassingly?) taken by surprise by the Khmer Rouges's violence. It ran so much against the grain of what any student of the area had learned and could normally expect from the Khmer ethos. History, with the might of its contingency, painfully shattered images of all-smiling, easygoing people, gentle in their manners and smooth in their social interactions. Somehow, Norodom Sihanouk's princely and debonnaire image too had been deposed. And thus, despite all that which separates Cambodia, historically and culturally, from the Philippines, it seems reasonable to wonder—which, of course, we have already begun doing—whether the latter's front of social ease, emphasis on smooth interpersonal relations, and the like does not, in fact, hide a latent, and thus far repressed, sense of violence that, given the proper context, could burst forth any moment.

But there is also, perhaps, an even more compelling reason to mention *The Killing Fields* when speaking of the recent past of the Philippines. During the brief but intense electoral campaign in preparation for the elections of February 7, 1986, which, in the end, were to bring about Ferdinand Marcos's fall, violence came to the very fore of actuality. I am not referring here to the real thing, neither to the "goons"[20]—as they have come to be known—nor to their exactions, but to an altogether different machination, the manipulation of the idea of violence. This is something that was manipulated over and over again in the Philippines throughout the mid-1980s, with the intemperate speeches of Juan Ponce Enrile,[21] with the real and imaginary, at any rate rumored and repeated, threats of military coup at each absence of President Corazon Aquino, and with the sort of permanent suspense that it created in Filipino affairs. Even though I have no special wisdom that allows me to foresee the future (neither to anticipate the loyalty of the armed forces nor to predict a military coup), I cannot help but perceive the strength that the idea of violence—the idea of it and its ideology—possessed and continues to possess throughout the Philippines.

At any rate, it was certainly an innovation on the part of the Marcos's campaign management to bolster his political appeal by representing *The Killing Fields* to the electoral masses. It was not shown as mere entertainment so as to capture the attention of an audience before the advent of a political speaker. It was meant by Marcos's political machine as an element of its propaganda, as demonstrated by the deliberate effort on the part of the KBL—Marcos's party—to give it a maximum of public exposure. Undoubtedly, this effort was facilitated by the fact that the film was recent, that it had a mass-audience appeal and that it had just arrived on the Philippine market.

In addition to these preconditions intrinsic to the film, there were others that were intrinsic to the Philippine situation itself, in the multiplicity of its local variants. For the sake of electoral efficiency, the film had to be shown almost everywhere and to almost everyone. The film was shown not only in Manila and other cities throughout the archipelago but also even in remote localities still without electricity or theaters where it was necessary to organize special runs on privately owned battery-operated videocassette recorders (VCRs).

This was, indeed, the case on Siquijor. On this impoverished island where electricity had barely arrived to the town centers, the political machine of the KBL party was in full swing. Its effort to deliver, by hook or by crook, as usual, impeccable electoral returns, in line with the wishes of Malacañang Palace,[22] included the screening of the film. This was made possible by militant VCR owners who, by virtue of being part of a relatively wealthy bourgeoisie, had evidently quite a bit at stake in the process.

The wealthiest KBL members and the most active Marcos supporters certainly had something to lose were Marcos not returned to office, not the least of which included their grip on local power, their total dominance and control of the local economy, and their social glamor. They were also the ones who were the most likely to own a VCR. In effect, the local bourgeoisie being as entrepreneurial as could be expected, had already begun to exploit for commercial purpose the possibilities offered by the VCR. As early as 1984, one person ran a video show on large screen every Saturday night, using a generator-operated VCR. The passage from a commercial use to a political one was as easy and painless as the passage from recreational to commercial had been.

It may not be immediately obvious to everyone why or how such a film could possibly bring grist to Mr. Marcos's political mill. The convoluted reasoning behind this ran something like this.

The first part of the film, which focused on the American entanglement, was not considered to be more than preambular. Even though its importance was played down, it still made—just in case someone paid real attention to it—two astute but not so subtle points. On one hand, it (not so much the film itself, but its electoral manipulation) was directed against the Americans. They had practically forced the issue of an election in the Philippines and were reminded that their previous interference in the domestic affairs of another Southeast Asian country had been ill-fated. On the other hand, it could not fail to strike, for domestic consumption, an anti-American note, and thus a nationalistic one, destined to resound as an ideologically perfect chord in the ears of the Philippine electorate.

But the ideological pièce de resistance was to be found in the second part of the film as it depicted in full colors the gore and horrors of the communist takeover. Here the dialectic of electoral representation and fictional representation reached quasi-perfection. For, in a fabulous ellipse, it stated that given the Cambodian precedent, a vote for any form of opposition whatsoever was an endorsement of the communists, who—no doubt, and the entertained electorate was encouraged to entertain no doubt whatsoever about that—would do here what they had done there, and, therefore, Marcos and Marcos only (with the help of his party, the KBL) could save the Philippines from total disaster. The film, in this particular context, had the merit of brandishing a highly simplistic but immediately identifiable scarecrow. The alternatives could not be clearer. It was to be either the vague promises offered by the KBL or the suggested certitude of a bloodbath, that is either Marcos's bliss or the Reds' blitz. Of course, this was never specifically stated, since obviously the film made no such claim, but this was precisely the strength of this form of propaganda, its indirectness, to say nothing of its insidiousness.

In the end, I gather that it backfired, or at the very least that it remained too inefficient an argument to have swayed enough votes in the hoped for direction, since Mr. Marcos lost. In the *barangay*, the threat of violence had not been entirely lost. Perhaps the subtleties of the plot had been missed by many spectators who, because of their lack of education and political sophistication, knew precious little about Cambodia. But the fact that the film was manipulated for political ends and that it contained a veiled threat had not escaped their attention. Once more they reacted passively to the film, which had neither mobilized them politically nor demobilized them. Instead, they turned to another solution, one with which we are now familiar, namely, derision. And, indeed, as late as September 1986, when I revisited Siquijor briefly, one of the young men who had gathered together for the slaughtering, plucking, and further preparation of a chicken in my honor pointed at the bloodstain on the ground, at the scattered feathers and at the dead bird, invited me, laughingly, with an ample movement of the arm, to contemplate "the killing fields."

Of course, a complete study of violence would require and indepth examination not only of the threats—that is, of the virtuality of violence—but also of its actuality, as the *barangay* peasants experience it. In addition to the all-too-human murders and assassinations, the supernatural world—which brings its toll of deaths, which causes sicknesses and accidents, which allows curses and bewitchings of all sorts—would have to be scrutinized.

In the ethnographic case that I have documented above with several examples, I believe I have shown that the mere threat of violence, "always already,"[23] stands beyond its mere virtuality, as it is itself a form and a use of violence. In that sense, threat is necessarily a use (and more often than not, an abuse) of force, because it is always given, that is imposed from a political above to a political below, and because its contrasts immediately with the persuasion to which a discussion between equals could pretend.

If martial law, birth control, and the political manipulation of *The Killing Fields* constituted, in the experience of the Visayan peasants, different—if not disparate—threats made by "the government," all three also represented instances of violence. Violence, in this case, was not seen as the exercise of force, but as its abuse. And it was experienced as an abuse not so much for any intrinsic quality that it might have—since, in a real but circular way, each activity was well within the law—but because the legitimacy of the power from which it emanated had begun to wane.

Interestingly, threats necessarily index the weaknesses of a present and refer to the promise of a future. Martial law was decreed in order to end a political turmoil, and promised a "new society" that the KBL was to deliver. Family planning was a response to a population explosion and was to be a solution to overpopulation and poverty. And the screening of *The Killing Fields* indicated a political danger and forewarned of total destruction. But if threats also entail the carrot as well as the stick, they cannot convince. A decree is not an argument.

Confronted with such violence, the Visayan peasants responded like most peasants do, that is, neither with enthusiasm nor with rebellion but with increased passivity, cynicisms and witticisms included. And this may be why, at least in the *barangay* I know best, those who a few months before could speak of "Our beloved President Marcos" could, as early as September 1986, and without batting an eye, call upon the smiles of "Our President Cory." And yet, in the same breath, the same people, as depoliticized as ever, could answer my "What has changed since my last visit?" with a smile and these words: "Sigi gihapon, pinobre tanan" (it goes on, we're still poor).

In order to analyze the distinctive character of violence in a specific Philippine province, I have carefully avoided what I would like to call the "frontal attack" method. If I have not produced a mugshot imagery, if I have not exhibited the dreadful evidence of battered or mutilated bodies, if I have not focused on the lamentable results of violence, it is because these images—powerful as they might be on occasion—beg for a systematically deferred interpretation of what they illustrate. Instead of looking deliberately for actual instances of conflicts and violence, I have chosen to draw from my daily experiences on the island of Siquijor. The notes and memories that I have kept of the encounter were sufficient, I believe, to document the general social, historical, and cultural context in which conflicts and its resolutions—violent or not—emerge.

Following the dominant Visayan mode of behavior, I have thus preferred to be indirect in my treatment of violence, and to focus, on its setting, that is, on the general conditions for its genesis. On one hand, I have presented the negations and narrations whereby violence presents itself as a pervasive condition of existence on the island. On the other hand, I have documented the experience that the islanders have acquired of an idea of political violence, its trace—a mental scar—as they carry it in their heads.

Ideas and deeds exist only in dialectical relationship. So does violence, which is a habitus in the sense that Bourdieu (1977: passim) gave to this phrase, at once structured and structuring: structured because the idea of violence results from historical events, stored as the memory of past deeds, of past encounters, of past frustrations; and structuring because the idea of violence informs human actions, determines the acceptability, even the banality of violence, if not the ability to erase the scandal of its occurrence. A solid grasp on current events and the institutional analysis of sociopolitical structures are, indeed, necessary to explain, or better to interpret, the occurrence of violence. Yet, as the case of Siquijor illustrates, this remains insufficient because violence is represented, manifested, and manipulated on many different levels and in many different arenas, and because violence is informed and constructed by a variety of factors that transcend the *hic et nunc* of its occurrence.

NOTES

Earlier versions of the two main parts of this chapter were written independently and presented at two different symposia organized by Dr. Carolyn Nordstrom on the theme of communal violence: in December 1986 in Philadelphia, Pennsylvania, at the 85th Annual Meetings of the American Anthropological Association and in Phoenix, Arizona, at the 87th Annual Meeting of that association.

Field research in the Philippines was made possible in 1979 by a Summer Grant from the Graduate School Research Fund of the University of Washington (Seattle) and in 1980/81 by a Fulbright-Hayes Research Fellowship administered by the Philippine-American Education Foundation (Manila), while I was affiliated with the Department of Sociology and Anthropology, Silliman University (Dumaguete) and with the Cebuano Studies Center, University of San Carlos (Cebu City). Ethnohistorical research in the archives of Spain, the Vatican, and the Philippines was supported in 1982/83 by two consecutive grants respectively from the Social Science Research Council and from the Spanish-American Friendship Treaty as well as by a leave of absence with pay from the University of Washington. I revisited the Philippines, all too briefly to my taste, in the summers of 1983 and 1986 to attend conferences organized by the Joint Committee on Southeast Asia of the Social Science Research Council. Substantial revisions to these papers were made during 1987/88, while I was a member of the School of Social Science at the Institute for Advanced Study in Princeton, New Jersey, under a fellowship from the National Endowment for the Humanities. To all these institutions, I express my gratitude.

Finally, I wish to thank Jean Comaroff, Michael Cullinane, E. Valentine Daniel, Elinor Dumont, Reynaldo C. Ileto, Charles F. Keyes, Dorinne Kondo, JoAnn Martin, Resil B. Mojares, Carolyn Nordstrom, Sally A. Ness, and Edgar V. Winans for their critical comments.

1. Jamin's words flow better of course in the original, which reads as follows: "L'hétérogénéité des phénomènes auxquels se rapporte la notion de violence suffit à démontrer qu'elle n'est pas un concept sociologiquement opératoire; son caractère protéiforme et polysémique la rend presque indéfinissable."

2. Returning from several years as a political expatriate in the United States, Benigno "Ninoy" Aquino, Jr., an opposition leader, was murdered on August 21, 1983 while under the "protection" of government security personnel, as he stepped down from the plane that had brought him back to Manila International Airport. This incident marked the beginning of a crisis that precipitated the end of the Marcos regime in February 1986. It also allowed against all odds for the coming to

power of "Ninoy's" charismatic widow, Corazon Aquino, as President of the Republic of the Philippines.

3. Magellan never completed the first navigation of the globe. He let himself be dragged into a local conflict between Humabon, who ruled on the island of Cebu—he converted quickly to Christianity and furthermore had recognized the suzerainty of the Spanish king—and his enemy Lapu-Lapu, who ruled on the neighboring island of Mactan. Magellan and a number of his companions died in the ensuing engagement.

4. Muslim piracy and the pillaging of coastal towns under Spanish control was particularly active during the eighteenth to nineteenth century. On this topic, the interested reader could profitably consult Warren (1981).

5. In 1744, on the island of Bohol in the central Visayas, a Spanish friar refused to bury a police constable on consecrated ground. His brother, Francisco Dagohoy, led against the Spaniards a rebellion that was to give Bohol a practically independent regime until 1829. Unfortunately, there is, to my knowledge, no book-length treatment of the Dagohoy rebellion.

6. The nationalist revolt that broke out in August 1896 marks the beginning of the Philippine armed struggle against Spain's rule.

7. In the course of World War II, the Japanese occupied Manila as early as January 2, 1942. General MacArthur landed on the island of Leyt on October 20, 1944, but fighting in the Philippines went on until the surrender of Japan on September 22, 1945 (Agoncillo 1965; Hartendorp 1967).

8. *Huk* is an abbreviation of *Hukbalahap*, itself an abbreviation of the Tagalog phrase, *Hukbong Bayan Laban sa Hapon* (People's Anti-Japanese Army). Founded in 1942, it was a guerrilla force. In 1946, it was renamed *Hukbong Mapagpalaya ng Bayan* (People's Liberation Army). The best source on this topic is Kerkvliet (1977).

9. The New People's Army (NPA) is a Marxist-Leninist revolutionary guerrilla movement operating in the northern Philippines (mainly Luzon, but also some of the Visayas; Negros, for instance). On the topic of Philippine insurgency, the interested reader may wish to consult Kessler (1989).

10. The Moro National Liberation Front (MNLF) created in 1969 is essentially a Muslim armed movement operating in the southern Philippines (Mindanao, Sulu, and Palawan) and reacting to the Christian encroachment of territories traditionally held by Muslims.

11. In a well-known but now often decried study of Philippine values origi-nally written in 1960, Lynch was the first to identify "smoothness of interpersonal relations (or SIR)." He defined it in the following way (1984:31):

SIR may be defined as a facility at getting along with others in such a way as to avoid outward signs of conflict: glum or sour looks, harsh words, open disagree-ment, or physical violence. It connotes the smile, the friendly lift of the eyebrow, the pat on the back, the squeeze of the arm, the word of praise of friendly concern. It means being agreeable, even under difficult circumstances, and of keeping quiet or out of sight when discretion passes the word. It means a sensitivity to what other people feel at any given moment, and a willingness and ability to change tack (if not direction) to catch the lightest favoring breeze.

12. Philippine municipalities are made up of several *barangay* or dispersed villages and one *poblacion*, designated as "town" in the local English usage.

13. On the issue of language, see Dumont (1991).

14. The supplement is but the trace of the operation of *différance* (see Derrida 1973, passim).

15. On Visayan souls, see Dumont (1987).

16. In the administrative lingo of the Philippines, province-islands are is-lands that are large enough to have the status of a province and small enough to constitute only one province. Among the Visayas, Siquijor, Bohol, and Cebu are province-islands, but not Negros, which is divided into two provinces: Negros Occidental and Negros Oriental. Siquijor was inaugurated as a province on January 8, 1972.

17. The Declaration of Martial Law on September 21, 1972 had brought political life to a halt. Shortly before the election of April 7, 1978, Marcos orga-nized his own political grouping, the *Kilusang Bagong Lipunan* (KBL), or in Taga-log, lit. new society movement.

18. Imelda Romualdez Marcos was appointed Governor of the newly created Metro Manila Region on November 6, 1975. By the autumn of 1978, she cumu-lated the latter function with the newly created cabinet post of Minister of Human Settlements.

19. King of Cambodia from 1941 to 1955, head of state from 1960 to 1970, Prince Norodom Sihanouk was deposed by the pro-American Premier Lon Nol and formed a government in exile in Beijing, after which war raged between the Lon Nol forces and Pol Pot's Khmer Rouges, who captured Phnom Penh on April 17,

1975. Over a million people were to lose their lives in executions and enforced hardships under Pol Pot's regime.

20. Goon squads, presumably under unacknowledged yet precise orders, carried out a number of political assassinations of a number of opponents to the regime in addition to creating a general sentiment of physical insecurity for political dissenters.

21. Juan Ponce Enrile was for years Marcos's Defense Secretary. A staged attempt against his life had been the pretext chosen by Marcos to declare martial law on September 21, 1972. Enrile's defection on February 22, 1986 played a crucial role in the collapse of the Marcos regime and in the installation of Ms. Aquino on February 25, 1986, in whose cabinet he kept his post as Defense Secretary until November 23, 1986 in the aftermath of a failed coup that he allegedly engineered. On August 28, 1987 a military rebellion led by one of Enrile's protégés, Colonel Gregorio B. ("Gringo") Honasan, erupted and was crushed the next day. Among the now enormous albeit uneven literature that related the February 1986 events in the Philippines, I have found the account given by Fenton (1986) lucidly written and particularly helpful.

22. In Manila, Malacañang Palace is the official residence of the head of state.

23. I borrow freely this "always already" from Derrida (1977, passim.)

WORKS CITED

Agoncillo, Teodoro A.
1965   *The Fateful Years: Japan's Adventures in the Phi-
        lippines, 1941-45*, 2 vols. Quezon City: R.P. Garcia
        Publishing Company.

Bourdieu, Pierre
1977   *Outline of a Theory of Practice*. Trans. R. Nice.
        Cambridge and London: Cambridge University Press.

Derrida, Jacques
1973   *Speech and Phenomena*. Trans. D. Allison. Evanston,
        Ill.: Northwestern University Press.
1977   *Writing and Difference*. Trans. A. Bass. Chicago:
        The University of Chicago Press.

Dumont, Jean-Paul
1987   "A Sheaf of Souls: Siquijor Reinterpretations." Paper
        presented at the Symposium on Soul in East and
        Southeast Asian Folk Religions, 39th Annual Meetings of
        the Association for Asian Studies on Boston, Mass.,
        April 10-12, 1987.
1991   "Language and Learning in a Visayan Rural Community,"
        In *Reshaping Local Worlds: Formal Education and
        Cultural Change in Rural Southeast Asia.* C. F. Keyes,
        et al., eds. New Haven: Yale University,
        Southeast Asia Studies, Monograph 36, pp. 70-88.

Fenton, James
1986   "The Snap Revolution," *Granta* 18:33-169.

Harthendorp, A.V.H.
1967   *The Japanese Occupation of the Philippines*, 2 vols.
        Manila: Bookmark.

Jamin, Jean
1984   "Une ethnographie de la violence est-elle possible?"
        Etudes Rurales 95-96: 16-21.

Kerkvliet, Benedict J.
1977   *The Huk Rebellion: A Study of Peasant Revolt in the
        Philippines.* Berkeley, Los Angeles, London: University
        of California Press.

Kessler, Richard J.
1989   *Rebellion and Repression in the Philippines.* New Haven
        and London: Yale University Press.

Lynch, Frank
1973   "Social Acceptance Reconsidered." In *Four Readings on
        Philippine Values*, F. Lynch and A. de Guzman, eds., IPC
        Papers no. 2, 4th ed., revised and enlarged, pp. 1-68.
        Quezon City: Ateneo de Manila University Press.
1984   "Social Acceptance Reconsidered." In *Philippine Society
        and the Individual: Selected Essays of Frank Lynch,
        1949-1976*, A. A. Yengoyan and P. Q. Makil, eds.,
        Michigan Papers on South and Southeast Asia, no. 24,
        pp. 23-91. Ann Arbor: The University of Michigan,
        Center for South and Southeast Asian Studies.

Scott, James C.
1985   *Weapons of the Weak: Everyday Forms of Peasant Resistance.* New Haven and London: Yale University Press.

Warren, James Francis
1981   *The Sulu Zone, 1768-1898: The Dynamics of External Trade, Slavery, and Ethnicity in the Transformation of a Southeast Asian Maritime State.* Singapore: Singapore University Press.

TEN

Manila's New Metropolitan Form

NEFERTI XINA M. TADIAR

I HAVE ALWAYS EXPERIENCED METRO MANILA AS A GENERALLY FLAT CITY.
Ostensibly because of flooding problems, it has no underground transport system, nor do the majority of its houses have basements. With
the exception of commercial office buildings, hotels, and condominiums, most of its structures are no more than a few stories high. Moreover, there is no single public monument from which a view of the
entire metropolis can be seen. As such, most people have no access to
an aerial perspective. I, like most residents, maneuver around the city
without a mental aerial map (without, even, a sense of North, South,
East, and West); instead, I get around with images of seriality, that is,
routes that I can trace by imagining the flow of adjoining objects on
particular pathways.[1] This is the kind of fluency one develops in a
congested, view-constricted space like Manila. One might call it imaginary urban tunneling, except that all the tunnels are aboveground.
And when one moves through this saturated space, submerged in the

inundation of people and matter, it is like swimming underwater in a shallow metropolitan sea.

A New Metropolitan Form

Since the toppling of the Marcos dictatorship and the much-touted restoration of democracy by the Aquino administration, which replaced the Marcos regime in 1986, a new metropolitan form that is altering the face of the metropolis and the experience of its spaces has emerged: "flyovers." The construction of flyovers, that is, overpasses at major interchanges, is the response of the Department of Public Works and Highways (DPWH) to the massive congestion of traffic caused by an ever-increasing population (estimated to be around 8 million). It is, in other words, a state as well as corporate[2] measure to cope with the vehicular and human flooding of the city, naturalized like the water floods the city periodically experiences as an "over-spill of growth." The significance of flyovers, which are a new form of the built environment, extends beyond the decongestion of traffic (which, in fact, also has significant social effects). As Neil Smith writes, "the production of space also implies the production of meaning, concepts, and consciousness of space which are inseparably linked to its physical production" (77). Congruently, one immediately observes that this new metropolitan form radically alters the cityscape, providing moving, expansive aerial perspectives not hitherto available to the greater urban population, thereby altering the space experienced by commuters and pedestrians alike. Apart from producing height and depth in a relatively flat space (relative, that is, to modern industrialized cities), the flyovers displace mechanisms of orientation that rely on contiguity and concrete detail and demand a more abstract system of finding directions, such as that employed by motorists on U.S. freeways. To inquire into the effects of this new metropolitan form *on* subjectivity is, however, to imply that the relation between physical production and the production of meaning is one of cause and effect. Even with the invocation of human practice as the mediator between material production and consciousness, the theoretical division of phenomena into these spheres curtails an analysis of the multiple ways in which this urban form inserts itself into metropolitan lives.

Anthony D. King argues that "physical and spatial urban form actually constitute as well as represent much of social and cultural existence: society is to a very large extent constituted through the buildings and spaces that it creates" (1). Flyovers constitute a particular social order, but not merely as physical structures affecting collective human consciousness and actions. Nor do they merely represent, they *are* a system of representation: a medium. In other words, this metropolitan form is a mode of material as well as symbolic production. It is a mode of regulation and control but also a medium of desire which helps to produce the effect *of* subjectivity. Hence it is the site of political conflict and struggle, where different systems of value and practice intersect. It is not therefore isolable from either the discourses that proliferate around it, or from the practices in which it participates and the conditions in which it is engaged. In fact, I argue that this form of built environment is only an *attempt* on the part of the state in conjunction with private investors to institute a form of social order. Collective movements, in this case, in the form of the vehicular and human flooding creating traffic, are also attempts to shape a society that can accommodate them. Users of the streets act as a form of pressure, forces which structure the social and urban space, indirectly through the state responses they provoke, but also directly through their presence and activity. Flyovers are a metropolitan form intended to accommodate some of these pressures.

Stand-still traffic is perhaps one of the most talked-about (at least among the middle and upper classes), most widely-experienced of urban problems in Metro Manila. It is hence not surprising that flyovers, as the solution to it, should also generate as much discussion as the vehicles they are trying to mobilize. The discourse, in other words, is as responsible for the urban construction as is the traffic itself. One might say it is itself a form of traffic. Indeed, this "public work" is the product of numerous social demands, the loudest of which have been calls for solutions to "the traffic problem." As one columnist of the *Manila Chronicle* still complains even after all the flyovers have been built:

Manila's streets are scenes of anarchy in more ways than one. Sidewalks seem to be running out of fashion. Rather, they are transformed into commercial or residential purposes which take priority over the needs of pedestrians. This is proven by the car repair shops, stores, eateries, playgrounds, garbage dumps, and shanties that sidewalks are used for themselves [sic] without a second thought. Naturally pedestrians end up walking on the streets or roads, competing with vehicles. With the unsurprisingly large number of private vehicles in the city due to the lack of efficient public transportation and the equally large number of public transport vehicles, it is obvious that there are not enough streets to contain both with ease, plus pedestrians. Add to the conventional vehicular traffic the unconventional types that also are part of the traffic such as tricycles, wooden pushcarts of scavengers, delivery persons or vendors, animal-drawn transport, plus bicycles and motorcycles, and the recipe for chaos is almost complete. What gives it the finishing touch is the absolute absence of discipline or adherence to rules of communal interest, traffic rationality, safety, and thoughtfulness. (Ongpin, "Traffic" 5)

The traffic problem as this writer sees it lies in two things: excess and lack—among other things, excess of people and vehicles, lack of discipline and law enforcement. The terms of this account, excess and lack, are the points at which other discourses that exert force on metropolitan organization converge. In this discourse, the urban excess is constituted mainly by pedestrians pushed off their proper place, the sidewalk, by illegitimate activities, "unconventional" vehicles, and motorists who would have taken public transportation if not for its inefficiency. Excess hence refers to the by-products of maldevelopment and mismanagement, to what is designated as informal production, that is, people who engage in activities recognized as non-productive, unregulated and, hence, illegitimate according to the standards of the national economy. It is to this surplus population which engages in "unconventional" forms of livelihood and its own by-products that the chaos of the streets is attributed. Anarchy, chaos, and the lack of "traffic rationality" are here inextricably related as forces that have brought about the new structuring of street space by means of flyovers.

The massive migration of people from the provinces to the metropolis is not, as many accounts would have it, simply due to the growth of the national economy, nor is it due to the natural attraction that the big city holds for the countryside. It is, rather, an eruption of the contradictions of the nation's, and correspondingly, Manila's development.[3] "Manila's development has been sustained by the economic surplus extracted from its hinterland" (Caoili 8). The surplus population found in the city is the human form of this economic surplus, that is, the labor from which profit is extracted and accumulated as capital (the capital that comes to the nation's capital). The pools of unregulated labor flowing into Manila's streets and corroding the urban structure might hence be viewed as this disgorged rural labor come to find and claim its capital. But rural migrants are also fleeing from the ravages of development—the migration is at the same time an exodus. Apart from the intolerable levels of exploitation they have suffered in the countryside, especially in agricultural industries controlled by feudal capitalists, they have also suffered the ravages of the armed resistance against national development, that is, against the economic organization supporting the ruling classes. Much of the urban poor therefore can be rightly viewed as refugees. Their "refuge" is the streets of Manila, paths strewn with waste—refuse like themselves—which many of them live off. In other words, the human flood engulfing Manila is a wave of capitalism's contradictions demanding accommodation.

It is not then merely the power of capital that has brought about this state of the metropolis. It is also resistance and antagonism. As Aprodicio Laquian, one of Marcos's Presidential Action Officers on Housing and Urban Developments, shows, centralized urban plans for Manila have been blocked in the past as well by popular movements and collective entrenchment. The implementation, for example, of the "Major Thoroughfares Plan for Metropolitan Manila," prepared by the National Urban Planning Commission in 1945, was partially prevented by the financial expenditure demanded by the Hukbalahap rebellion which was taking place in the countryside against U.S. colonialism and U.S.–sponsored national rule. Additionally, the plan's implementation was obstructed by the "unplanned development" brought about by the migration of people fleeing this war in the rural areas. And the master plan for the city prepared by the National Planning Commission in 1954 had to be confined to the suburban areas surrounding Manila because of the de facto development and congestion of the city itself (638-640). Laquian, however, concludes that the lack of planning and control which has resulted in the city's main problems, "transportation, peace and order, housing and floods," is due to fragmented local governments and particularist politics. A "single metropolitan authority" that will override the latter is therefore his proposed solution to Filipino excesses (644).

That solution was realized with the imposition of Martial Law. Supported by the World Bank and its developmentalist plans for the Philippines, President Marcos integrated the four cities and thirteen municipalities that comprised the Greater Manila Area, and created the Metro Manila Commission (MMC), a "supralocal metropolitan government" headed by the First Lady Imelda Marcos, on November 7, 1975 (Ruland 28). Metro Manila "was thus ruled by the principle of concentration and unification of powers in a single body and, as a result of the composition of that body, in actual fact a single person" (Ruland 30). In its bid to join the international community of advanced nations, the Marcos regime launched a program of economic development that was export-oriented and foreign-capital-dependent. To attract foreign investments, it built five-star hotels, an international convention center, a cultural center, specialized medical centers, and numerous other "beautification projects," all under the supervision of the MMC. "Since Martial Law, the efforts of the First Lady have been focused on making Manila a center for the 'jet set' and the 'beautiful people'" (Doherty 25). This meant the eradication of unsightly structures such as slums. Consequently, every international visit or event held in Manila resulted in the eviction of squatters or the relocation of their shanties from the site of the event or the routes to be taken by Imelda's guests. Hence, although the city was Imelda's personal domestic showcase, it was "beautified" for the eyes and pleasure of foreigners and to attract the flow of foreign capital. In her vision, Manila was to be "the city of Man," the practical definition of which excluded the urban poor.[4]

The urban poor, however, help to sustain the very same economy in behalf of which they are marginalized. Scavengers, for example,

are cheap, casual labor working for the large waste recycling industry— "they work for the organization but are not part of it" (Abad
284). It is on this informal economy that multinational corporations
increasingly depend to keep labor costs low and to underwrite the
reproduction of its consumers. As informal workers, the urban poor
embody the contradictions integral to the ruling classes' political and
economic power. They are at once marginalized and essential. Without Martial Law to contain or repress them, these contradictions are
relatively freer to surface. Hence, the "crises" (the same problems
Laquian perceived before the Martial Law, but now intensified) that
seem to have erupted during the Aquino administration, in its desire
to restore democracy and encourage private enterprise, that is, to
restore free market capitalism, are in fact merely the greater continuing crisis that is Philippine development manifesting its full-blown symp-
toms.

The current crisis, as it realizes itself in all the problems that
Manila is experiencing as a "dying city," might be viewed as a necessary crisis for the renewed expansion of global capital, or the crisis
that has necessitated a makeover of capital's infrastructure for greater
and more efficient accumulation. It is, according to this view, still part
of the global crisis of the 1980s that has brought about the transformation of the dominant mode of global production into flexible production. In other words, the desires that fueled the Marcos's beautification projects and urban streamlining for development are the same
desires fueling government political and infrastructural projects today. The continuity of the state's function can be gleaned from the
highly-publicized role Manila's newly-elected Mayor Alfredo S. Lim
has taken upon himself. Lim's scum-cleaning (anti-prostitution, anti-
pornography, anti-graft, anti-crime) campaigns, which have propelled
this retired, bemedalled policeman into politics, might be seen as continuous with Marcos's slum-clearing projects to the extent that their
respective metropolitan gentrification drives stem from desires determined by an identification with global capital.[5]

Capital, however, requires different strategies for the containment of its contradictory and antagonistic elements. During Martial
Law and under the centralized power of the metropolitan government, these strategies entailed military control, direct domination, and

bodily repression and territorial confinement—such as erecting walls to hide slums, relocating squatters, and imprisoning and torturing members of urban resistance movements (including squatter organizations). After 1986, with the new administration's renewed vows to democracy and its decentralization of metropolitan government, stratification strategies are more a matter of channeling flows in the way that the flyovers channel traffic, lifting the middle and upper classes who drive private cars out of the congestion created by the "urban excess." Indeed, Imelda's desire to remove these "eyesores" is achieved with flyovers to the extent that the height and distance they provide render Manila an aerial sight—a space deprived of detail and content and reduced to abstract textures from which one can extract a particular kind of aesthetic pleasure. From this suspended pathway the city looks greener because the foliage of walled-in neighborhoods becomes visible, and the roofs of shanties look like variegated pieces of mosaic or a collage, especially because movement blurs marks of decay and makes details of the corroding urban landscape and its trash disappear into a "postmodern" spectacle of the heterogeneity and fragmentation of its pronounced uneven development.[6] Of course, this transcendent perspective is not legitimately available to the lower classes who, as pedestrians and public transportation commuters, are routed through crowded ground-level streets.

Smith asserts that "what (capital) achieves in fact is the production of space in its own image" (xiii). Flyovers, on this view, produce space in the image of transnational capital. Michael Sorkin writes of one transnational capitalist, the CEO of Citicorp, as being "a true Baron Haussmann for the electronic age, plowing the boulevards of capital through the pliant matrix of the global economy" (xi). The new boulevards of capital which transcend space and time with 800 telephone numbers, credit cards, modems, and faxes are, so to speak, electronic flyovers. The figure of speech is not merely a happy coincidence. Flyovers attempt to realize the transnational conceptual space occupied by what Sorkin calls the new city (the postindustrial city which he compares to television), by allowing the subjective experience of "the dissipation of all stable relations to local physical and cultural geography, the loosening of ties to any specific space" (xiii). In this sense, they aspire to achieve the shape of non-cities, i.e., "ultra-urban" places that end up by transcending the definition of "city" or "nation" (Daniele 133). A flyover is, as Lim described Makati, a business and commercial district in Metro Manila, "a place that has no history and no memories for the race of Filipinos" (5). As such, it can serve as the site of transnational identification. Just as one might identify with and through a city or nation, one might identify with that which transcends geographical places, i.e., the international community.

But flyovers realize the transnational conceptual space of this community not only by serving as a site of symbolic identification, but also by concretizing the socio-economic network of the national bourgeoisie, that is, of the classes with access and links to the transnational economy. They are not representations of this transnational economy—they are its means of production. Flyovers connect major shopping areas, foreign-invested malls, commercial and business centers, and exclusive residential neighborhoods, channeling consumption to corporate-owned spaces and goods, and integrating its managerial class. In its differentiation of urban space—enabling middle and upper classes better, more efficient means of commuting as well as raising them out of their urban immersion in the contradictory conditions of their economic upliftment—the flyover restructuration is a part of the process of reproducing uneven development, "the systematic geographical expression of the contradictions inherent in the very constitution and structure of capital" (Smith xi). In other words, flyovers physically realize the new division of labor in which First World-Third World or core-periphery relations are being produced within rather than among nations.[7] On this view, it is the network, rather than any downtown center, which constitutes the core space of the national economy.

Traffic and the Economy

As media and circulatory pathways become increasingly important to the production of global capital, so do they become increasingly important to its articulation. Hence, the same language is used to describe economic investments and traffic movement: flows, bottlenecks, channeling, and regulation are all terms deployed in the discourses of economy as well as traffic. As one columnist makes explicit: "Traffic is a metaphor for the economy. Can a society that cannot control its streets be expected to manage its monetary system?" (Samson 5). But the relationship between the two is more than metaphorical, for in fact, both partake of the same logic. "Traffic management is practice for economic management. If we can't succeed in regulating the flow of vehicles and pedestrians, can we expect to do better with savings and investments?" (5). In other words, both traffic and the economy are governed by a system of values and practices predicated upon the regulation of "flows."

The economic strategy of liberalized regulation or deregulation of industries and capital flows advocated by businessmen as well as international investors and banks (such as the International Monetary Fund) is deployed in the management of traffic by using flyovers to replace traffic lights and traffic police at interchanges. Flyovers in fact demonstrate well the new strategies of management that accord with the transnational mode of production: *the paths themselves become the means of regulation and decentralized control.* Thus the economic trend towards privatization is merely the internalization of mechanisms of control—an ascribing to private initiative in a self-regulating system of production and circulation: the global economy. If the flyovers are like freeways, they are free only in the sense of the free market. Flows are liberalized ultimately to the benefit of capital expansion. This is the meaning of democraticization: the process by which state control is replaced by the delimiting and channeling of desire.[8]

The system of representation constituted by the discursive articulation of the flyovers is also an economy of desire, for which the traffic system and the national economy are privileged figures. But the traffic field as well as the economic field are not prefabricated, self-regulating systems—they are sites of political contestation and struggle. In other words, roads and streets are sites of intersubjective as well as intercollective encounters and relations which produce conflicting articulations of space. Congestion and chaos are two complex results of contradictory articulations of space, for example, which the state attempts to override by building flyovers. It is in this sense that traffic is constituted by various social movements;[9] it is in a very literal sense in which collective action can be understood—in terms of pedestrians, cars, passenger jeepneys, street hawkers, and vendors, etc. The particular movements of the "urban excess" are articulatory practices which participate in the production of urban space. It is not therefore the lack of attributes of power such as planning, will, discipline, strict law enforcement, political firmness, and inner strength on the part of the state of its "citizenry" or adherents, that has brought about the chaos and decay which has become the monument of the city.[10] Rather, it is the crisis of conflicting desires and social practices, caused by the intensification of the constitutive contradictions of capital.

Such contradictions are visible within the state itself to the extent that the national and local metropolitan governments, now no longer united as they were during Martial Law, pursue ostensibly conflicting paths of development: while the national government leans towards deregulation and privatization (building flyovers, "depoliticizing" power rates), metropolitan governments tend towards totalitarian control and centralized policies (shutting down businesses, censoring sexual entertainment). However, overriding these different state strategies is an impelling desire for upward mobility.

Desires for Unhampered Flows

The state understands traffic as it understands the economy—as a system of practices upon the efficiency of which the nation's development depends. As one headline evidences—"Smoother Quezon City Traffic Flow Seen"—the building of flyovers is predicated upon a desire for greater efficiency, smoother flows, etc. The desire for these qualities is consonant with the desire for development and modernization. Hence it is a desire with a more general significance. "There are several specific institutions, particular areas of endeavor, which in microcosm tell a cautionary tale of how and why things don't work in this country. Traffic is one of them" (Puno 11). Like almost everyone writing for the newspapers, this writer calls for management and control—that is, for the attributes of power whose lack in the state is constantly bemoaned by the middle and upper classes. The ultimate consequences of the latter's frustration with the "problems" of Manila can be gleaned from an only half-ironic article entitled, "Fascist Tack to Traffic":

Our plan for traffic is intimately tied into our scheme for managing the metropolis . . . The central problem, as we see it, is a lack of proper enforcement, which may even be a blessing, considering the stupidity of some of the traffic regulations and the inadequacy of the infrastructure. The roots of this problem are that Manila is a largely laissez-faire state. Entry into the city is completely unregulated, and the population is growing at a rate that has long since outstripped the availability of resources.

Some of the measures we have outlined may seem to be overly authoritarian, even fascist [the writer recommends, among other things, the handcuffing of jaywalkers to center island railings, the erection of chain barriers to trap traffic violators, and the deployment of a military-like Patrol and Pursuit squadron]. *We believe that such regulations need to be stringent as a reaction to the current chaotic conditions. Manila drivers—and pedestrians—need to be shown that we are serious about imposing order in the streets. (Ongpin, "Fascist Tack" 1)*

As a state response to this hegemonic call (the "we" voice of this article) for channeling, regulation, and order, flyovers achieve in traffic what is attempted for the rest of the city with the various campaigns or "drives" of local autonomous city governments.[11] On the occasion of Manila's 422nd anniversary, Mayor Lim promises his constituency: "We shall clear up the streets and unclog the thoroughfares to allow the city to breathe again—and let the lifeblood of its commerce flow freely once more to give life to our city" (30). What Lim articulates, for which he has become immensely popular among the middle and upper classes, is a desire for what Sigfried Giedion views as "the fundamental law of the parkway—that there must be unobstructed freedom of movement, a flow of traffic maintained evenly at all points without interruption or interference" (824). The "meaning" of highways identified by Giedion is in fact what flyovers in Manila manage to convey: "the liberation from unexpected light signals and cross traffic, and the freedom of uninterrupted forward motion" (825). In other words, the desire for this unhampered flow and speed (as well as the progress implied),[12] which produces and is produced by the flyovers, is the same desire that Lim acts on.

Flyover Dreams

The desire articulated by this new metropolitan form, however, does not emanate from a subject outside of that articulation; rather, the articulation itself helps to produce the effect of subjectivity, that is, the desiring subject. Driving on one of these freeways produces the experience of being a free, mobile unit (what Giedion calls "the space-time feeling of our period" [826][13])—a self that can transcend the human mass, that is, the corporeal excess and chaos which constitutes Manila's "laissez-faire" state. In other words, this liberalized flow or "drive" allows one who is afforded the privilege of overseeing the city to occupy a self removed from face-to-face confrontations with its social contradictions, which are heightened in congested moments (creating eye-gridlocks with the "eyesores" Imelda tried to eliminate such as beggars, street children, scavengers, street hawkers, and the urban poor in general). Since Martial Law, there have in fact been many state "drives" to rid the metropolis of squatters, scavengers, and waste, and to clear the streets of vendors, tricycles, jeepneys, and provincial buses, which obstruct the movement of the metropolis's citizenry— "drives" to clear pathways for the city's privileged subjects to move freely. Flyovers fulfill this task, providing a relatively exclusive, suspended network which allows the ghettoed, privileged, metropolitan subjects to "breathe"—granting them, in the language of capital, (upward) "mobility."

Indeed, the effect of subjectivity that flyovers help to produce is that of a mobile cell ("the lifeblood of commerce") in free-flowing circulation—an *I* occupied by a free-floating consciousness. Manila's hegemonic consciousness is constituted by the organization of these discrete, mobile selves, by that suspended network which images the conceptual space of transnational capital. It becomes clear that the collective *I* employed by metropolitan residents speaks as this consciousness which views the metropolis as a space to be made its own: "We want spaces that we can live and grow in, spaces responsive to our needs and our lifestyles. Safe, secure, comfortable, and ultimately, beautiful to us who will inhabit it" (Cruz 16). Such is the desire of metropolitan subjects on "the road to that dream house in Lim's dream city" (Cruz 16), a desire to inhabit, which is consistent with being cells, discrete entities that occupy space. This desire to inhabit is predicated upon the modern Western house, with its characteristics of verticality, concentration, and centrality, qualities that also shape the individual self. Gaston Bachelard observes that "the house is one of the greatest powers of integration for the thoughts, memories, and dreams of mankind" (6). The metropolitan subject who finds his or her desires congruent with Lim's is captivated by this power of the house. The mankind whose dreams he or she buys into, however, is the same mankind for whose development and progress the dreams and desires of countless others continue to be sacrificed.

It is in the image of the Western house, its rationally designed and partitioned spaces, and its "valorization of a center of concentrated solitude," that Metro Manila is once again being envisioned. Except that the valorized center has become multiple and mobile, demanding a new kind of metropolitan house. In this blueprint, flyovers perform the function of corridors leading to and from the exclusive, walled-in neighborhoods where the upper strata are ensconced. One might view this new metropolitan form as a network house, a decentralized spatial system resembling an archipelago whose islands are interconnected by bridges. I say islands because subdivisions where the paradigms of the Western house with its solid, monolithic structures, geometrically-defined, and partitioned spaces as well as its attention to housing content have most completely applied, are surrounded by a sea of "unplanned development." In these areas inundated by poverty and its haphazard production of space there is no other way to go but up and that is what flyovers do—they secure centers or spaces of concentration by building elevated horizontal links among them. Such is the architectural structure that enables the new metropolitan selves to circulate as and dwell in discrete cores of being.[14]

In "The Housing of Gender," Mark Wigley observes that the role of the architect as defined in classical architectural theory ("a privileged figure for cultural life") "is, after all, no more than the principle of economy. The propriety of place derives from the elimination of all excess" (352). Indeed, both state projects—the flyovers and Lim's "clean up drives"—are predicated on this principle of economy; that is, they are part of the process of subjecting the metropolis to an economic regime intended to streamline its spaces. Lim's over-all project might therefore be viewed as "cleaning house." In fact, during the last local elections, Lim touted a broom as part of his campaign image. That the image associated with him used to be a gun (he used to be depicted as Clint Eastwood and John Wayne) only underscores the continuity between his purification drive (not to mention his "Clean and Green Campaign") and Imelda's beautification projects—both are dedicated to the task of sweeping away urban refuse. For the dream house of the metropolis, or the house that the metropolis through its subjects is dreaming into being, depends on the elimination of the urban excess from its spaces.

State Bulimia

The job of eliminating this excess is carried out by the state through its various campaigns to clean up the city. This excess is a corporeal excess from which metropolitan subjects must be removed as a condition of possibility of their discrete, mobile selves. It is this detachment from the fleshly (the bodily masses) that Manila's desire requires and that the flyovers' reduction of concrete places to fixed, abstract names reinforces. In fact, Lim's determination to "clear up" the streets is merely another expression of his consuming "drive" "to rub out Manila's image as the flesh center of Asia" (Romero D-8). This tourism-sponsored identity of Manila is created, in fact, by the flesh trade, that is, the thriving prostitution industry which first received an enormous boost from the Marcos regime in the latter's scheme to attract foreign investment and interest through "tourism." Lim's "clean-up drive" has hence been comprised mainly of raids in the red-light district, Ermita, and the shutting-down of clubs, bars, and other "entertainment" establishments in the same area. But the flesh and the desires they arouse—desires which this purification process attempts to eradicate—include the graft and corruption pervading the bureaucracy and police as well, for their motivating "base instincts" are merely another form of the corporeal excess. Such is the refuse of the government's streamlining efforts.

But this regime to which the state subjects the city might be characterized as bulimic. That is, the various "drives" of the government are carried out in spurts, followed by binges of laxity, indulgence, and negligence. This inconsistency is what is constantly decried as the "lack of strict enforcement" and "lack of will" on the part of the state. Sally Ann Ness, an American ethnographer who spent some time in the Philippines doing field work, observed this "sporadic nature by which rules were tightened and relaxed in a seemingly endless fashion" (53). While Ness naturalizes this characteristic as part of the cultural rhythm that pervades other aspects of society, the law-abiding classes consider it a deplorable cultural habit of weakness that is a legacy of our colonial past. But the bulimic character of the state's purgings is not unrelated to the stomach purgings of women afflicted with what is taken as a pathologized complex. This bulimic behavior is an effect of the contradiction between ideal images and illegitimate desires, both of which are promulgated by dominant ideological apparatuses. The pathologization of this contradictory behavior solidifies it as a psychological and cultural condition which attracts numerous efforts and institutional programs to cure or address it, such as the public clamoring for consistency of the state's "drives," that is, the strengthening of its will.

However, in the case of the national "disorder," the state's lack or weakness of self-discipline and will (which is viewed as a trait of its emasculation) is produced by a conflict between ideal national images and illegitimate capitalist desires. This conflict can be gleaned from Lim's purifying regime. Lim's anti-prostitution drive is, for example, in actuality merely a purging of the entertainment establishment's contents, that is, female prostitutes, stripteasers, and "hospitality girls." The option of converting the bars and clubs into "legitimate" businesses which he offers to the owners (who are almost exclusively foreigners), is, however, hardly considered an option. As one club owner complains: "people come here because of the beautiful girls. You remove them and nobody will come anymore" (qtd. in Romero, D-8). True enough, the foreign-capital-dependent economy depends on these women as well as on an almost exclusively female labor force in other industries to attract foreign investments (the somebodies who need to come). The desire for these flows of foreign investments is in fact what has led to the prostitution of the country and the image of Manila as a "flesh center" which Lim wants to rub out.

The ambivalent relation between Manila's excess, composed of its informal labor, and the state which attempts to control or eliminate it, is clarified by George Yudice's comparison of the informal economy to irrationality. As Yudice argues, "'Irrationality' is born of the guiding (market) 'rationality' of modernity" (3). Just as irrationality is produced as well as contained by rationality, so is the "irrational" urban excess produced as well as contained by the "rational" regime of the state. Thus, on the one hand, this excess must be disavowed or contained to preserve the country's moral value; on the other, it must be released and exploited to increase the country's surplus value.

The bulimic behavior of the state might be seen as a conflict of identification which results in a conflicted relation to the urban excess it is trying to eliminate; or put another way, the bulimia of the state makes manifest its conflicted relation to the metropolitan body. If by body is meant "the concrete, material, animate organization of flesh, organs, nerves, muscles, and skeletal structure which are given a unity, cohesiveness, and organization only through their psychical and social inscription as the surface and raw material of an integrated and cohesive totality" (Grosz 243), then the metropolitan body might be understood as the totality of corporeal labor inscribed by modes of production and symbolization such as that articulated by the flyovers. On this view, Manila's metropolitan body can be understood as the immense pool of surplus cheap labor—the sea—surrounding the archipelago edifice system of the upper strata. The liquidity attributed to the informal sector is not merely a figure of speech—it refers both to the liquidity of its petty cash and the liquidity of its spatial practices which corrode the solid infrastructures (such as the fences pedestrians wear away in their insistence on jaywalking). Indeed, part of the liquidity of the urban excess lies in the nature of its labor. As Smith asserts: "The particularity of labor implies the particularity of its spatial attributes" (86). Much of this labor has been characterized as "homework" in that it consists of work that is either an extension of conventional domestic work or "women's work" or work carried out at home. Also the street becomes the site of both work and residence. In all cases, this informal work might be viewed as a perversion or transgression of modern divisions of public and private spaces and activities, as well as the Western notion of home which is predicated upon this division. It is hence not surprising that the urban excess creates living-spaces whose boundaries are mobile and porous, nor that their movements ignore the private as well as public boundaries erected by others. In fact, the prostitution of informal workers whose casual services are procured on a contractual basis demands the periodic dissolution of the boundaries of their selves, bodies, and homes in exchange for subsistence.

The realization of the urban excess in terms of the informal sector's liquidity and the female sexuality in which it traffics allows a sex-gender reading of the state's conflict of identification. Wigley notes that in the dominant cultural logic of Western architecture "women lack the internal self-control credited to men as the very mark of their masculinity. Their self-control is no more than the maintenance of secure boundaries. These internal boundaries, or rather boundaries that define the interior of the person, the identity of the self, cannot be maintained by a woman because her fluid sexuality endlessly overflows and disrupts them" (335). Western perceptions of colonial bodies, including those of Filipinos, have historically affixed this debased fluid, feminine sexuality onto the latter, and have thereby served to erect masculine ideals embodied in the nation-state. The nation-state becomes the instrument with which the ruling classes produce and contain the feminine sexuality which it has displaced onto its labor. The excessive and fluid sexuality attributed to women as well as to colonial bodies is housed and contained in a feminized national body that hence becomes the jurisdiction of a masculine nation-state. The house which is ostensibly produced by the need to control this feminine sexuality but is also the means by which that sexuality is produced is the paradigm of the nation as well as the metropolis.

Lim's regime to achieve his dream city, the metropolis as house, is indeed an effort to eliminate this threatening fluid sexuality to the extent that the objects of his purging are women and feminized labor. As Wigley shows: "The building itself is subjected to the economic regime it enforces. Just as the house is a mechanism for the domestication of women, it is itself understood as a domesticated woman" (352-53). Imaged as just such a house, Metro Manila is thereby produced as a domesticated female body and the metropolitan state as the controlling and self-controlled masculine order to which it is submitted. These gendered identities, however, are secured only at the level of the nation. For at the level of the international community, that is, in the eyes of global capital, the Philippines is feminized global labor, and that includes the state. The ambiguity and ambivalence of Manila's gendered identity hence stems from its vacillation between identifying with global capital and identifying with global labor.

Lim's proposed plan "to give life to" Manila, to let it breathe again, and to "let (its) lifeblood . . . flow freely," manifests the construction of the city as an organic body. But the configuration of this metropolitan body is also contradictory and ambivalent depending on its point of identification—the point from which it sees itself or from which it is seen. For while capital demands an "open-economy"[15]— meaning a feminine, permissive, and porous metropolitan body,[16] a national identity based on masculine ideals of power and self demands a centrally-controlled, self-protective economy—meaning a contained and discipline metropolitan body. In other words, the metropolitan state is hailed to *be* this body at the same time that it is hailed to *possess* (and control) this body; to be a pliant, porous, feminine people, or a strong-willed, self-disciplined, masculine nation-state. Such is the gender trouble of the state, one that is completely predicated upon the heterosexual political-libidinal dynamics of capitalism and nationhood.[17]

The state's conflict of identification and its consequently ambivalent attitude towards its metropolitan body is part of the reason that the urban excess is neither eliminated nor contained but rather, discharged—displaced from the spaces and structures of the upper strata and permitted everywhere else, flooding the rest of the metropolitan area.[18] The state's ambivalence towards the urban excess demands a new mode of regulation other than that which relies on "older" centralized strategies of containment and eradication such as those used by Marcos. In the prostitution of the metropolitan body, the Marcos regime's pimping strategy was territorial, involving the parcelling out of natural resources (including property rights, which has resulted in these foreign-owned prostitution establishments) to centralized monopolies. Lim's strategy is more a matter of deterritorialization in that it drives prostitutes to work informally, that is, unregulated by syndicates of pimps and clubs. Lim's efforts actually encourage the decentralization of prostitution and its related "graft" activities, such as drug dealing. By deregulating the trafficking of commodified female sexuality (tendered by prostitutes) and other illegitimate substances, such efforts also see to the perpetuation of this trafficking in liquid form. This is not unlike the function of flyovers in relation to the urban excess. For flyovers mediate between the formal and informal economies and between the state and the urban excess, accommodating their respective "rational" and "irrational" modes. Thus, Lim's authoritarian drives are coextensive with the mode of production of flyovers; they each retain the excesses of Manila by displacing them into the neglected tarn of the metropolis.

Fluidity

The demands for deregulation and free flows made by the new mode of production articulated by flyovers show that a certain kind of fluidity is congruent with modernization and development. It is important hence to distinguish between the organizing and organized mobility of capital and the ostensibly unorganized liquidity of labor. As infrastructural supports of this new mode of production, flyovers negotiate between these two kinds of flows, accommodating both by channeling them through different spaces. What flyovers make manifest in effect are the metropolis's conditions of fluidity, upon which they are predicated and by which they are produced. The image of Manila as it is realized by the performance of the flyovers is as a sea of fluids separating into channeled flows of mobile particles and a stagnating lake of liquid excess. In other words, in the configuration of the metropolis as an archipelago, a body of fluidity dotted with congealed, scattered centers, there are no spaces of interiority for the repression of contradictory desires—Manila has no unconscious. Flyovers bring the upper strata into *relief*, detaching them from the lower strata but not masking the latter, securing domination through bypasses and overpasses rather than through enclosure and censorship. The stratification of metropolitan space is, in other words, not a mat-

ter of masking, containment, and repression, but rather, of accommodating and channeling flows—not a matter of centrality and rationally-
ordered spaces, but of decentralized cores and winding pathways.
What in fact this new mode of production reveals in its emergence to
accommodate the metropolis's "rationality" and "irrationality" (whose
polarization in the psyche Bachelard imaged as the polarization of the
attic and cellar in the house), is their fluid and symbiotic coexistence.
Metropolitan stratification can hence be seen as a matter of velocities
of solid and liquid elements rather than as merely a matter of inside
and outside.

These conditions call into question the deployment of modern,
Western theories and epistemologies of urban space, subjectivity, and
sexuality to understand metropolitan formations like Metro Manila.
As Wigley recognizes: "Sexuality in the age of psychoanalysis is the
sexuality of the interior. Each of the new regimes of classification—
perversion, fetishism, homosexuality, voyeurism, etc.—presupposes the
institution of some kind of 'closet' that masks them, a supplementary
realm of withdrawal" (388). It is not that such theoretical regimes are
inapplicable to Philippine conditions. That is, it is not a matter of
dismissing these theories of space and subjectivity as irrelevant or
immaterial to some radically different formation, but rather a matter
of viewing them as historical forces (modes of production) among a
multiplicity of forces impinging on and impelling the conditions of
Philippine social formations. One must recognize that there are other
regimes besides the sexual-economic regimes of capital which the
metropolitan body is subjected to, among them the regimes of First
World theories. Indeed, I have tried to show that the epistemologies
of modern, Western formations—the "metaphysics of being" implied
by paradigms of the house and the body—are instruments which are
used in the attempts to stratify Metro Manila through the desires of
and for development.

Flyovers, themselves, introduce a verticality and depth to the
city which is endemic to these epistemologies. Hence while this new
metropolitan form might be seen to displace and delimit modern paradigms and structures of containment as well as the constructions of
sexuality and subjectivity which they help to make, it also deploys
them. In fact, part of the innovation of flyovers lies in the way they

insert themselves in this heterogeneous metropolitan body to become the coordinating mechanism of its various modes of production. In other words, as a new metropolitan machine regulating Manila's metropolitan life in behalf of capital, the flyover network requires, produces, and exploits these conditions of fluidity.

The fluency and fluidity that characterize the social as well as spatial practices of the urban excess, however, cannot be reduced to properties ultimately functional for capital. In other words, such qualities are not merely a residual mode of production that participates in the reproduction of uneven development. The mobility and porousness of boundaries of self and body that might be observed among larger sectors of the population, for example, would have historical determinants that include but are by no means limited to the exigencies of colonialism and capitalism. For Ness, who observed fluency and fluidity in so many other aspects of Philippine cultural life, they belong in the realm of the pre-economic: "Sources from which activity tended to develop and into which activity dissolved still appeared to be fluent, not solid, mobile, not stable . . . Fluency of all kinds, as opposed to strength or single-minded determination, for example, was tacitly recognized as of primary importance for coping with the environment in a variety of ways"(41). Although this account tends to be culturally essentializing, as does much other ethnographic writing, it does bring out a crucial dimension of this fluidity, which is its significance for "coping with the environment." If one recognizes that this environment consists of fundamentally oppressive socio-economic and sexuality-gender structures, one will also recognize "coping" as a matter of resistance to such structures. Moreover, "coping" is a persistence in, or better, insistence on practices that are on some level disharmonious to capitalist development and subjectification (even though on another level they might be "accommodated" by the state); it is also simply life-enabling, both collectively and individually. In other words, this fluency and this fluidity are forms of social and individual subsistence as well as resistance.

Take for example the unregulated movements of jeepneys (passenger vehicles originally made from surplus American jeeps after the second world war). Their unruliness stems from the "informality" of their functioning which serves the interests of its users. Jeepneys are unruly not only because their drivers want to make as many trips as possible and because this is a way for them to act on and express a certain antagonism towards the "private classes," but also because they stop anywhere along their route where passengers indicate. There are many functional and structural characteristics of the jeepney which render it a more collective mode of transportation, and that is part of the reason that it has been valorized, as well as aestheticized as the Filipino cultural symbol *par excellence*. This essentializing practice exemplifies the proclivity of the national bourgeoisie for isolating objects with very concrete significance in daily lives and imbuing them with the capacity to embody cultural identity. In *Perfumed Nightmare*, however, Filipino filmmaker Kidlat Tahimik presents the jeepney not as a reified national icon but as a living artifact realizing the desire to forge a life out of the ravages of oppression and domination. As his main character declares: "We have turned the vehicles of war into vehicles of life." In short, the fluidity that characterizes jeepneys as well as the urban excess of which they are a part, is not an "authentic" cultural trait, rather, it is a mark of the desire to live.

This desire might be seen to extend over the metropolis in general. As a colonial body for nearly five hundred years, Metro Manila is also a testimony to its own "coping" with the exigencies of global capital. Its chaos, its horizontality, its porous surfaces, and its fluidity, as well as the forms of subjectivity such conditions enable, are expressions of the desire of its population to survive—evidence that it is not a "dying city" but, rather, an enduring one.

NOTES

1. This mode of orientation is necessitated by the widespread practice of locating through contiguity (with concrete landmarks) rather than through transcendent vectors and abstract signs. In Manila, generally unused street signs are often obscured or absent. Also, large monuments and landmark buildings built by the Americans lose visual prominence as one becomes buried in the density of one's surroundings. In any case, all Manila's major centers of activity (government, commercial, residential) have nomadically changed locations periodically, while historical structures have either deteriorated beyond recognition or have been destroyed by human and natural forces, with the result that attempts to represent the city with any single monument invariably fail. A greater collective signifier might be the experience of moving through the thickness of the city, through its crowds and traffic, its dirt and pollution, and its relentless assault on one's senses.

2. F. S. Cruz, the company contracted to build the flyovers, was the same company in charge of Imelda Marcos' project reclaiming land from Manila Bay mainly for the purpose of erecting international cultural centers.

3. Arturo Escobar shows how the "imaginary of development" through which planners and economists in the Third World have inscribed and produced their reality has been subjected to numerous critiques: "Development has been the primary mechanism through which these parts of the world have been produced and have produced themselves, thus marginalizing or precluding other ways of seeing and doing" (22). Many such critiques, however, focus on "the ways in which the Third World is constituted in and through representation. Third World reality is inscribed with precision and persistence by the discourses and practices of economists, planners, nutritionists, demographers, and the like, making it difficult for people to define their own interests in their own terms—in many cases actually disabling them to do so" (25). Aside from ignoring the incredible scale of systematic violence used to underwrite these "discourses and practices," such critiques also ignore the efforts and activities of "the masses" (that is, the nationally marginalized) in shaping or influencing the policy actions of the "people" (that is, the global representatives of the nation-state).

4. Doherty gives a comprehensive account of the systematic oppression of squatters in spite of Imelda's avowed concern for the urban poor, and the numerous projects intended to benefit them. The meaning of this exclusion, of course, is that the poor are not members of the race of Man. The gendered humanity for which

Manila is built aligns the urban poor with a femininity which must be contained in order that the metropolitan body can be enjoyed by those to whom it belongs.

5. The present administration's obsession with reaching NIC (Newly Industrialized Countries) status is clear evidence of this identification.

6. This is in no way to characterize Manila, a city of what used to be known as the Third World, as post modern. Rather, because the particularity and significance of Manila as a socio-historic-economic formation threatens to disappear in the face of third world cities discursively realized as such in first world nations (such as L.A.—the quintessential postmodern, third world *and* global city), it is all the more important to show that such categories and their discursive power, the desires upon which they are predicated as well as their material hardware, are reproduced rather than found in places like Manila. To argue this differentiation is important not only to engage the specificity of Manila but also to show that this specificity reveals a certain aporia in first world theories (that is present especially when these attempt to analyse the internal third world as a way of understanding global phenomena), an aporia that stands in for conditions endemic but invisible to late capitalists societies.

7. See Appelbaum and Gereffi.

8. As Jonathan L. Beller writes: "transnational industry attempts to narrow the people's choices until democracy means acquiescence to the world-economic system, that is until it means nothing at all" (15).

9. "Social movements constitute an analytical and political terrain in which the weakening of development and the displacement of categories of modernity (for example, progress and the economy), can be defined and explored" (Escobar 28). Thus, the urban excess and its structuration of Metro Manila can also be viewed as displacing or at least challenging the dominant epistemological categories of metropolitan experience, as well as prevailing epistemological categories of gender and sexuality.

10. "Our city's monument is decay" (Villalon 16).

11. That the 4 cities and 13 municipalities have been called "fiefdoms" manifests the political structure of the metropolitan government. In other words, metropolitan politics has reverted to the fragmentation and particularism that Laquian deplored before Martial Law. Clearly, however, this kind of "feudal" politics is now completely compatible with the prevailing mode of transnational production.

12. EDSA (Epifanio de los Santos Avenue), the main thoroughfare stretching across the entire metropolis and now overlaid with the most flyovers, is in fact

the product of this modernist valorization of movement, as well as of modernization itself. Constructed by the Americans (as Highway 54), it was a later partial
realization of the 1904 urban plans for Manila drawn up by Daniel H. Burnham the
Chicago architect who worked on designs in Washington, D.C., Cleveland, San
Francisco and Chicago. The plans for Manila included a system of broad thoroughfares, diagonal arteries and rotundas (rather than traffic lights) superimposed on
the medieval narrow streets built by the Spanish colonial government. The great
emphasis Burnham's urban designs placed on monuments and expansive avenues
demonstrated his own participation in and support of the imperialist project of his
government to the extent that they were predicated on the belief in the civilizing
influence of artifacts of power. As he asserted: "Make no little plans, for they have
no power to stir man's minds" (qtd. in Mumford 402). Flyovers are not so much
modeled on an imperialistically imposed metropolitan form as much as produced
by an identification with a compelling metropolitan desire: the desire for modernization and capitalist development. However, this infrastructural form is not merely
produced by particular desires but more importantly, is constitutive of those desires.

13.   "Our period" refers to the age of monopoly capitalism of first world
nations, and hence its "space-time feeling," to the experience of modernity. Therefore, what Filipinos (as the bourgeois nationalists proudly assert themselves to
represent) experience in their own period is, rather, a space-time feeling *for* the
modernity of capital. It is not accidental that urban life in Manila is pervasively
characterized by its own residents as modern. On the other hand, what makes it
postmodern is the conscious relation it maintains to an already realized and extant
modernity, that is, to the ideology of modernity and modernization imported from
advanced capitalist nations.

14.   As I have tried to argue, these are what flyovers *attempt* to accomplish.
The height afforded by these structures, however, might also enable the emergence
of other subjectivities. The significance of this consciousness-formation for subaltern subjects cannot be underestimated. In "Oberpas," a short story by Tony Perez,
a young gay man mired in depression and self-loathing after his love is rejected,
gains the desire to continue living as he contemplates the expanse of his life and of
his self from the top of a pedestrian overpass. Metropolitan forms such as flyovers
and overpasses become new sites of experience, spaces in which one can lift oneself out of the mire of one's existence to reflect upon one's life or to dream of
alternative ones. Perhaps because of the slower movement, pedestrian overpasses
might be more conducive to such reflections. The flyovers, however, are now also
being appropriated by the urban poor.

15.   This is characterized by the "stress on export development . . . , the
liberal importation of foreign goods, the attraction of more foreign investments,
unhampered repatriation of profits and capital, unhindered access to foreign ex-

change, and free or floating exchange rate for the Philippine peso" (Canieso-Doronila 8).

16. The profitability of this porousness and its relation to commodified female sexuality can be gleaned from a caption accompanying an article on global prostitution: "Poverty, political chaos and porous borders have turned prostitution into a global growth industry" (*Time Magazine* 1). The similar construction of women and children as porous—obedient orifices open to sexual exploitation—shows the complex relations between national identity and sexuality. I discuss some of these relations in "Sexual Economies in the Asia-Pacific."

17. This is in no way to suggest that the oppressive structures of capitalism, patriarchy, and homophobia are the same or equivalent, merely that on the level of the nation state, they are cooperative or at least congruent. But even on that level, the contradictions between economic profit and state morality demonstrate the tenuousness of that cooperation. The equivalences made from a dominant perspective (for example, between femininity and class) are undone in specific contexts of oppression, in which particular lines of differentiation or systems of value (for example, the sex-gender system) are deployed over and above others.

18. The other part of the reason for the continued and pervasive presence of this urban excess is, of course, its own desire. In other words, the state's bulimia is also induced by the *resilience* and *will to survive* of the informal sector which constantly defies state injunctions and state terrorism to return to the streets.

Works Cited

Abad, Ricardo G. "Squatting and Scavenging in Smokey Mountain." *Philippine Studies* 39.3 (1991): 263-86.

Appelbaum, Richard P. and Gary Gereffi. "Power and Profits in the Apparel Commodity Chain." Unpublished manuscript.

Bachelard, Gaston. *The Poetics of Space.* New York: Orion, 1964.

Beller, Jonathan L. "Winning the Heart of the Military-Industrial Complex." *Manila Chronicle* 8 June 1993.

Canieso-Doronila, Maria-Luisa. "Educating Filipinos for the World Market." *Manila Chronicle* 20 June 1993.

Caoili, Manuel A. "Metropolitan Manila Reorganization." *Philippine Journal of Public Administration* 29.1 (1985):1-26.

Colomina, Beatriz, ed. *Sexuality and Space.* New York: Princeton Architectural Press, 1992. Vol. 1 of *Princeton Papers on Architecture.* 1 vol. 1992.

Cruz, Larry J. "Dream House." *Metro* July 1992.

Daniele, Daniela. "Mapless Cities: Urban Displacement and Failed Encounters in Surrealist and Postmodern Narratives." Diss. City University of New York, 1992.

Doherty, S. J., John F. *The Philippine Urban Poor.* Honolulu: Philippine Studies Program Center for Asian & Pacific Studies, U of Hawaii, 1985.

Escobar, Arturo, "Imagining a Post-Development Era.? Critical Thought, Development and Social Movements." *Social Text* 10.2-3 (1992): 20-56.

Giedion, Siegfried. *Space, Time, and Architecture.* Cambridge: Harvard UP, 1982.

Grosz, Elizabeth. "Bodies-Cities." *Colomina* 241-54.

King, Anthony D. *Urbanism, Colonialism and the World-Economy: Cultural and Spatial Foundations of the World Urban System.* London: Routledge, 1990.

Laquian, Aprodicio. "Manila." *Great Cities of the World; Their Government, Politics, and Planning.* Eds. William A. Robson and D. E. Regan. vol. 2. London: Allen & Unwin, 1954. 605-44.

Lim, Alfredo F. "A Vision for Manila." *Panorama* 20 June 1993

Mumford, Lewis. *The City in History.* New York: Harcourt, 1961.

Ness, Sally Ann. *Body, Movement and Culture: Kinesthetic and Visual Symbolism in a Philippine Community.* Philadelphia: U of Pennsylvania P. 1992.

Ongpin, Ma. Isabel. "Traffic, traffic traffic." *Manila Chronicle* 17 June 1993.

Ongpin, Rafael A.S.G. "Fascist Tack to Traffic." *Manila Chronicle National Weekly* 25 December 1992.

Perez, Tony. "Oberpas." *Cubao 1980 at Iba Pang Mga Katha: Unang Sigaw ng Gay Liberation Movement sa Pilipinas.* Manila: Cacho, 1992. 184-89.

Puno, Ricardo V. "Southexpressway Revisited." *Philippine Star* 6 June 1993

Romero, Lindablue F. "Fear and Loathing in Ermita." *Philippine Daily Inquirer* 6 June 1993.

Ruland, Jurgen. "Metropolitan Government under Martial Law: The Metro Manila Commission Experiment." *Philippine Journal of Public Administration* 29.1 (1985):27-41.

Samson, A. R. "Traffic and the Economy." *Manila Chronicle* 23 Feb. 1993.

Smith, Neil. *Uneven Development.* Oxford: Blackwell, 1984.

Sorkin, Michael. "Introduction: Variations of a Theme Park." *Variations of a Theme Park.* Ed. Michael Sorkin. New York: Noonday, 1992. xi-xv.

Tadiar, Neferti Xina M. "Sexual Economies in the Asia-Pacific." *What's in a Rim?* Ed. Arif Dirlik. Boulder: Westview, 1993.

Time Magazine 141.25 (1993).

Villalon, Augusto F. "Manila Malaise." *Manila Chronicle* 17 June 1993.

Yudice, George. "Postmodernity and Transnational Capitalism in Latin America." *On Edge: The Crisis of Contemporary American Culture.* Eds. George Yudice, Jean Franco, and Juan Flores. Minneapolis: U of Minnesota P, 1992 1-28. Vol. 4 of *Cultural Politics.* 4 vols.

INDEX

C

Cacique Democracy, 3, 15, 16, 17, 18, 19, 27, 31, 155
Caciques, provincial, 9
Cailles, Juan, 57
Calamba, 56, 57, 64, 75, 76, 78
California, 41, 45, 125, 157, 163, 181, 185, 188, 210, 211, 213, 214, 215, 217, 256, 283
Callboy-*bakla* relationships, 200
Cambodia, American intervention in, 271
Camp Wallace, 54
Campomanes, Oscar V., 159
Cannell, Fenella, 223, 256
Capital, 8, 11, 17, 31, 56, 136, 157, 179, 204, 224, 227, 228, 240, 289, 290, 291, 291, 292, 293, 294, 295, 297, 300, 303, 304, 305, 306, 307, 310
Capitalism, 18, 43, 135, 188, 291, 303, 306, 310, 311, 313
Capitalism, free market, 291
Capitalists, feudal, 289
Casper, Linda Ty. *See* Ty-Casper, Linda
Catholic Church, 137, 195, 216
Catholic Church, critique of the, 137
Catholicism, 256, 263
Catholics, 262
Cebu City, 7, 8, 29, 278
Censorship, colonial, 136
Central Bank of the Philippines, 12
Chamberlain, Weston P., 109, 110, 111
"Charing," 199

Chiang Kai-shek, 21, 22
Chiang Kai-shek, Madame, 21
"Children of the Ash-Covered Loam," 179
Chinese, 3, 4, 5, 6, 7, 8, 33, 34, 55, 75, 119, 160, 185, 227, 239
Chinese mestizos, 4, 119
Cholera, 51, 52, 53, 54, 55, 56, 57, 58, 59, 60, 61, 62, 63, 64, 65, 66, 67, 68, 69, 70, 72, 73, 74, 75, 76, 77, 78, 79, 80, 81, 104, 111, 118
Cholera epidemic, 52, 58, 65, 72
Civil service, 12, 21, 110
Clark Field, 21, 42
Class origins, common, 201
"Clean and Green Campaign," 299
"Cleaning house," 299
Clerical dominion, 6
Clifford, James, 252, 256
Climate, Philippine, 97, 110
Climograph, 88, 89
Cojuangco, Corazon. *See* Aquino, Corazon
Cojuangco, Eduardo 'Danding', 4, 21
Cojuangco, José, 16, 28, 29
Cojuangco, José 'Peping', 4, 33
Cojuangco, Melecio, 3, 35
Colonial history, reinterpretations of, 169
Colonial inequality, 95
Colonial law, Spanish, 6
Colonial mentality, 228
Colonial policy making, 88
Colonial warfare, 59

Guide to photos on front cover:

Left to right, from top left
Billboard, *Cubao Intersection (Ibabaw);* Movie billboard (Ruffa
Gutierrez and Robin Padilla), *Shaw Blvd.;* Sultan Kudarat and
the Citibank Bldg., *Makati;* Dollar coin; Movie billboard, *Shaw
Blvd.;* Detail, Installation by Santiago Bose, Baguio Arts Fest;
Tutuban Station Mall, *Divisoria;* Bonifacio Monument,
Kalookan; Detail, Bonifacio Monument, *Kalookan;* Detail,
Dollar bill; Movie billboard (Bong Revilla), *Cubao;* Stained
glass window of a *Bahay Kubo* (R. C. Sunico Collection); Ruins
near San Agustin Church, *Intramuros;* Ortigas flyover, *EDSA;*
Philippine flag, *Rizal Monument;* Carlos III of Spain, *Manila
Cathedral Plaza;* Detail, Bonifacio Monument and movie
billboard (Ronnie Ricketts), *Kalookan*

Photographs by Ramón C. Sunico